CHRIST and the CHURCH

alba house  A DIVISION OF THE SOCIETY OF ST. PAUL
STATEN ISLAND, NEW YORK 10314

Rene Latourelle, SJ

CHRIST and the CHURCH

SIGNS OF SALVATION

Translated by: Sr. Dominic Parker

Originally published under the title *Le Christ et L'Église*: *Signes du Salut* by Desclée & Cie, Tournai, Belgium and Bellarmin, Montreal, Canada.

Library of Congress Cataloging in Publication Data

Latourelle, René.
  Christ and the church.

  Translation of Le Christ et l'église, signes du salut.
  Includes bibliographical references.
  1. Jesus Christ—Person and offices. 2. Revelation. 3. Church
4. Vatican Council. 2d, 1962-1965. I. Title.
BT202.L3713   232   73-39673
ISBN 0-8189-0241-8

Nihil Obstat:
    Austin B. Vaughan, S.T.D.
    Censor Librorum

Imprimatur:
    James P. Mahoney
    Vicar General, Archdiocese of New York
    January 20, 1972

CONTENTS

INTRODUCTION   3

CHAPTER I: THE SECOND VATICAN COUNCIL
         AND THE SIGNS OF REVELATION   9

   1. *Christ, the Sign of revelation*   10
   2. *Christ's miracles*   12
   3. *The Church, the Sign among the nations*   15
   4. *Christian witness*   18
      The Council's declarations   19
      New terminology and a new perspective   23
   5. *Martyrdom, the supreme witness*   28
   6. *A mutation: from the nineteenth century to the
      twentieth century*   29
   7. *Towards a renewal of the theology of the signs*   33

CHAPTER II: THE ECONOMY OF THE SIGNS OF
          REVELATION   39

   1. *The signs and our call to salvation*   41
   2. *Signs of God, signs for man*   44
   3. *The signs and the message of salvation*   48
   4. *The comparative intelligibility and efficacy of the signs* 51
   5. *The action of the signs throughout history*   55
   6. *Signs and Counter-signs*   58
   7. *The present age and eschatology*   62
   8. *The interconnection and convergence of the signs*   65
   9. *The unity of the signs in Christ and the Church*   69
  10. *The total sign: Christ in the Church*   72

CHAPTER III: CHRIST, THE SIGN OF REVELATION,
ACCORDING TO THE CONSTITUTION
DEI VERBUM   75

1. Literary and doctrinal antecedents   76
2. The signs and Christ's witness   81
3. The signs and Christ's Person   86
4. Christ's glory and the Father's witness   89
5. The dialectic of the sign   93
6. Men confronted by the sign   99

CHAPTER IV: THE CHURCH, THE SIGN OF THE
COMING OF SALVATION IN JESUS
CHRIST   105

1. From the First Vatican Council to the Second   108
2. Contemporary points of resistance to the sign
   of the Church   115
3. Towards a way of approach   125
4. The Church as a mystery of faith   127
5. Paradoxes and tensions in the Church   131

CHAPTER V: THE PARADOX AND TENSIONS OF
UNITY   133

1. A complex and demanding unity   133
2. Faithfulness to the message and constant adaptation
   to time   135
3. Unity of faith and theological pluralism   138
4. Wounded unity and ecumenical desire   144
5. Unity and catholicity   152
6. The Church universal and the local Churches   154
7. Internal unity and missionary unity   158
8. Unity pursued and always in flight   159
9. Conclusion   161

CHAPTER VI: THE PARADOX AND TENSIONS OF
TEMPORALITY   163

1. *The threat of Judaism* 165
2. *The weight of the Roman Empire* 172
3. *The enslavement of the Church by feudalism* 177
4. *The greatness and ambiguity of medieval Christendom* 180
5. *The modern nations and neo-Caesarism* 184
6. *The Renaissance, humanism and cultural insertion* 187
7. *The nineteenth century and lack of insertion* 192
8. *The twentieth century: in search of new forms of presence and engagement* 198
9. *Conclusion* 207

CHAPTER VII: THE PARADOX OF SIN AND HOLINESS IN THE CHURCH. *THE PROBLEM AND WAYS OF APPROACH TO IT* 211

1. *The declarations of the magisterium* 211
2. *The nature and dimensions of the paradox* 214
3. *Ways of approach* 216
The first way of approach: the biblical conception of holiness 217
The second way of approach: the great images of the Church 220
The third way of approach: the reflection of theologians 227

CHAPTER VIII: THE PARADOX OF SIN AND HOLINESS IN THE CHURCH. *THEOLOGICAL REFLECTION* 243

1. *The dogmatic point of view* 243
The holiness of God's initiative 243
The holiness of response 246
In what sense can the Church be called "sinful"? 251
2. *The Church as an observable reality* 254

CHAPTER IX: DISCERNING THE SIGN OF THE CHURCH 265

1. *The dialectic of the sign*   265
2. *Men confronted by the sign*   272
3. *Conclusion*   283

CHAPTER X: THE WITNESS OF LIFE   285

1. *The contemporary appeal of the sign of holiness*   286
2. *The testimony of twentieth century converts*   291
3. *Holiness from the point of view of faith*   298
4. *Observable characteristics of holiness*   304
5. *The dialectic of the sign of holiness*   309
6. *The efficacy of the sign and subjective conditions*   313

INDEX OF PROPER NAMES   321

CHRIST and the CHURCH

The Problem of the Signs of Revelation

To pose the problem of the signs of revelation and salvation in Jesus Christ is equivalent to posing a problem of interpretation, to posing indeed the first and most important problem of Christian hermeneutics, that of the very *meaning* of Christianity.

For the Christian claim presents itself to the eyes of contemporary man as something at once scandalous and meaningless. He is not only asked to admit that a God exists (which is already a very great deal), but to believe that this God has emerged from his mystery and intervened in the course of human affairs through a series of events culminating in the life, death and resurrection of Jesus Christ; and he is invited to recognize that this irruption of God into human history and the living word which he addresses to men is the event *par excellence,* the only good news there is or may be.

To recognize this good news as the truth of man is to declare that our destiny goes beyond the frontiers of earthly existence and that we are called to an eternal destiny, to a very sharing in the life of God, in communion with the Father, the Son and the Spirit; it is to declare that Christ is the Son of God incarnate in the womb of Mary, that he actually rose from the dead and that we shall one day rise from the dead with him and be judged by him. To recognize the *Christian* claim as true is to allow that history has not brought us and will never bring us anything more important than Jesus Christ; for in him we have

[3]

been given salvation and there is now no other salvation for which we can hope.[1]

There is indeed at the heart of Christ's witness to himself this assumption that he is the equal of God and can claim the very prerogatives of Yahweh over the law, over institutions and over consciences. Neither more nor less, Christ by his words and by his behavior, has put himself on the same plane as God: the Father's Son, the Father's equal, sharing his secrets and his power, like him the master of life and death, demanding in his name ultimate sacrifices, laying bare consciences and pronouncing upon them, as universal Judge, the sentence of salvation or loss. Christ has constituted himself the center and object of religion. And it is undeniable that the great motive of the Jews' hostility towards him was this claim to equality with God (Jn 10:33; Mk 14:60-64).

To recognize the Christian claim is, moreover, to allow that Christ has founded a Church, as the sacrament of his saving presence among men, that he has entrusted to this Church his words and his sacraments in order to enlighten and sanctify men, and that he has given to this Church his own Spirit, the Holy Spirit, to direct it, prevent it from failing and uphold it until the end of time.

There is in the Christian claim, let us say so openly, something unheard of, something even of a provocation. Before giving any credit to pretensions such as these, contemporary man reacts with the same reflexes as the Jews did: he asks for signs (Jn 6:30-31). Before rushing into the adventure of faith, an adventure which involves life and death and his deepest desires about them, he wants quite legitimately to know who it is he is trusting himself to. He wants to be convinced that God has really entered history, and that Christ is really the manifestation of this God in human flesh. For if faith is a complete surrender of the self to God, it is not an abdication of the self into unconsciousness, leaving man deprived of his nature so that he has to fall back on fideism, unable to establish the human rightness of his choice. To undertake committing himself as ab-

1. Constitution *Dei Verbum*, n. 4.

solutely as this a man must have valid *reasons*, which can if necessary be made explicit in a coherent, discursive way. For if revelation is an act of God, faith is an act of man, and the same God who invites a man to make the decision of faith is the God who, in creating him, meant him to have a choice conformable to his dignity as a free and intelligent creature. The language of God's revelation does not destroy the language of his creation.

Classical apologetics expresses this legitimate demand of man and human reason in the face of the message of the gospel by explaining that we must be able to establish the *credibility* of the Christian revelation, or, from the point of view of the believer as it were, the *reasonableness* of the option of faith. The Christian assertion, though of things in themselves hidden and mysterious, is nevertheless *believable*, because we have "very certain signs of the divine origin of the Christian religion." [2] These signs—miracles, prophecies, the message itself, the presence of holiness, the resurrection of Christ—are for man motives of credibility. If we rely on them, and on the certainty founded on them, that is the certainty that God has spoken to men, the choice of faith is not made blindly or imprudently, but is a completely rational act of recognition, a human choice, made by an intelligence which has reasons for making it and by a will which decides to make it in the light of these reasons seen as valid.

In language more familiar to man today, and also more evocative, we might say that the problem of man confronted with the message of the gospel presents itself as a problem of *meaning*. The question is, has the central Christian statement that God is present and manifested in Jesus Christ any *meaning?* Is it a coherent, acceptable, intelligible statement? Are there any indications in history that an event as astonishing as this has occurred? And what degree of consistency have these indications? And more than this, is it true that Christ through his life and what he says to us really *mediates meaning*, in what concerns man and the mystery of man? Is it true that in him

2. DS 3009, 3539, 3876.

and through him man comes to situate himself, to understand himself, to achieve himself and even to go beyond himself? And finally, is the claim of the Church to be among men the sign that salvation has come in Jesus Christ, a claim that can be sustained? Is it a claim for which there is any valid support to be found in facts? Is it a claim for which there is any critical justification in the eyes of men today? And if it is true that Christ has sent his Spirit into the world to transform the heart of man into the heart of a son, how is the Spirit of Christ manifested in a concrete way in history through his effective presence in the Church?

This present book, as will be apparent, touches on the classical problem in fundamental theology, the problem of the signs of revelation, but from the point of view of an inquiry into the meaning of Christianity and the meaning of what the Christian says.

The first chapter stresses how the Second Vatican Council, by a process of personalization and interiorization which is characteristic of its work, has brought back all the signs of revelation to Christ and the Church, as to two shining points of focus, in which all the particular signs converge and emit their light. Chapter 2 tries to show how the signs of revelation, far from being gaps in the coherence and intelligibility of a world which man is coming better and better to understand in its totality, constitute on the contrary an economy of the highest degree of intelligibility, marvellously adapted to a revelation which comes to us through the mediation of sense and history, and marvellously adapted also to the inner nature of man to whom this revelation is made. Chapter 3, with the support of the constitution Dei Verbum, presents Christ as at once the epiphany of God in the flesh and the sign of the authenticity of this epiphany. The six following chapters are devoted to the sign of the Church. Here again the sign is to be sought not so much in a series of absolute attributes, manifesting directly the Church's transcendence, as in an ensemble of paradoxes and tensions the secret of whose intelligibility has to be discovered. The last chapter explores at a deeper level one aspect of the sign of the Church, the evidence of holiness of life, the sign *par excellence* of the supernatural which transforms the human condition, the very light cast by this transformation which the gospel has brought about.[3]

So this preliminary study touches on only two of the signs of Christianity, Christ and the Church. A study of the whole would have to go on to re-examine and consider each of the particular signs implicitly contained in the two fundamental signs studied here. Here I have set out only to illustrate a *perspective*, proposed by the Second Vatican Council, and a *method* for treating the problem of the signs of revelation in the right way.

---

3. Chapter I appeared in *Gregorianum*, 49 (1968): 225-252. Chapter 2 appeared in *Sciences Ecclésiastiques*, 19 (1967): 7-31. Chapter 3, after appearing first in *Gregorianum*, 47 (1966): 685-709, was reshaped and developed. Chapter 10 appeared first in *Gregorianum*, 46 (1965): 36-65, and has similarly been reshaped. The other chapters are all published here for the first time.

CHAPTER I

The Second Vatican Council and the Signs of Revelation

The Second Vatican Council, which revitalized so many doctrinal themes, was also the Council of "the spiritual renewal of signs": the "signs of the times," and especially the signs of salvation in Jesus Christ.[1] Between the First and Second Vatican Councils a profound change took place, a change from a perspective of object to a perspective of person, from a perspective which looked at things from outside to a perspective which looked at them from within. *Dei verbum* and *Lumen gentium* constitute the main evidence of this process of personalization and interiorization.

The constitution *Dei verbum* stressed the personalist and Christocentric character of revelation, and at the same time personalized the presentation of signs. The great sign of revelation in history is Christ himself. A better understanding of the sacramental structure of revelation (in both word and deed) and of the economy of its transmission through the centuries (by the *life* of the Church as well as by her teaching) has made us grasp all the importance of the Christian life as a sign that salvation has come into the world. From Pentecost to the par-

---

1. G. Martelet, *Les Idées maîtresses de Vatican II* (Paris, 1966), p. 131.

ousia, the great sign of the setting up of the kingdom in Jesus
Christ is this very transformation of man into a new creature,
into the Father's son. *Lumen gentium,* by binding closely together again the gospel and life according to the gospel, has
interiorized and personalized the reality of signs.

It is the aim of the present chapter to stress the importance
of this teaching of the Council on the signs of revelation. The
chapter begins with an inventory of texts, emphasizing changes
in perspective and the motives by which they are inspired; then
it indicates the course taken from the nineteenth to the twentieth
century in the presentation of the signs; and finally it tries to
show how the Council can be the point of departure for a profound renewal in the theology of the signs.

1. Christ, the Sign of revelation

The originality of the constitution *Dei verbum* in what concerns the signs of revelation is that it presents Christ as being
at the same time the supreme Revealer and the supreme Sign of
revelation, the Mystery and the Sign of the Mystery.[2] It is
true that earlier documents[3] also reattach the signs of revelation to Christ himself, but they relate them specially to his
teaching. Just as the divine origin of the teaching of Moses and
the prophets was attested by the miracles which they performed and the predictions which they made, so Christ's miracles
and prophecies attest the divine origin of his message and his
mission.

This way of presenting signs, valid for the revelation of the
two Testaments as a whole, does not take sufficient account of
the *unique case* which Christ represents in the history of revelation. Christ is God's representative, not as a mere prophet or

---

2. R. Latourelle, "Le Christ Signe de la Révélation selon la Constitution
Dei Verbum," Gregorianum, 47 (1966): 685-709: J. Ratzinger, in: *Das
Zweite Vatikanische Konzil,* Vol. II, *Lexikon für Theologie und Kirche,* p.
511.

3. For example, the encyclical *Qui pluribus* in 1846 (Denzinger-
Schönmetzer, n. 2779), and the First Vatican Council in 1870 (Denzinger-
Schönmetzer, n. 3009).

human Messiah, but in virtue of being the Father's Son, sharing with the Father Wisdom and Power and Love. Hence Christ's miracles are the works of the Son as they are the works of the Father. They witness to the fact that Christ is among us with the power of Yahweh. "As the Father raises the dead and gives them life, so also the Son gives life to whom he wills" (Jn 5:21). To see Christ's action is to see the Father present in the Son, exercising through the works of the Son his own creative and saving work (Jn 14:9-10); it is to see at once the Son and the Father whom he reveals.

If Christ is God among us, "signs" are not exterior to Christ and his revelation: they emanate from this personal center which is Christ, and their purpose is to lead men to identify this personal center as divine. It is Christ as a whole who is the Sign of the Mystery constituted by him, and he is himself the Sign which demands to be deciphered. All the partial signs (miracles, prophecies, "message," holiness, resurrection) can be understood only if they are referred to Christ who addresses them to us: they are the manifestation of his being in its divinity.

The Council grasped and described perfectly this specificness of revelation in Jesus Christ. In a mere single phrase, pregnant with meaning, *Dei verbum* presents Christ as being the Sign which at once reveals God and reveals himself *as God.* "It is he then—to see him is to see the Father (cf. Jn 14:9)—who through his whole presence and the manifestation which he makes of himself, through his words and his actions, his signs and his miracles, but especially through his death and glorious resurrection from the dead, and his sending of the Spirit of truth, gives to revelation its complete fulfillment and the *confirmation* of divine witness, attesting to the fact that God himself is with us to save us from the darkness of sin and death, and raise us up to everlasting life." [4]

So Christ, the incarnate Word, is at once the epiphany of

---

4. "Quapropter Ipse, quem qui videt, videt et Patrem (cf. Jn 14, 9), tota suiipsius praesentia ac manifestatione, verbis et operibus, signis et miraculis, praesertim autem morte sua et gloriosa ex mortuis resurrectione, misso tandem Spiritu veritatis, revelationem complendo perficit ac testi-

the Father and the veiled epiphany of the Son's glory. Through the *same realities* of his life, he is the Revealer of the Father and witnesses to himself as such. Christ reveals through his works, but there is in his works, particularly in his miracles and resurrection, a deployment of power, witnessing to the fact that in him the power of Yahweh is in operation. Christ reveals through his words, but there is in his teaching such wisdom, such depth, such consonance with the mystery of God and the mystery of man that this teaching appears as the doctrine of the Father, the word of the Father, as Christ affirms. Christ reveals the Father's love, but there is, in his acts of mercy and forgiveness, in his attitude towards sinners, in the gift of himself even to the sacrifice of his life, the expression of a charity which is its own witness that in the charity of Christ we have known the charity of God. This radiance of power and wisdom and love, which is, properly speaking, the glory of Christ, attests that he really is *God-with-us,* come among men to deliver them from sin and raise them up to everlasting life. It is by his Incarnation that the Son manifests the Father and his saving design; it is also by means of the Incarnation that men identify Christ as the Father's Son. Christ's mode of action announces his Godhead. In him the witnesses of being and acting answer to each other as realities of the same magnitude. We are aware that the signs arc inseparable from the Person whom they aim, by means of the characteristics observed, to identify and make known. Christ is of himself the Sign of the authenticity of the revelation which he is in Person.[5]

2. Christ's miracles

Chapter IV of the schema *De deposito fidei pure custodiendo* contained five paragraphs on the signs of revelation[6]: the first

---

monio divino confirmat, Deum nempe nobiscum esse ad nos ex peccati mortisque tenebris liberandos et in aeternam vitam resuscitandos" (Constitution *Dei verbum* on Revelation, n. 4).

5. R. Latourelle, "Le Christ Signe de la Révélation selon la Constitution *Dei verbum,*" *Gregorianum,* 47 (1966): 704.
6. Paragraphs 23, 24, 25, 26, 27.

on exterior signs in general; the second on miracles and prophecies; the third on the resurrection, the messianic prophecies and Christ himself; the fourth on the sign of the Church; the last on interior signs. Of these paragraphs the Council retained only the third, on Christ, giving it, moreover, a different orientation. The other paragraphs were omitted, no doubt because they were judged merely to duplicate the teaching of the First Vatican Council, which is very definite and already known.

The rare texts of the Second Vatican Council which speak of miracles are characterized by the fact that they always reattach these closely to the person of Christ. We have already noticed how the constitution *Dei verbum* assigns to the same realities in Christ's life (miracles and the resurrection for instance) a function which is revelatory and confirmative at the same time.[7]

In the constitution on the Church and in the decree on the missions, miracles are bound up with the theme of the *kingdom*. "Above all," observes *Lumen gentium,* "the kingdom manifests itself in the very person of Christ, Son of God and Son of man, who came to serve and to give his life as a ransom for many."[8] The kingdom of God shines before the eyes of men "in Christ's words and actions and presence.... Similarly the miracles of Jesus are a proof that the kingdom has come already upon earth" (LG 5). Cures and exorcisms are signs that the

---

7. Constitution *Dei verbum* on Revelation, n. 4.

8. Constitution *Lumen gentium* on the Church, n. 5. From now on the following abbreviations will be used for conciliar texts: *Dei verbum* on revelation, DV; *Lumen gentium* on the Church, LG; *Sacrosanctum Concilium* on the liturgy, SC; *Gaudium et spes* on the Church in the modern world, GS; *Ad gentes* on missions, AG; *Christus Dominus* on the pastoral office of bishops, CD; *Presbyterorum Ordinis* on the life and ministry of priests, PO; *Optatam totius* on the formation of priests, OT; *Perfectae caritatis* on the renewal and adaptation of the religious life, PC; *Apostolicam actuositatem* on the apostolate of the laity, AA; *Unitatis redintegratio* on ecumenism, UR; *Orientalium Ecclesiarum* on the Eastern Catholic Churches, OE; *Dignitatis humanae* on religious liberty, DH; *Gravissimum educationis* on Christian education, GE. The figure which follows the abbreviation refers to the official numbering of sections in the conciliar texts.

prevailing power of Satan is in dissolution, and that the reign of God has arrived. Wherever Christ is, the power of salvation and the life of the living God are at work.[9] The decree *Ad gentes* develops the same theme: "Christ went about all the towns and villages curing every kind of sickness and infirmity as as a sign that the kingdom of God had come" (AG 12).

The decree on religious liberty stresses the objective value of the signs of revelation as well as the freedom allowed to man when he is confronted by them. God invites him to faith and salvation, but does not coerce him in any way. "This is to be seen at its highest in Christ Jesus, in whom God perfectly manifested himself and his ways with men. For Christ, our Lord and Master, gentle and humble of heart, invited and drew his disciples to him with patience. Certainly he *supported* and *confirmed* his preaching by miracles, but it was to arouse and strengthen the faith of those who heard him, not to exert coercion over them" (DH 11). In a note on this passage the decree refers to the encyclical *Ecclesiam suam* of 6 August 1964.

In this encyclical Paul VI suggests that the dialogue of salvation and revelation is the prototype of the dialogue of the Church with the world. Describing its characteristics or properties, he observes that it was a dialogue of unheard of importance, since it was salvation which was at stake, and yet it was a dialogue in which there was an infinite respect for human freedom: "The dialogue of salvation constrained no one to accept what it offered; it was a formidable call by love which, if it constituted a fearful responsibility for those to whom it was addressed, still left them free to correspond with it or to refuse it." [10] Apropos of this, moreover, the encyclical points out that the signs of revelation do not curb man's freedom, but are offered to him rather as a *help* to a free and meritorious assent. The dialogue of salvation, continues the encyclical, "adapts the

---

9. R. Latourelle, *Théologie de la Révélation* (third edition, Bruges and Paris, 1969), pp. 470-472: trans., *Theology of Revelation* (Alba House, New York, 1966), pp. 391-2.

10. Paulus VI, *Ecclesiam suam*, AAS 56 (1964), 642.

quantity (Mt 12:38f) and demonstrative force (Mt 13:13f) of its signs even to the demands and spiritual dispositions of its hearers so as to help them to assent freely to revelation without taking from them the virtue of doing so." [11]

It is the first time that the magisterium of the Church has stressed *to this degree* the respect for human freedom in the economy of signs. God has multiplied the indications of his intervention in history, yet with discretion, leaving to man both freedom and merit, in responding to the message of salvation as in responding to the signs by which the divine origin of this message is attested. The signs are not compulsions, but God's *gifts* and *helps*. Their confirmatory value is real, but their way of acting on man does not violate his liberty. They invite him to, and sustain him in, the free trial and decision of his faith.

3. *The Church, the Sign among the nations*

In *Lumen gentium* the Council stresses the Mystery of the Church rather than the Church as a motive of credibility. Since the First Vatican Council, whose work remained unfinished because of contemporary circumstances, we have indeed felt in urgent need of an account of the Church which would envisage her not merely as an historical fact but as an object of faith, an account which would try to fathom the Mystery of her being through an investigation setting out from the twin sources of revelation and her own life in the Spirit. In the depths of her Mystery, the Church is the sacrament or sign of salvation, for she represents and communicates the grace of salvation. She is the very salvation of Christ in the visible form of a social body. She makes this salvation present and effective, and it is her theandric structure which lies at the basis of her capacity to become a motive of credibility. When her visibility becomes as it were luminous, that is to say when the glory which shines in the face of Christ is reflected in the Church, then she becomes the transparent Sign of her divine origin.

---

11. *Ibid.,* 642-643.

At first sight, and simply from a terminological point of view, this theme of the Church as the sign among the nations does not seem to have any considerable place in the conciliar documents. Sometimes it is a question of very general indications. For instance speaking of the separated Christian communities, the Council reminds Catholics of their heavy responsibility in this matter and urges them "to purify and renew themselves so that the sign of Christ may shine more brightly in the face of the Church" (LG 15; quoted in GS 43).

Other passages allude directly to the text of the previous Council.[12] The constitution on the liturgy for example declares that "since the liturgy daily builds those within the Church into a holy temple in the Lord, a dwelling place of God in the Spirit (Eph 2:21-22), until they become fully mature with the fullness of Christ (Eph 4:13), it strengthens in a marvellous way their power to make Christ known, showing the Church to those outside her as a sign lifted up before the nations (Is 11:12), beneath which the children of God who are scattered abroad may be gathered together in unity (Jn 11:52) until there is only one fold and one shepherd" (SC 2). So liturgical life, and especially sacramental life, sanctifies Christians, and when this holiness shines in them, it makes of the community united in love a sign which draws towards it those who see it.

In the constitution on the Church, the Council, again referring to its predecessor, remarks that in the saints "God manifests to men in a living way his presence and his countenance. In them God himself speaks to us, gives us a sign of his kingdom and draws us powerfully towards it, so great is the cloud of witnesses by which we are surrounded (Heb 12:1)

---

12. "Ecclesia per se ipsa, ob suam nempe admirabilem propagationem, eximiam sanctitatem et inexhaustam in omnibus bonis foecunditatem, ob catholicam unitatem invictamque stabilitatem magnum quoddam et perpetuum est motivum credibilitatis et divinae suae legationis testimonium irrefragabile. Quo fit, ut ipsa veluti signum levatum in nationes (cf. Is 11, 12) et ad se invitet, qui nondum crediderunt, et filios suos certiores faciat, firmissimo niti fundamento fidem, quem profitentur" (Denzinger-Schönmetzer, nn. 3013-3014).

and so great is their testimony to the truth of the gospel" (LG 50. Cf., Denzinger-Schönmetzer, n. 3013).

The decree on missions asks all Christians to undertake the responsibility of spreading the gospel throughout the world. "Their first and most important duty in spreading the faith is to live deeply their own Christian life. For their enthusiasm in the service of God and their love for others will bring a new breath of spiritual life to the whole Church, so that she will appear like a sign lifted up before the nations (Is 11:12), the light of the world (Mt 5:14) and the salt of the earth" (Mt 5:13; AG 36).

Finally the decree on ecumenism stresses that the living unity of Christians "in professing one faith, in celebrating divine worship in common, and in brotherly concord among themselves" makes the Church "like a sign lifted up before the nations" (UR 2). The division of Christians on the contrary "is a scandal to the world," and "does harm to the holy cause of preaching the gospel to every creature" (UR 1).

In these conciliar declarations certain characteristics of the sign of the Church, as it was described by the First Vatican Council, are left in the shade or even omitted altogether—the wonderful spread of the Church, for instance, or her unshakable stability. The sign of the Church is brought back in practice to the sign of *unity in charity*. When the inner life of the Church, and especially her sacramental life and the life of the theological virtues, becomes intense, then she draws men's eyes toward her and becomes for the world the sign of the setting up of the kingdom of God, the sign of the coming of salvation in Jesus Christ. In reality the Second Vatican Council let slip no element of the sign of the Church as described by the First: it retrieved them all, but in concentrating them and reducing them to their essentials. For the unity it describes is a *dynamic* unity, which works towards the bringing together of all peoples, and which time cannot dissolve.[13] So it recovers the First Vatican Council's

---

13. A theme especially developed in *The decree on missions* and *The decree on ecumenism*.

notions of Catholic unity, admirable propagation and stability.
The charity of which it speaks is an active and ingenious charity,
eager to serve all men; and it is a charity which reaches its
perfection in the heroism of the saints. So the notions of eminent
holiness and fruitfulness in all good are recovered too. The
Church is a community of love brought together by Christ and
his Spirit in unity and charity. This community is a sign of
the coming of salvation among men in the measure in which
it reflects in our world the unity of love in the life of God, the
life which is both one and three.

4. *Christian witness*

If the letter of the text in which the First Vatican Council
proposes the Church as "a great and perpetual motive of credibility" is not to be found in the Second, except in the form of
brief and concentrated references, we must not for that conclude
that this sign has been devaluated. It is the contrary which is
true. But anxious not to fall into the verbal triumphalism
so often denounced in the course of its sessions, and more conscious than ever of the misunderstandings, mistakes and sins
of the members of the Church, the *Council of the Church*, which
is also the Council of *ecumenism* and of *mission*, went to the
essential thing. The sign of the Church, definitively speaking,
is the sign of unity in charity. And the Church in question is
not an abstraction, situated somewhere outside Christian people
themselves: it is the whole People of God and those who make it
up.

The process of *personalization,* which has reattached all the
signs of historical revelation to the personal center which is
Christ himself, has been equally called into play in the case
of the sign of the Church: it is Christians themselves by their
life of holiness, and communities of Christians by their life
of unity and charity, who pose the sign of the Church. It is
by living perfectly their condition as sons and daughters of
the Father, redeemed by Christ and sanctified by the Spirit,
that Christians will make others understand that the salvation
proclaimed and merited by Christ is really among us, since

man's disobedient and rebellious heart is changed into a filial and obedient heart. The Spirit has been given; for the new man, the Christian, lives and acts under the influence of the Spirit.

This concentration and personalization brought about by the Second Vatican Council is recorded in a new term: *witness*. What its predecessor understood by the sign of the Church is henceforward to be sought in the category of witness. Once this transposition has been made, it is obvious that the sign of the Church, far from being the poor relation among signs, is valued more than ever before. The theme of witness is in fact one of the major and privileged themes of the Council. As a *leitmotif*, it reappears in all the constitutions and in all the decrees. Just as Christ's disciples are called by God, each one, according to his state, to a holiness whose perfection is that of the Father (LG 39-42), all are equally called to *witness*, through the transformation of their lives, to the reality of the salvation given in Jesus Christ (LG 35 and 12; GE 2). The word *witness* recurs more than a hundred times in different conciliar documents. Add to this number all the equivalent expressions, such as "an authentically Christian life," "faithfulness to the gospel," "a perfect living of the Christian life," "the example of life" and so on, and there is no doubt that in the eyes of the Council, *witness* is, for the Christian, an obligation no less important than that of *sanctifying himself*.

The Council's declarations

Witness should take a form at once *individual* and *common*. It is the *People of God* in its entirety which must diffuse its living witness through a life which is intensely that of the theological virtues (LG 12). But "since the People of God lives in communities, especially in diocesan and parish communities, and it is in these communities that it is in a sense visible, it is also to these communities that it belongs to witness to Christ among the nations (AG 37 & 6; CD 30). In mission countries, "the whole of the young Church should give a single, steadfast and living witness to Christ, so that she may be a clear sign of the salvation which has come to us in Christ" (AG 21). When she leads "a life worthy of the calling to which she has been called," she "becomes a sign of God's presence in the world" (AG 15).

Every Christian grouping is asked, according to its own social situation, to live the gospel, and so to make known that salvation has touched the human race to transform it and give it new life. Bishops and pastors are to present to the world an image of the Church which will enable men to judge of the truth and force of the gospel. "In union with religious and with all the faithful of their dioceses, they are to give proof in word and deed, that the Church, by her very presence with all the gifts she brings, is an inexhaustible source of those energies of which the world today stands in greatest need" (GS 43). *Parish priests* in particular "are so to preach the word of God that their people, rooted in faith, hope and charity, grow up in Christ, and the Christian community bears the witness of love which was the Lord's commandment" (CD 30). *Priests* "are to offer to all a living witness to God" (LG 41). They "should, by their everyday behavior and their care for others, present to believers and to unbelievers, to Catholics and to non-Catholics, the face of a truly priestly and pastoral ministry and bear witness to all men of the truth and the life which is Christ" (LG 28; PO 3). Let all *religious,* declares the Council, "by integrity of faith, by charity towards God and their neighbor, by love of the cross and hope of the glory which is to come, spread the good news of Christ through the entire world, so that their witness may be seen by all men, and our Father in heaven glorified" (PC 25).

The *laity* are called to this same witness of holiness of life. Each one of them "is to be a witness before the world of the resurrection and life of the Lord Jesus Christ, and a sign of the living God" (LG 38). If the laity "are consecrated a royal priesthood and a holy nation (I Pet 2:4-10), it is to make all that they do a spiritual offering, and to bear witness to Christ everywhere upon earth." [14] In their homes husbands and wives

---

14. AA 3; see also 2, 6, 13, 14, 17, 29, 31; LG 31, 35; GS 43; AG 21.

are to be witnesses of the faith and love of Christ, to each other and to their children (LG 35). The Christian family "by its example and witness is to convince the world of sin and give light to those who seek the truth" (LG 35). *Teachers* in schools "are to bear witness, by their life as well as by their teaching, to the one Master, who is Christ" (GE 8).

It is in mission countries above all that the life of Christians in unity and charity becomes an especially impelling sign; for then the whole Church as the presence and manifestation of Christ is concentrated there. The first among them, the *missionary*, "by a life which is authentically that of the gospel, by great patience and forbearance, by gentleness and genuine charity (2 Cor 6:4f.) must bear witness to his Lord, even, if need be, to the shedding of his blood" (AG 24). In this rôle of witness, the *laity* have the same responsibility as the missionary himself: "for all Christians, wherever they may be, are bound to make known by the example of their lives and the witness of their speech the new man they have put on in baptism, and the power of the Holy Spirit who, in confirmation, has given them strength" (AG 11).

This general theme of witness is often defined in terms which make its object and orientation more precise. The most common of these are charity, humility, service, unity and poverty.

Since the Church is a mystery of communion, Christians are asked to bear "the witness of *charity* which is the Lord's commandment to us" (CD 30; LG 42). Charity to one's neighbor, when it is genuine and effective, may be called *service*. So the Council sees service, like witness, as something to which all the different groups of Christians are obliged: bishops (LG 24), priests,[15] religious (LG 42, 46), the laity (AA 1; GS 93). The constitution *Gaudium et spes* calls to mind in the same breath the Church's mission to witness, to save and to serve. The Church "has only one end: to continue, under the inspiration of the Comforter the work of Christ, who came into the world to bear

---

15. PO 1, 2, 11, 15, 16. In section II the decree says that the life of priests should give "a clear and manifest witness to the spirit of service and to an Easter joy in the risen Christ."

witness to the truth, to save not to condemn, to serve not to be
served (GS 3). Finally, rightly concerned to remove the scandal
created by the divisions among Christians, who are all members of the religion of charity, the Council insists on the witness
of *unity* which Christ's disciples should give. Several constitutions
and decrees reflect this desire for unity which is at work in the
Church: the unity of Catholics among themselves (*The constitution on the Church*), the unity of all Christians (*The decree
on ecumenism*), the unity of all men in Christ (*The decree on
missions*), the unity of the whole human family (*The constitution on the Church in the world*). "All the baptized . . . are
assembled in one, in order to bear unanimous witness before
the nations to Christ their Lord" (AG 6). Their division, on
the contrary, "is a scandal to the world, and puts an obstacle
in the way of the most holy of all causes, that of preaching the
gospel to every creature" (UR 1).

So, in the thought of the Second Vatican Council, the great
sign of the coming of salvation into the world is the life of unity
and charity lived by Christians themselves, the witness of a
genuinely filial life. Yet, on the other hand, the Council gives
only the most summary indications of the *nature* and *dynamism*
of this witness.

In one series of texts, it appears that to witness to Christ
is to live intensely the life of the theological virtues. The holy
People of God "diffuses its living witness above all by a life
of faith and charity" (LG 12). The laity are asked "to make
Christ known to others principally by the witness of their own
lives, by the light of faith, hope and charity which they shed
around them (LG 31; AA 4). In another series of texts the
same theme is taken up again, but in a more detailed way.
Speaking of the apostolate of the laity in "the context of their
work, their profession, their studies, their place of residence,
their leisure activities, their social life" the Council declares that
"the laity fulfill this mission of the Church above all by that
agreement between their life and their faith which makes of
them the light of the world" (AA 13). In *The constitution on
the Church*, it says that "the laity become heralds of the faith
in things hoped for (Heb 11:1), if they resolutely join a life

of faith to the profession of faith" (LG 35). Finally, in *The decree on the missions,* the Council says that "all Christians, wherever they may be, are bound to make known by the example of their lives and the witness of their speech the new man they have put on". (AG 11).

The Council, that is, describes witness as an existential accord between faith professed and faith lived. Witness is born of faith accredited by holiness of life. When he really witnesses, a man *commits himself to what he says,* freely and deliberately implicates himself in it. To witness then to his faith in Christ is to do as the apostles did, to proclaim the gospel as the truth and salvation of mankind, and at the same time to surrender to Christ, recognized as the supreme value, his own day to day existence.

It is in the same strain of sober matter of fact that the Council speaks of the dynamism of witness as a sign. On the one hand it recognizes the authenticity and demonstrative value of witness as a sign. In the lives of the saints, says *Lumen gentium,* God "gives us a sign of his kingdom and draws us powerfully towards it, so great is the cloud of witnesses by which we are surrounded (Heb 12:1) and so great is their testimony to the truth of the gospel" (LG 50). Nevertheless this sign does not in any way violate man's freedom: it acts by attraction, drawing him towards it as a good. In *The decree on the laity,* the Council remarks that the laity, by the witness of their life, "*dispose* men's hearts unconsciously to the action of saving grace" (AA 13); they "*draw* men to faith and to God" (AA 6); they "lead men on towards Christ" (AA 4). The Council does not explain beyond this the action of witness as a sign.

New terminology and a new perspective

What is new in the conciliar declarations is not the doctrine itself, but the way of expressing it: there are new words and a new emphasis. Yet this new terminology is indicative of a new perspective and new preoccupations in the Church.

The doctrine itself is the traditional doctrine. The God of

the Old Testament, proclaiming the dispensation to come, had already declared through the mouth of Ezekiel, "A new heart I will give you, and a new spirit I will put within you ... I will put my spirit within you" (Ez 36:26-27). This new Spirit is the Spirit of love, who makes us live in charity, the Spirit of the Father and the Son. Christ himself proposed this life of charity as the sign by which the true disciples of the kingdom he had just founded would be recognized. "A new commandment I give to you, that you love one another. Even as I have loved you, that you also love one another. By this all men will know that you are my disciples, if you have love for one another" (Jn 13:34-35; 17:22-23; 1 Jn 4:7). "God is love, and he who lives in love lives in God and God in him" (1 Jn 4:16). It is through love that man is holy as God is holy. The early Church, faithful to the Lord's commandment, was defined as a community of charity: "The multitude of believers had but one heart and one soul" (Acts 4:32). When the Church spread through the Graeco-Roman world, she included slaves and free men, rich and poor, the ignorant and the learned, representatives of all professions and all races (Phoenicians, Syrians, Persians, Egyptians, Africans, Asiatics and so on). Always the same characteristic distinguished the Christian community: charity.

The Church has never ceased to regard the union of Christians in charity as the sign *par excellence* of the coming of the Word of salvation into the world. But the terminology which serves to express this idea varies with the theological preoccupations of the time, and with the men who live and express the ideal. So the Greek fathers, whose theology stresses wherever possible the divinity of Christ, see the perfection of Christian life as a deiformization. The Latin fathers see holiness in the exercise of the theological and moral virtues. For the Middle Ages, sensitive as they were to the humanity of Christ (a St. Bernard or a St. Francis for instance), the perfect Christian was the one who imitated Christ in his earthly life. St. Ignatius of Loyola insists on the seeking and fulfilling of God's will, on submission to Christ and to his Spirit. St. John of the Cross sees holiness in the transforming union, with Christ, with God.

Bérulle sees it in imitating Christ's *states*. For St. Francis de Sales the perfect Christian is the one whose life is an example to his neighbor.

To indicate this holiness of life through which God gives us a sign of the setting-up of his kingdom in Jesus Christ (LG 50), the Second Vatican Council uses, in preference to all others, the expression, *witness of life,* and speaks of *living witnesses* to Christ. This privileged use of the category of witness is to be understood, it would seem, in the context of the Council's teaching on revelation, and in relationship to the mentality of man today.

We have already noticed the Council's obvious concern to *personalize* revelation, and consequently the signs of revelation. But there is more to the matter than that. In stressing the value, among signs, of the witness of life, the Council is following its own teaching on the *economy* of revelation. The constitution *Dei verbum* indeed describes revelation, in its historical sense, as an economy sacramental in structure, that is, an economy characterized by a deep and indissoluble union of *events* and *words* (DV 2). God intervenes in history, and tells us the meaning of his intervention; he acts, and comments on the meaning of his action. *Dei verbum* applies to both the Old and the New Testaments this general structure of revelation. "God reveals himself in words and in action, to the people of his choice" (DV 14). Under the new covenant, Christ is at the same time the Event, and the Interpreter *par excellence* of the Event. In him, revelation reaches its objective climax, since he is the Mystery in person, and also its climax as an economy. Christ, the epiphany of the Father, reveals "through his words and through his works," which are precisely and in the proper sense the words and works of God in human form (DV 4).

Since revelation is essentially the revelation of the personal Mystery of God through the works and words of the Word made flesh, its *transmission* is accomplished according to the same economy. Just as revelation in Christ was a *doing* and a *teaching*, so its transmission by the apostles was at the same time a *teaching* and a *life*. The apostles obeyed Christ's commandment to preach the gospel to every creature, by transmitting "through oral preaching, through example and through institutions" what they "had learnt from the lips of Christ when they lived with him and saw him act" (DV 7). Because the revelation Christ brought was the revelation of the Mystery of his life as the Son, and of the mystery of our adoptive sonship in him, this revelation could not be simply verbal and notional: it had to take the form of a *witness of life*.

What is transmitted to the People of God by the apostles, *Dei verbum* stresses, moreover, "includes everything which contributes to the holiness of its life and the increase of its faith, so that the Church is perpetuated in her doctrine, in her life and in her worship, and transmits to each generation all that she herself is and all that she believes" (DV 6). What is transmitted is much more than a teaching; what is transmitted is a *life*. This life has been communicated to the Church so that the whole Church, clergy and laity, may live it and perpetuate it through the centuries. It is the whole Christian People which is asked "to maintain, to exercise and to profess the faith which it has received" (DV 10). It is the whole Christian community which must, by its faith *professed* and *lived*, assume the responsibility for the faithful transmission of the faith.

In this way the economy of words and deeds continues until the parousia. Preaching and witness of life are inseparable. The category of witness is closely bound up with the very economy of revelation, in its structure and in its transmission through the centuries. When witness becomes luminous, that is to say, when the gospel and life according to the gospel coincide, witness becomes a *sign*. Witness of life possesses then a double function: it is a *means* by which revelation is transmitted, and a *sign* that the gospel is really the word of salvation, since it saves men and makes them holy. The sign of the gospel itself and the sign of life lived according to the gospel, by the mutual support which they give to each other, constitute a new unity, a new sign, whose dynamism is the result of the interaction of the dynamism of each.

The recourse on the part of the Council to the category

of witness is a manifestation also of its concern to speak in a language which corresponds to the way in which the man of the twentieth century thinks and feels. This man, formed as he is in the context of personalist and existentialist thought, has a revulsion against holiness conceived as the platonic reflection of an abstract idea. If holiness has any meaning at all for him it is as an experience of total and active consecration to God and to men. But to speak of holiness in terms of witness is precisely to suggest that it involves the whole of a man and the whole of his life in a commitment to another person, that is to God in his Son, Jesus Christ; and it is to suggest the supreme hazard, the giving of a man's life to the point of martyrdom. Looked at from this point of view, holiness is truly a *sign*, but at the level of the person. The sign is in the very transformation of a man into a new creature, given life by the Spirit of God.

This sign of the coming of salvation in the witness of a life totally committed certainly seems to be the one which exercises most influence over man today, because it answers best to his mentality. Twentieth century man is jealous of his *autonomy*. He wants to be free to choose, and to refuse. He has a horror of a religion in which he can discern the least appearance of constraint. And what characterizes witness as a sign is precisely its discretion: it acts by attraction, without doing violence to anyone's freedom. Again, twentieth century man is the man of *efficiency*. In his eyes men and institutions are worth what their results are worth. He has a loathing for proclamations and speeches. What he asks for are actions, facts. And in the witness of a life which is authentically Christian, gospel and life answer for each other. Life itself proves the title of the good news: the human condition can be changed because it has in fact been changed.[16] And in the end, though in his mastery over techniques and over the material universe, contemporary man may seem omnipotent, he is at the same time psychologically *fragile*. Before suffering and death he is in fear and agony (cf. Camus,

---

16. R. Latourelle, "La testimonianza della vita segno di salvezza," in: *Laici sulle vie del Concilio* (Assisi, 1966), pp. 389-394.

Sartre and Sagan). That is why meeting with an existence which radiates love and peace and joy, in spite of suffering and death, excites of itself in him a secret desire to share this fullness of life.

It may be added finally that in a pluralist and secularized society, where there exist less and less those zones of organized Christian life once constituted by medieval Christendom and by the Catholic nations of the modern world, witness *of life* takes on a singularly urgent character. Where the Church as an institution has been driven out or is absent, she is found again in the life of the Christian. It is he who, by his *style of life*, much more than by his words, must bear witness to the presence of salvation in the world. By his love and service of his neighbor, by the different way in which he lives their common situation, he should lead men to ask themselves what is the spirit which inspires him, and where its source may be. It can happen then that meeting Christ in this living witness may penetrate to the innermost depths of those who surround him, and lead them on to the experience of salvation in Jesus Christ.

5. *Martyrdom, the supreme witness*

In the way of witness, martyrdom represents the point of furthest advance; for it is the sign of the greatest love. The Council returns several times to the necessity and value in the Christian economy of this supreme witness.

Like Christ, the good Shepherd who has given his life for his sheep, the *apostles* and *martyrs* have given "the supreme witness to faith and charity" (LG 50). In the same way, *priests* must be "ready to go as far as the supreme sacrifice after the example of those who even in our own time have not hesitated to give their lives" (PO 13). The *missionary*, by a life wholly conformed to that of the Church, "must bear witness to his Lord, even, if need be, to the shedding of his blood" (AG 24). All *Christians*, as disciples of Christ, should be ready for this same witness. "Since Jesus, the Son of God, manifested his love by giving his life for us, no one shows greater love than

he who gives his life for Jesus and for his brothers (cf. 1
Jn 3:16; Jn 15:13). To give this supreme witness to love before
all men and especially before their persecutors, some Christians
have been called from the earliest times and will always be
called . . . . And if martyrdom is granted to only a few, all
nevertheless should be ready to confess Christ before men,
and, in the midst of the persecutions which are never lacking
to the Church, to follow him in the way of the cross" (LG 42).

The Church recognizes that Catholics are not alone in
giving this witness of martyrdom. For the Spirit of Christ gives
strength to all his true disciples. It is this Spirit who, through
his sanctifying power, has given to certain members of the
separated communions "the strength to go even to the shedding
of their blood" (LG 15). *The decree on ecumenism* suggests
for its part that we should recognize and appreciate "the authentically Christian values which have their source in our
common heritage and are to be found among our separated
brethren" (UR 4). It would therefore be contrary to the spirit
of the Council to consider sanctity and martyrdom as the
monopoly of the Catholic Church.

About the value of martyrdom, the Council's teaching con-
tains two distinct affirmations: martyrdom is the greatest manifestation of charity, and at the same time it is an extraordinary
gift. It is a sign of love and a signal grace: "Martyrdom, in
which the disciple is assimilated to his Master through freely
accepting death for the salvation of the world, and becomes
like his Master in shedding his blood, is considered by the
Church a signal grace and the supreme proof of charity" (LG
42). A man could not derive within himself the strength for
a witness as pure, a self-giving as complete as this, without a
special grace to make him strong and to carry him beyond
himself.

6. *A mutation: from the nineteenth century to the twentieth
   century*

After this inventory of texts from the Second Vatican Coun-

cil on the signs of revelation, let us try to plot the path taken
since the nineteenth century, and particularly since the First
Vatican Council.

1. A preliminary point to be established concerns the very
realities stressed as signs. The First Vatican Council, like the
anti-modernist oath, which reiterates its doctrine, emphasizes
the historical signs of revelation, the *miracles* and *prophecies*
of Christ, the prophets and the apostles. After Christ, the
Church is the great and perpetual motive of credibility. The
signs emphasized by the Second Vatican Council are above all:
(a) Christ, "through his whole presence and through his manifestation of himself"; (b) the Church or, still more concretely,
the witness of life given by Christians, right up to the heroism
of sanctity and martyrdom. The signs in the cosmos and in
history are not denied, but the "moral miracle," that is to say,
the transformation of man into a new creature, is stressed in
a way hitherto unknown. This emphasis on witness of life among
the signs of revelation is in keeping with the Council's teaching
on the economy of revelation and its transmission through
the centuries. It is because revelation is a matter at once of
words and of deeds that its transmission is accomplished by a
witness in which words are united to life.

2. When one passes from the nineteenth to the twentieth century
one passes from a perspective of object to a perspective of person. The very fine text of the encyclical *Qui pluribus* enumerates
all the many and striking signs which are evidence "that the
Christian faith is the work of God." [17] For the First Vatican
Council and the anti-modernist oath, miracles and prophecies
serve to establish on a solid basis "the divine origin of the
Christian religion." [18] The encyclical *Humani generis* remarks
that "there exist a great number of striking external signs which
allow us ... to prove the divine origin of the Christian religion." [19]

---

17. Denzinger-Schönmetzer, n. 2779.
18. *Ibid.*, nn. 3034 and 3539.
19. *Ibid.*, n. 3876.

In all these texts the testimony of revelation is regarded from an *objective* point of view: the divine origin of the doctrine of salvation is confirmed by exterior signs. Only the sign of the Church, as proposed by the First Vatican Council, escapes from this perspective: the Church "in herself," it says, that is to say, in her whole presence and her manifestation through the centuries, is a sign of her divine mission.[20] The Second Vatican Council extends to all the signs this *personalist* perspective. The two great signs of revelation are personal centers, that is, Christ and the Church. All the historical signs of revelation are reattached to Christ, and all the signs which are landmarks in history from Pentecost to the parousia are reattached to the Church. It is the luminous glory of Christ's life and words and actions which testifies that he is God among us, and in the same way it is the multiform and paradoxical light which shines from the Church in her members which testifies that she is of God. From this personalist point of view it is more easy to understand why signs must be presented in a synthetizing and *catholic* way. It is the totality and convergence of signs in Jesus Christ and in the Church which witness to the presence of salvation in our world. The signs emanate from Christ and from the Church like rays of light from the same focal point. They testify by their multiplicity, their diversity and their unity that the salvation proclaimed by Christ and preached by the Church is a reality of history.

3. A very considerable evolution is suggested by the words used. The encyclical *Qui pluribus* uses *argumenta;* the First Vatican Council and the anti-modernist oath use *argumenta, facta divina, signa, motivum credibilitatis, testimonium;* the encyclicals *Humani generis* and *Ecclesiam suam* say *signa;* the Second Vatican Council says *signa, testimonium.* These multifarious words express the diverse aspects of the one reality. But it is noticeable, nonetheless, that the term *argumenta* tends to disappear, while *signum* becomes the privileged term.

---

20. *Ibid.,* n. 3013.

And this is rightly so; for *signum* conforms more to biblical usage, and it well expresses the essential *rôle* of the reality involved, which is to manifest a divine intention.

4. This evolution in the words used is indicative of a deeper awareness, a more profound grasp which is precisely a grasp of consciousness. One cannot speak of signs of revelation without speaking also of the human subject to whom they are addressed. And in the respective importance attributed to these two poles, *personal* and *objective*, one can notice in the documents of the magisterium a progressive increase in flexibility. Under the influence of the currents of contemporary thought (personalism and existentialism), and of the human sciences (psychology, sociology and anthropology), the Church in the twentieth century and twentieth century theology are much more attentive than before to the human condition. In nineteenth century documents,[21] attention is directed above all to the objective reality of the signs, with a tendency to magnify their power of persuasion over the human subject. This tendency emerges particularly in the encyclical *Qui pluribus*.[22] The First Vatican Council remarks discreetly that miracles and prophecies are signs "adapted to the intelligence of every one," which can be interpreted as meaning that they can be understood by every one, just as well by simple as by cultivated minds.[23] In

---

21. For instance, the encyclical *Qui pluribus* and Vatican I.

22. The encyclical states for instance that from the signs of revelation "humana ratio luculentissime evinci omnino debet, divinam esse Christi religionem." The signs manifest such wisdom and such power "ut cuiusque mens et cogitatio vel facile intelligat, christianam fidem Dei opus esse." And finally: "humana ratio ex splendidissimis hisce aeque ac firmissimis argumentis clare aperteque cognoscens, Deum ejusdem fidei auctorem exsistere, ulterius progredi nequit, sed quavis difficultate ac dubitatione penitus abjecta ac remota, omne eidem fidei obsequium praebeat oportet, cum pro certo habeat a Deo traditum esse, quidquid fides ipsa hominibus credendum et agendum proponit" (Denzinger-Schönmetzer, nn. 2779 and 2780).

23. R. Aubert, *Le Problème de l'acte de foi* (third edition, Louvain, 1958), p. 169.

the twentieth century the attention given to the human subject who perceives the signs becomes preponderant. The encyclical *Humani generis* insists on the importance of intellectual and moral dispositions. If these dispositions happen to be lacking, a man confronted by the signs will find it difficult to perceive their brilliancy and meaning; he may even offer resistance to the invitations of grace. The encyclical *Ecclesiam suam* observes that the signs of revelation are not restrictions upon our freedom, but God's gifts and helps to enable us to adhere more easily to the message of salvation, without however taking from us the virtue of this adherence. The Second Vatican Council expresses itself in the same sense. This respect for human freedom and this discretion in speaking of the action of signs on man are among the characteristic marks of its teaching in this matter.

7. *Towards a renewal of the theology of the signs*

There is, in the conciliar texts and in the orientations to be found there, a *tout-ensemble* of indications capable of bringing about a profound renewal in the theology of signs.

1. An authentic theology of signs must have as its axis the fundamental signs of Christianity, Christ, the Church and the message of salvation itself. All the particular signs (miracles, prophecies and so forth) are only the multifarious rays of light which these fundamental signs emit. If it is true that the Second Vatican Council did not speak explicitly of the message of the gospel as a sign, as it did of Christ and of Christian witness, the whole work of the Council says clearly enough how much importance is attached to the gospel as a sign. "The Church is perfectly aware that her message is in accordance with the deep life at the heart of man" (GS 21); she knows that "the mystery of man can be really solved only in the Mystery of the incarnate Word" (GS 22). The Council undertook and carried on its work only because it was confident that the gospel, by the light which it throws on the Mystery

of God and the mystery of man, already witnesses to the divine character of its Source.[24]

2. The Second Vatican Council stressed the value of the witness of holiness of life, and rightly so; for the time of the Church is the time of the Spirit. At the time of revelation in the historical sense of the word, the great sign was the gift of the gospel itself, and the presence among men of the incarnate Word, with the three-fold designation of power and wisdom and holiness. Now that the gospel is proclaimed and the Spirit given so that men may live by it, the great sign of salvation is life according to the gospel: it is the transformation of man as an individual into a new creature given life by the Spirit, and the transformation of man in society into a unity of love. Christianity should be able to show that Christ has really saved mankind, and that the grace merited by him is really capable of making us children of the Father, living a filial life under the guidance of the Spirit. It is not enough to assume that salvation has, in the event, arrived, but that it is intangible, that holiness has been given us, but that, paradoxically, nothing betrays its presence from the outside in the behavior of those to whom the Spirit has come. Holiness, on the contrary, should exist and be manifest in fruits "of love, joy, peace, patience, kindness, goodness, faithfulness, gentleness and self-control" (Gal 5:22). In the same way, the Church cannot be content to state that she has received from Christ the means of sanctifying men, without being able to sanctify them. If the Church were to preach an abstract ideal, never lived and never to be met with, she would destroy the gospel and destroy herself. The more she talks about salvation the more she is bound to

---

24. John XXIII, in inaugurating the Council, commented that the Church "considers that she is responding better to the needs of our time by bringing more clearly into the light of day the wealth of her doctrine than by uttering condemnations." And again: the Church "is opening the rich resources of her doctrine, so that in the revealing light of Christ men may become fully aware of who they are, of their own worth and of the end they are seeking."

produce witnesses to salvation.[25] In this respect we should give
to the sign of the Church and the sign of holiness of life a very
much greater importance than we have done in the past. There
is room in fact, in the theology of signs, for methodical reflection
on the action of the Spirit in human souls and in the concrete
life of the Church.[26]

3. If, after all, all the signs come back to Christ and the Church,
one sees immediately how artificial it is to treat signs twice,
under two separate headings, as has been done up to now
in most of the manuals of apologetics: first in an abstract criteri-
ology, and then a second time in application to the case of
Jesus. To tell the truth the first treatment constantly takes for
granted what is going to be said in the second. More than that,
it is the second treatment which authorizes, and is the basis of,
the first. For signs of revelation *in general* do not exist. The
economy of signs is an economy of *fact*: it belongs to that wholly
gratuitous and unpredictable economy through which God saves
man by means of history and the Incarnation, and it prolongs
this economy in an economy of signs which is homogeneous with
it. It is by taking as the point of departure the signs in *fact*
given in Christ and the Church that a true theology of signs
càn and must be worked out. Reflection on how signs may be
discerned, what sort of certainty they lead to and their relationship to one another has no meaning unless it is based on observed facts. A semiology founded on a *phenomenology* will
also have more respect for the dynamism peculiar to each sign.
Up to now the physical miracle has been turned into a sort
of prototype, to which all the other signs have been accom-
modated; as the miracle was a going beyond physical nature,
so prophecy was a going beyond the intellectual order and
holiness a going beyond the moral order. Reflection founded
on facts would allow us to show more respect for the originality

25. K. Rahner in: *Écrits théologiques IV* (Bruges and Paris, 1966),
pp. 57-60: the English translation is *Theological Investigations* IV (London, 1966; New York, 1967).

26. K. Rahner, *Est-il possible aujourd'hui de croire?* (Paris, 1966),
p. 207. English translation, *Faith Today* (London, 1967).

of each sign. And this way of treating signs as *unified* in Christ and the Church would allow us also to avoid useless repetition.

4. If all the signs are brought back to Christ, the personal and saving Presence among men, and to the Church, the Sacrament of salvation through the centuries, signs are no less signs of *presence* than signs of power. They appear as particularly luminous focal points, in which sanctification and salvation are manifest. In them salvation seems concentrated and operative. In them there is apparent a completeness of scope, in which message answers to life and life to message. The presence of this plenitude of salvation among men may enable the personal source of this light to be identified.

5. Signs are not detached from their "message," any more than they are detached from their personal source: the Council closely united dogmatic vision and apologetic vision. It was one of the weaknesses of the old apologetics that in practice it cut all connections between signs and the gospel. Yet "the miracles authenticate the doctrine and the doctrine the miracles," as Pascal long ago observed.[27] If, that is, the message has need of signs to attest to its divine origin, it is in the message that the signs receive their full signification. This *complementarity* of the two points of view (dogmatic and apologetic), is of its nature such as to renew the whole theology of signs. So in the multiplicity of its aspects the miracle appears as a tangible ànd living commentary on the word of salvation. The resurrection of Christ becomes "thinkable" and intelligible only in the light of the Christian synthesis. In the same way, if one has first grasped that in founding his Church, Christ wanted to assemble and unite in love men dispersed and divided by sin, and that he gave to this Church as her principle of cohesion and expansion the very Spirit who unites the Father and the Son, it will be more

27. Pascal, *Pensées* (ed. Brunschvicg), fr. 803. Of the many translations of the *Pensées*, not all use the Brunschvicg text and arrangement, but in those which do the fragment numbering remains the same.

obvious that the ecclesial society may transcend the limits of space (Acts 1:8), of time (Mt 28:20) and of human particularity (Mt 28:19). One will be able to understand how such a society, inserted within the fabric of human societies, could strike the eyes of men with unaccustomed brightness. The dogmatic vision of the Church seeks in the light of faith for the secret of her external glory, while the apologetic vision, contemplating first her outer splendor, poses the question of its source, and searches for an explanation commensurate with the phenomenon observed. They are two complementary points of view: the mystery of the Church illumines what amazes in the facts, while the tangible phenomenon awakens us to the presence of the mystery.

6. In *The constitution on the Church* and *The decree on ecumenism*, the Council has honestly recognized that there exist in the separated Christian communities incontestable spiritual riches, which are the authentic fruit of the Spirit of Christ. In relation to our present subject of study, for instance, there are the exercise of charity carried to the heroic point of holiness and martyrdom, a sincere desire for unity and a unity in action among all the disciples of Christ, as well as a lively missionary enthusiasm for extending to all the peoples of the world the blessing of the gospel. If theological thought wishes to take account of these facts, it will have to make *still more* various and flexible the traditional argument drawn from the "moral miracle." It will have to avoid giving the impression, in its language or its reasoning, that the Catholic Church is alone in *signifying* the coming of salvation into the world. For the gospel, faith, hope and charity, holiness, martyrdom and the other kinds of spiritual good which exist in the separated communities, all belong to the *Christian* heritage, and are to be found in the separated communions in different degrees, in the measure in which these live the life of Christ and his Spirit. It will be, then, rather a matter of showing, with great respect for the truth, that the Catholic Church manifests herself among Christian communions as a more complete, more perfect sign, particularly in her fruits of holiness, as contrasted with signs which,

though real, are partial and less perfect. She represents a *fullness* of sanctification and salvation, which does not seem to be realized to this degree in the other communities which bear the Christian name—a delicate and complex demonstration this; for it is in the measure that the Church is the luminous and transparent Sign of Christ that she becomes a Sign among the nations.

7. One last element of renewal which the Second Vatican Council has brought to the theology of signs is the very lively attention which it gives to contemporary man and contemporary sensibility. The Council has been at pains to show that if the signs of revelation come from God they are meant for man, in order to help him to understand that salvation is here and that the gospel has come to throw light on the mystery of his existence. If the signs did not appear to be made for man, or intended to orientate his mind towards the new life which Christ has brought, how would revelation itself not seem to be something foreign to the human being it sets out to save? A theology of signs which wants to be *en-situation-historique* will be able to discern in contemporary mentality at once its privileged points of access and its points of peculiar resistance. Such a theology will be sensitive to the way man today expresses himself. In this respect a solid knowledge of contemporary literature and philosophy seems to be indispensable to a theological approach to signs.

If theological thought were willing to take into account all these indications from the Council, explicit or implicit, in the literal or in the full sense of the texts, the renewal in the theology of signs which would follow would have all the appearance of a revolution.

CHAPTER II

The Economy of the Signs of Revelation

In speaking of the mysteries of the inner life of God and his saving purposes, human intelligence cannot adduce necessary and demonstrable reasons. God's initiatives are part of the mystery of his love. That God, for instance, should have willed to reveal himself to man and save him by means of the Incarnation and the cross, and that he should have willed to prolong this economy of the Incarnation through an economy of signs homogeneous with it—all this depends on his unpredictable love.

But contemporary man finds it difficult to accept the idea of God's intervening in his history under the form of Incarnation, and in nature under the forms of miracle and resurrection from the dead. Whether this resistance arises in the name of philosophy or in the name of science, it is not peculiar to the non-believer: it affects the believer as well.[1] As a man of his time, the believer, like the unbeliever, is marked by the scientific spirit. And the more the influence of science pervades the atmosphere about him, and penetrates into the sanctuary

---

1. J. Lacroix, *Le sens de l'athéisme moderne* (Paris, 1958), p. 54: trans., *The Meaning of Modern Atheism* (London, 1965). J. B. Metz, "L'incroyance, problème théologique," *Concilium*, n. 6 (1965): 63-81: trans., in English edition.

of his personal life, the more difficult he finds it to escape
from the mentality which the progress of science inspires. The
idea of divine intervention in the midst of cosmic regularity
seems to him something highly *unsuitable,* even impossible.[2]

A direct answer to this attitude and the objections to which
it gives rise often merely exasperates the forces of resistance.
What is irritating to contemporary man is the sort of *unintelligi-
bility* which the miraculous introduces into a world which has
its own intelligibility. To admit the miraculous, under any
form at all, is to admit the co-existence of the unintelligible
and the intelligible. In that case is it not the most urgent thing
to make plain the sovereign intelligibility of God's designs, to
show that the economy of salvation is a higher economy, in
which the rupture of the phenomenal order of things itself
becomes the expression of the order of grace offered by God?

If it in fact appeared that the signs of revelation are not
elements of incoherence in an order which has its own proper
consistency, but organic elements of an admirable economy
of wisdom and goodness through which God as it were lays
siege to man in order to make him understand that salvation
is at hand; if it appeared further that this economy is marvellously adapted to the economy of a revelation which comes to us
by way of history and the Incarnation, as well as to the inner
nature of man, to whom it is addressed; and if finally it appeared
that this economy is no less wonderful than that which connects
the mysteries of revelation with one another, would not man
be bound to show himself less hostile to the idea of a possible
intervention by God in the cosmos and in history? If God's

---

2. This is a difficulty which Bultmann often expresses in different
ways. For example: "one cannot make use of electric light and radio,
call, in case of sickness, on medical aid and modern clinical practice,
and at the same time believe in the New Testament world of spirits and
miracles. Anyone who thinks that for his own part he can, must realize
that in exhibiting this as a Christian attitude, he is making the message
of Christianity incomprehensible and impossible for our time." (R. Bultmann, "Neues Testament und Mythologie," in *L'interprétation du Nouveau
Testament,* trans., O. Laffoucrière (Paris, 1955), p. 143. Cf. also *Theology
of the New Testament* (London, 1965).

gifts were presented in this way as having a character of intelligibility and harmony (harmony among themselves, harmony with revelation, harmony with the nature of man) would he not be obliged to consider them with sympathetic attention, instead of rejecting them *a priori* as not fitting into the category of the things he has foreseen? To strive to show the *inner coherence* of the economy of signs seems then the most discerning and effective way of disposing man to a receptive and friendly frame of mind towards the unforeseeable interventions of God.

According to the documents of the magisterium, the signs of revelation are numerous, admirable, striking and solid.[3] In point of fact, they are not disparate facts, arbitrarily assembled, but organic elements of a wonderfully wise economy. The signs invoke one another, correspond to one another, fall into a hierarchical order and fit into an organic synthesis in which Christ is the principle of unity and intelligibility—of *radiance*. In contemplating this divine economy and its inner coherence, and the many bonds which link the signs with one another and carry them back to their first principle in Christ and the Church, one is aware of a new argument, capable of disposing the mind to recognize the facts which would lead to a certainty that this economy is *real*. Would not many objections and difficulties raised against and about the signs fall away of themselves if the signs were seen synthetically as multiple rays of light emanating from the same focal point? It is this profound intelligibility of the signs of revelation that I should like to illustrate by a series of reflections or successive approaches, which envisage the signs from different points of view.

1. *The signs and our call to salvation*

In the work of salvation, all is *grace*. And in revelation, which is the luminous fringe of salvation, that is, the communication to man of God's saving design in Jesus Christ, all is likewise grace: the news of salvation, the signs of God's intervention

---

3. Denzinger-Schönmetzer, nn. 2779, 2780, 3013, 3014, 3876.

in history and the ability to respond to God's call. Revelation, signs and faith are God's *gifts*. And these three realities are organically linked with one another, all three contributing to a single effect, the drawing of man to God through faith in Jesus Christ, the plunging of man in that great stream of life which makes him a new creature, a son of the Father, given life by the Spirit of love.

The signs, that is, with the exterior invitation of the gospel (Mk 16:15) and the interior attraction of grace (Jn 6:44; Acts 6:14), constitute a true *vocation* to faith. St. Thomas rightly observes that God invites man to believe by means of a threefold help: by an interior call, by the preaching of the gospel and by exterior signs.[4] The First Vatican Council, in its description of faith, brings together the three terms, revelation, interior help from the Holy Spirit and divine signs.[5] In the perspective of the Second Vatican Council revelation and signs are connected with the gift of Christ, who is himself the Fullness and the Sign of revelation, while faith is connected with the gift of the Spirit, who enlightens man's mind and moves his heart.[6]

The signs, consequently, are to be situated in a context of salvation and grace, and are not intelligible except in this context. Man in the concrete, man as he exists in history, cannot stand before the signs as before an external and objective reality which is of no concern to him. The signs confront him with the problem of an intervention by God in history, an invitation given to man and a decision which involves the whole of his

4. "Adjuvatur autem a Deo aliquis ad credendum tripliciter. Primo quidem per interiorem vocationem, de qua dicitur Jn 6, 45: omnis qui audivit a Patre, et didicit, venit ad me; et ad Rom 8:30: quos praedestinavit, hos et vocavit. Secundo, per doctrinam et praedicationem exteriorem, secundum illud Apostoli ad Rom c. 10:17: fides ex auditu, auditus autem per verbum Christi. Tertio, per exteriora miracula; unde dicitur 1 Cor 14 quod signa data sunt infidelibus ut scilicet per ea provocentur ad fidem" (Quodl. 2, q. 4, a. 6). Cf. S. Th., 2a 2ae, q. 2, a. 9, ad 3; In Jo. 15, lect. 5.

5. Denzinger-Schönmetzer, n. 3009.

6. *Constitutio dogmatica de divina revelatione*, c. 1, nn. 4-5; R. Latourelle, "La Révélation et sa transmission selon la Constitution *Dei verbum*," *Gregorianum*, 47 (1966): 21-23.

existence.[7] In a context of this sort the recognition of the signs and of their value normally takes place in a climate of grace; for if the signs are gestures on the part of God, made to man with the intention of saving him, they are imbued with grace. Is it conceivable that God, having established an economy of revelation and supernatural faith, intrinsically ordered to a supernatural end, should give man signs of this economy without helping him to read them aright? It would be contrary to God's wisdom and goodness to call upon men to orientate their lives and their thinking towards a supernatural end, and then at the same time refuse them the very aid which would help them to reach it.[8] This effective, historical presence of grace obviously does not mean that human reason left to its own devices would be incapable of perceiving the signs and their value.[9] Theological reflection can indeed show that nothing in the dialectic which leads from the sign to the thing signified is strictly beyond the power of reason. What is meant is simply that in point of fact the grace of God is at work the moment there is any question of a salvation which is properly speaking supernatural—not only in revelation and faith but in the signs as well. The signs are addressed to reason, but to reason enlightened and sustained by grace. It is grace which helps a man to read the signs aright and to perceive their relationship to his own personal salvation, just as it is grace which gives him the courage to face the choice with which their perception inevitably presents him.

Exterior revelation, interior help and exterior signs constitute as it were three calls to salvation, calls which are not isolated from one another but interconnected, echoing and

---

7. J. Alfaro, *Fides, Spes, Caritas* (ad usum auditorum, Romae, 1963), p. 409.

8. G. De Broglie, *Les signes de crédibilité de la révélation chrétienne* (Paris, 1964), pp. 6-8: trans., *Revelation and Reason* (London, 1965).

9. When the encyclical *Humani Generis* says that "there are a great many striking external signs which allow us, even with the merely natural light of reason, to prove the divine origin of the Christian religion" (Denzinger-Schönmetzer, n. 3876), it is speaking of external signs taken as a whole.

supporting one another. Grace sustains the whole process which leads from the gospel to faith. From outside, salvation comes to us through preaching accredited by signs, and from within through an obscure and indistinct attraction, which makes us perceive as personally addressed to ourselves the message and the signs which accompany it. This three-fold reality is a three-fold aid to faith and salvation. Faith is the one and indivisible fruit of this three-fold help: of the *gospel,* which proclaims salvation, of *grace,* which interiorly enlightens and strengthens us, and of the *signs* which accompany the message. So completely is the light of grace made for the gospel and ts signs, that to speak of one without the other would be impossible. It is grace which, by the connaturality which it infuses into us, opens our minds to an understanding of the gospel, and it is grace which makes us sensitive to the reality and the dynamism of the signs. On the other hand, without the gospel and the signs, we should not be able to know that salvation were offered to us, and offered to us by God.[10]

2.   Signs of God, signs for man

Whether we consider the economy of signs from the point of view of man for whom they are made, or from the point of view of God whom they reveal, the intelligibility of this economy seems extraordinary.

Designed for man and addressed to man, the signs of revelation attain to man in his entirety, and also the whole world which he inhabits. It might be said that God, in order to signify to man his own gracious and saving intervention in history, has made use of all the means of expression accessible to man in his condition as a spatio-temporal, individual and social being,

---

10. J. Alfaro, *Fides, Spes, Caritas,* pp. 409-410; R. Latourelle, *Théologie de la Révélation* (third edition, Bruges - Paris, 1969), pp. 187-188: trans., *Theology of Revelation,* (Alba House, New York, 1966), p. 150; L. Monden, *Le Miracle, signe de salut* (Bruges - Paris, 1959), pp. 84-85; G. De Broglie, *Les signes de crédibilité de la révélation chrétienne,* pp. 5-6: trans., *Revelation and Reason.*

composed of body and spirit. No dimension of man or of the universe has been neglected by God, in order to besiege man, and make him understand that God's Word has come into the world and that salvation is in our midst.[11] God's condescension, manifested in the Incarnation, has been continued even in the economy of the signs of revelation.

Three dimensions, and three only, define man in his present condition: time, space and humanity itself. Hence it is in nature, in history and in man himself that signs of God can become perceptible.[12] By miracles God makes signs in nature; by prophecy he makes signs in time; by holiness he makes signs in man himself. The transfiguration of nature by miracle, of history by prophecy, and of man, individually and socially, by sanctity, is the visible mark of the coming of the Word into the world, the reflection of the glory of Christ present among us as the Word of God. When God makes signs to man through history, nature and humanity itself, he so to speak exhausts the significative virtualities provided by the human condition.

But man is at once *individual* and *society*. It is fitting there-fore that there should be signs in man as an individual (sanc-tity or martyrdom) and as society (the sign of the Church). For since revelation has a *public* and *social* character, it is fitting that its sign should have this character also, so that men, conscious of their solidarity in salvation, should be no less conscious of it in the signs which manifest that this salvation has come. In this way an economy of revelation and *exterior*

---

11. Taking into account, however, what one might call God's habitual discretion in not violating man's freedom. The encyclical *Ecclesiam suam* points out that revelation, or the dialogue of salvation, "adapted to the demands and spiritual dispositions of its hearers even the number (Mt 12:38f) and demonstrative force of its signs (Mt 13:13f), so as to make it easier for men to consent freely to revelation, without at the same time losing the virtue of this consent" (Paulus VI, *Ecclesiam suam*, AAS 56 [1964] 642-643). Compare the Second Vatican Council's *Declaration on religious liberty*, n. 11.

12. C. Dumont, "Unité et diversité des signes de la Révélation," *Nouvelle Revue theologique*, 80 (1958): 133-158.

signs becomes for each individual a means of consciously parti-
cipating in the faith of all, and of strengthening his own personal certainty in the certainty of all.[13] And just as the faith
of each is supported by the faith of the community, within
the faith of the Church as a whole, so the possession in common
of the same signs becomes a support for the faith of all. This
possession in common—and the awareness of this possession
in common—of the same gospel accredited by public and permanent facts (such as miracles, resurrection, sanctity, prophecy,
Church) thus becomes a new argument for those who believe,
and a new sign for those who do not believe.

Finally, man is *body* and *spirit*: it is fitting therefore that
there should be signs which are addressed to both of these
aspects and which speak to all the human faculties. "Miracles
and truth are necessary," said Pascal, "because the whole man,
body and soul, must be convinced." [14] The first of all the signs,
the excellence of the Christian message itself, is addressed
principally to the mind. Because it comes from God, the gospel
bears traces of its origin (Jn 7:17). In the splendor and coherence of its content, in the light which it throws on the
mystery of God and the mystery of man, the message of salvation attests its divine character. While doctrine, like prophecy,
is for the mind, miracle addresses itself rather to the faculties
of sense. It should not for this—as the most carnal of signs—
be under-estimated; for it constitutes a language singularly
adapted to our human condition, and consequently a particularly
persuasive and pressing form of divine witness. More than any
other sign, it fits into the economy of God's condescension, God
who in order to embrace the whole of man, body and soul, becomes man himself, speaks to men in human language and addresses signs to them at their own level.

Through the Incarnation, the Word of God makes the human
body the instrument of his revelation, a mirror in which the
divine is reflected in the human. This body, and with it the

---

13. J. Clémence, "Le miracle dans l'économie chrétienne," *Études*
227 (1936): 577-589.
14. Pascal, *Pensées* (ed. Brunschvicg), fr. 806.

universe which is its extension, becomes the sign by which God enters into relationship with man. It is by means of corporeality that God communicates to us his design of salvation,[15] and it is by the same means that he attests the divine origin of this communication. The incarnate God does indeed remain enigmatic, veiled beneath the livery of a slave. But to help our poor eyes, inattentive to spiritual realities because fascinated by the world of sense, he allows something of his glory to appear, not only in his doctrine and his holiness, but also in the impact of his power over the cosmos.[16] And so not only man's dependence on the sensible but even his propensity towards it becomes the means of his return to God. God carries his condescension to the uttermost limit; for he uses our very weaknesses to raise our eyes to himself. Without being essential, miracle thus seems to be in perfect harmony with the economy of the Incarnation and the redemption, and in harmony also with the demands of our senses. It harmonizes too with the condition of a nature on which sensible objects exercise an almost irresistible attraction.

If we consider the signs from the point of view of God whom they reveal, they manifest the same coherence and intelligibility.

Although the Father, the Son and the Holy Spirit are one and the same principle of action, and the essential attributes of God are common to all three Persons of the Trinity, each Person acts according to effects which correspond mysteriously to what, in the inner life of the Trinity, the Father, the Son and the Spirit are. It is for this reason that power is specially attributed to the Father, for he is the Origin without origin; knowledge and wisdom to the Son, for he proceeds from the Father through the operation of his Understanding of himself; and holiness to the Spirit, for he proceeds from the Father and the Son as their mutual and common Love. But if God is omnipotence, truth, knowledge, wisdom, holiness and love, and God comes into the world, is it not natural that there should be in the

---

15. R. Latourelle, *Théologie de la Révélation*, pp. 436-438: trans., *Theology of Revelation*, pp. 360-363.

16. L. Monden, *Le Miracle, signe de salut*, pp. 31-33.

world signs of power, such as miracles and resurrection, signs
of knowledge and wisdom such as prophecy and sublimity
of doctrine, and signs of holiness, such as martyrdom and the
charity of Christ and the saints? And if Christ is God among men,
why should we be surprised that his presence in our midst should
be accompanied by manifestations of power, of knowledge and
of holiness? Christ is among men as the Father's Son, having
all the Father's power and love, and as the Father's Word,
the unfathomable abyss of knowledge and wisdom. Christ's
miracles, Christ's holiness, the sublimity of his teaching, the
keenness of the glance which pierces history and penetrates the
hearts of men, these are simply the reflections of his glory as
the Son of God, present among us with the power and wisdom
and holiness of the Son of God.

This glory of Christ is reflected also in the Church. "Just
as power and wisdom and goodness shine with a unique splendor
in God, whose Unity we adore in Trinity and Trinity in Unity, . . .
so also," said St. Robert Bellarmine, "God has made his chosen
friends and sons, the Fathers and Doctors of the Church, more
like himself, more pleasing and more admirable to men, by
making them at once powerful and wise and holy to an eminent
degree." [17] The signs of the Church, like the signs of Christ, are
reflections in our world of the world beyond.

3. *The signs and the message of salvation*

The signs are not extrinsic to the message, like a trade-mark
stamped on an object to identify its manufacturer. On the contrary there is a deep and rich harmony between the gospel
and the signs of the gospel, between the message revealed and
the signs of its divine origin. The gospel tells us that Christ is

---

17. "Quemadmodum in Deo, quem unum in Trinitate, et trinum in
unitate veneramur, tria quaedam singulariter eminent, potentia, sapientia,
bonitas; ita quoque, auditores, singulares amicos et filios suos, Patres ac
Doctores nostros, Deus, ut sibi quam simillimos et gentibus omnibus
suspiciendos atque admirabiles redderet, potentissimos, sapientissimos, op-
timos sanctissimosque esse voluit" (Robertus Bellarminus, *Concio 9 de
probitate Doctorum Ecclesiae* in the office of the feast).

the Son of God come into the world, to save man from sin and
death, to transform the meaning of his life by revealing to him
the love of God, and to make him a son of the Father, suffused
totally by charity, living and acting under the domination of
the Spirit. It is therefore proper that there should be in the
world signs which *express* this spiritual renewal announced and
effected by Christ. Now this is precisely what happens. Through
his preaching Christ proclaims the salvation which he accomplishes by his Incarnation and death on the cross. And at the same
time there arise a new creation, a new age, a new man, in
whom the Spirit lives and to whom the Spirit gives life.

Miracle, by its paradoxical transcendence of the order of
nature, appears as a sensible analogue of the revealed mystery
of our elevation to supernatural life. By the multiplicity of its
aspects and forms, it is a living and tangible commentary on
the word of salvation, the visible illumination of a message
which without it might remain too abstract, too purely intellectual.[18] Miracle is the transparency, through matter, of the new
invisible spiritual life which Christ proclaimed. "Visible miracles,"
wrote Pascal, "are images of those which are invisible." [19] Bodies
which have been healed and raised from the dead are expressive
likenesses of souls delivered from sin and filled with everlasting
life. The *mirabilia* accomplished in nature are the expression,
at a human level, of the *mirabilia* of grace. In saving man from
suffering and death, Christ signifies that he saves him still more
profoundly, from the corruption of sin. To quote Pascal again,
God "accomplished in the order of natural good the new creation
which he was to accomplish also in the order of grace, so that
we might judge that he could do the invisible, since he had
certainly done the visible." [20] Miracle thus becomes the dimension
in the flesh of a spiritual content, giving relief and color to the
word.

Just as miracle is the transparency of salvation in nature,

---

18. G. De Broglie, *Les signes de crédibilité de la révélation chrétienne,*
p. 110: trans., *Revelation and Reason* (London, 1965).
19. Pascal, *Pensées,* fr. 675.
20. *Ibid.,* fr. 643.

so *prophecy* is the illumination of history by the proclamation of the saving event: it is "the flowering of eschatology in the commonplace, factual chronicles of peoples."[21] In Christ, history possesses already its direction and end. And thanks to prophecy, this goal of human history enlightens the present. Prophecy announces that the essential event is still to come, and so the future invades the present and gives it meaning and consistency. Time present is a time of preparation, of watchful waiting, of hope and trust. Through prophecy, history is already oriented towards Christ. Prophecy thus establishes a new relationship among past, present and future. On the one hand, there is an analogy between things past and things to come: the final event will reproduce in greater beauty and magnitude the marvels of the past; and the types of the past (king, prophet, and priest) are rough sketches, early studies, of the awaited Messiah. And on the other hand, every partial fulfillment in the present of the promises of the past is the shadow in outline of a future already announced and prepared, each new fulfillment turning our hopes towards a more decisive fulfillment to come. All history is in flight towards the future. Israel tends towards the ultimate fulfillment of this eschatological history, without being able to foresee it or define it clearly.[22] But already prophecy appears as a figure, within history, of this definitive transformation brought into human history by the coming of Christ. The fullness of Christ fills the present time.

Finally *sanctity* is the tangible reflection of this transformation of man and society foretold by the prophets (Ez 36:26-27) and preached by Christ (Mt 5, 48). For if the gospel announces that man is saved by Christ, and that we are the children of the Father, regenerated and given new life by the Spirit, it is right that we should be able to see signs of this renewal of man and of society. But the saint is precisely the new man announced by the gospel, with a new heart and a new spirit

21. C. Dumont, "Unité et diversité des signes de la Révélation," *Nouvelle Revue théologique*, 80 (1958): 143.
22. Hans Urs von Balthasar, *La Gloire et la Croix*, t. 1, *Apparition* (Paris, 1965), p. 533.

within him, a man generated by God and moved by the Spirit. In him, gospel and life answer to each other and are in perfect harmony. He already lives fully, here and now, his life as son of God. The Church, for her part, in virtue of the Spirit who is the divine principle from whom her life comes, constitutes already in the midst of the earthly city a type or model of the heavenly Jerusalem, an anticipation, as it were, of the kingdom of the saints.

So the new *creation* signified by miracle, the new *time* signified by prophecy, the new *man* and the new *society* signified by the sanctity of the individual and by the Church, these are the signs of that transformation announced by the gospel and accomplished by the coming of the Word into the world. The Word of God is an operative and effective Word. At the same time as he makes known God's saving design, he leaves visible traces in the world of this newness in which God *re-creates* in a still more wonderful manner what he created at the dawn of time. He touches the whole of nature and history and man, so that the economy of signs prolongs the economy of the Incarnation, through which God leads man to invisible realities by means of the signs of the flesh, of scripture and of the sacraments.

4. *The comparative intelligibility and efficacy of the signs*

One can distinguish among the signs different levels of depth or *intelligibility,* as well as different degrees of *efficacy.* On the plane of intelligibility, the most striking signs are not necessarily the richest. On the other hand the most intelligible are not necessarily the most efficacious; and this efficacy itself varies with persons, circumstances and eras.

Miracle does not demand, in order to be grasped, any special intellectual preparation. It is, as the First Vatican Council put it, "adapted to the understanding of all," [23] to that of the simple, no less than to that of the more cultivated.[24] By its massive, almost brutal, character it forces itself upon our attention.

---

23. Denzinger-Schönmetzer, n. 3009.
24. *Ibid.,* n. 3539.

To be sure, miracle, like any other sign, cannot be perceived without certain antecedent subjective dispositions, but these are less numerous than for the grasping of many other signs. It is thus the most communicable of signs, "the most social" if one might put it so.[25] On the other hand it is not the deepest or purest of signs. By its exteriority it easily distracts the mind from its religious meaning; it is constantly threatened by magic or superstition.

Holiness is, as it stands, a richer and more fruitful sign than miracle; for it is indissolubly united with the person, and directly bound up with the message it communicates. It allows us to contemplate the gospel in action. It makes us see in fleshly beings like ourselves, the spiritual transformation which the gospel proclaims. But it presupposes, in order to be seen, not only the synthesis of many objective data, but, also and above all, the just appreciation of certain spiritual values, notably the victory of the Spirit over natural human weaknesses, as manifested in the life of Christ and the saints. It presupposes also more in the way of moral dispositions than does the discernment of miracle: sincerity, humility, magnanimity for instance.

The sublimity of the Christian message, the wonderful coherence of the mysteries with one another, the correspondence of Christianity with the aspirations of mankind, its excellence and originality in comparison with the teachings of other religions—all this is incontestably an authentic sign of Christian truth, but as can readily be seen, a sign whose intelligibility requires much more delicate perception. Transcendence of this kind is not easy to demonstrate or define. Who can say indeed that a given doctrine is really transcendent in comparison with another? In what does such transcendence consist? In the order of thought, who can say what the human mind can discover by itself? Where is one to fix its limits? If it is relatively easy to see the splendor of Christianity, to grasp its real and objective transcendence demands a relatively high degree of intelligence and an uncommon critical insight. Besides, a sign of this sort derives its force not simply from a complex multitude of data

---

25. L. Monden, *Le Miracle, signe de salut,* p. 86.

which must be considered synthetically, but also and principally from value judgments brought to bear on this. To effect the mental synthesis correctly, and to be able to appreciate the values manifested in it needs subjective dispositions of connaturality. It is indeed objectively that the message of the gospel in itself possesses incomparable excellence, but just as the merit of a work of art, however objective this may be, cannot dispense the critic from the necessity of a certain aesthetic sense, so the objectivity of the gospel's message as a sign cannot dispense those who are to judge it from possessing at least an inchoate connaturality with the things of God.[26]

In the case of *prophecy*, we must distinguish between *prediction* and *promise*. Even prophecy in the sense of prediction of a future event is a more spiritual and complex sign than miracle. It is more spiritual, because while miracle is an exception to the laws of bodily nature, prophecy is an exception to the laws of knowledge, and consequently makes less impression on the imagination and sensibility of the mass of men. It is more complex, because while miracle is realized in a single time and place, the sign of prophecy exists only in virtue of the perceived convergence of two independent and heterogeneous groups of data, drawn from different times and places, that is, the knowledge of the prediction made by the prophet and the knowledge of the event in which the prediction is fulfilled.[27] But if predictive prophecy, in the sense of the foretelling of a particular event, is a relatively easy sign to discern, prophecy in the sense of the *promise and fulfillment* of salvation in Christ manifests a much greater complexity; for it rises to a total vision of history. To grasp the sign of this prophecy of promise, one needs to be familiar not only with the message of the New Testament but with the entire economy of the Old: its events, institutions, persons and doctrinal themes. The understanding of the sign presupposes further an understanding of the prophetic language—sometimes literal but more often symbolic, a capacity

---

26. G. De Broglie, *Les signes de crédibilité de la révélation chrétienne,* pp. 63-64: trans., *Revelation and Reason.*

27. *Ibid.,* pp. 137-139.

to grasp the mysterious harmony between the two Testaments at the same time as the way in which the New leaves the Old behind, and finally a discernment of how Christ realizes the harmony by taking up, without losing any of them, all the essential elements of the promise. For the attentive mind able to grasp all these coincident aspects there is no doubt that such a vision can constitute a sign of inexhaustible intelligibility; it remains however a sign for the mature—accessible in practice to a relatively limited number.

The sign of Christ and *the sign of the Church,* as personal and virtually multiple signs, are both the most intelligible and the most efficacious of signs. By the radiance of his Person, through the sublimity of his teaching, the brilliance of his holiness and the power of his actions, Christ *signifies* that he really is what he claims to be, God present among men, and that his testimony is true, He is in Person *the Sign par excellence.*[28] In him the transformation of humanity through the infusion of grace becomes transparent to our eyes. He is the new Man, wholly alive in the Spirit.

Analogously, and with the necessary reservations, the same may be said of the sign of the Church. Just as Christ "signified" to the men of his time by the radiance of his whole Person as the incarnate Word, so the Church by the radiance of her being and action (expansion, Catholic unity, stability, permanence, holiness and fruitfulness in good works) *signifies* to men of all times that she has her mission and message from God himself. She shares in the glory of Christ. But the sign of the Church is more ambiguous than the sign of Christ; for if the Church is holy in her foundation and in a certain number of her members, she betrays, in many others, signs of weakness and sin. Her unity needs always to be protected and recovered; her catholicity is always more fully to come; her stability lies always under threat. *Paradox* is woven into the fabric of the Church. She has greatness enough to draw and hold the eyes of the well-disposed, and weakness enough to repel the proud and mean. The Church is great and glorious, not because of her

---

28. *Constitutio dogmatica de divina revelatione,* c. 1, n. 5.

earthly strength and achievements, but because the redemptive grace of Christ triumphs in her in spite of human weaknesses, because it is precisely in these weaknesses that the power of God is made known, and known in a visible way.[29]

5. *The action of the signs throughout history*

In this series of reflections on the economy of the signs of revelation, some consideration should be given to their relative efficacy throughout history, in the succession of human generations. For this efficacy varies with the centuries, and according to the human *milieux* in which the action of the sign takes place. This is not surprising; for if it is true that the signs are objectively given and lie in history, it is equally true that they are always addressed to a being *en-situation-historique*, belonging to a specific human environment. Now this situation and this environment vary with the centuries. The efficacy of a sign depends not only on the authenticity of the sign itself, but also on the receptiveness which it meets in a given historical environment. The variability of the human environment in the course of the centuries will have its repercussion on the action of the signs, which may be diminished or increased. For the sake of completeness it might be added that in the designs of God it would appear that certain signs are called to play a dominant *rôle* in one era rather than in another. We must take account then, in plotting the curve of variability in the efficacy of signs, of this double influence of the historical conjuncture and the providential action of God.

The argument from *prophecy,* for instance, which was evocative and convincing to a Jew of the first centuries, who saw in Christ the climax and fulfillment of a long series of promises recorded in scripture, where they had become the subject of his daily meditation, does not exert the same attraction upon the man of the twentieth century, who is unfamiliar with the

---

29. E. H. Schillebeeckx, *Le Christ Sacrement de la rencontre de Dieu* (Paris, 1960), p. 246: trans., *Christ: the Sacrament of the Encounter with God* (London and New York, 1963).

already distant history of the people of Israel. On the other hand, martyrdom, which, in the age of the open persecution of the Church, became the sign *par excellence* of the divine origin of Christianity, is again becoming, with the new forms of persecution against the Church in the twentieth century, the object of sympathetic and attentive reflection.[30]

Miracles have never ceased to happen in the Church, but it might be said that at certain periods their rhythm intensifies. To the people of the Jews for instance, accustomed since the time of the Exodus to the power of Yahweh and his sway over nature, Jesus proposed miracles first and foremost: these prodigies, evoking the *mirabilia* of the past, were designed to help men to recognize that Christ was present on earth with the power of Yahweh. The miracle is the striking deployment of this power, the articulate deed of the saving Word. In the nineteenth century, when technique seemed to have banished the supernatural, and determinism was imposing itself as an impalpable dogma, miracle reappeared. It was this naturalist, positivist and rationalist century which witnessed the miracles of Lourdes and of the Curé d'Ars. Miracle assumed social dimensions to meet a crisis of social dimensions.

In the twentieth century, under the influence of science and of a liberal theology impregnated with rationalism (that of Bultmann for instance), contemporary man disputes God's right to disturb the laws of the universe. Miracles still happen, as in the Middle Ages, but men's receptive capacity is less. The rigor of the historical and physical sciences has fashioned a scientific and critical mentality (in itself perfectly legitimate), which enters deeply into the character of the man of the twentieth century. Consequently the influence actually exerted by miracles has undergone a decline. The unsophisticated believe in marvels as easily as before, but the *milieux* affected by scienti-

---

30. K. Rahner in: *Écrits théologiques III* (Brussels-Paris, 1963), pp. 171-203: English translation, *Theological Investigations III* (London and New York, 1967).

fic culture are less open to the action of miracle than the cultivated *milieux* of previous centuries.[31]

The sign which seems to exert a special attraction over our
contemporaries is the sign of *sanctity*. While there are no fewer
physical miracles in our time than before, the man of today
is not so much impressed by God's intervention in nature
as by his presence and action in human beings. If God's
right to intervene in the cosmos is disputed, his power to convert
and transform the human soul is more readily admitted.

The sign of the Church, normally the richest and most attractive of signs, admits in the concrete of alternations of light
and shadow, according to the variability of the qualities which
go to make it up. Sanctity, unity and stability vary, and, in
the same proportion the efficacy of the sign will vary. The
splendor of the Church, and therefore her power to attract,
depend especially on her holiness. In the early centuries charity
seems to have been the sign *par excellence* by which Christ's
disciples were recognized (Jn 13:35). "The multitude of believers had but one heart and mind" (Acts 4:32). In this springtime of the Church the Spirit of Christ acted freely. The
shadows of egotism and hatred did not obscure his full light.
The life of the Church, as a pure glass, was the transparent sign
of the love preached and lived by Christ, even to the consummation of the cross. The freshness of grace breathed in
the new creation. In periods when the Church's holiness seems
to diminish, her radiance is dimmed. The two most serious
breaks with Rome took place, "the first, after a century and a
half of the papacy's degradation, the second, after a whole
series of pontificates steeped in a spirit showing little resemblance to that of the Body of Christ." [32] Now, in the twentieth

---

31. F. H. Lepargneur, "La nature fonctionnelle du miracle," *Nouvelle
Revue théologique,* 84 (1962): 291-292. On the other hand, present day
science is making more precise the line of demarcation between what
science will probably one day be able to explain, and what is basically
and permanently outside its competence. At the same time, science is

century, at the time of the Second Vatican Council, the sign of the Church seems to be experiencing a new visibility and a new force. The presence among men of this society which appeals to the intervention of God in Jesus Christ, which confesses its weaknesses and faults, which prays to the Lord in union with its separated brethren, which in a sincere longing for unity and charity corrects its past errors and labors to become holy, arouses men's interest and evokes their questioning. Once again the Church presents herself to the world as a standard lifted up among the nations.[33]

6. Signs and Counter-signs

Closely connected with the problem of the relative efficacy of signs in history is the problem of their partial or total inefficacy, by reason of factors which compromise or annul their action. Besides signs, there exist indeed *counter-signs,* or signs which negate.

For the gospel to be *sufficiently* proposed to men, its preaching must be accompanied by signs which solidly attest its credibility and divine origin. Is it then enough—for us to be able to speak of a sufficient proposal of the gospel, exerting a moral obligation to believe on those who hear it—that it should be preached and spread in a country with an account of the historical signs which accompanied its promulgation by Christ? One is tempted to say yes; for the signs which accompanied the promulgation of the gospel by Christ (holiness, miracles, resurrection and so on) certainly constitute a very solid divine testimony in favor of the divine origin of Christianity.[34]

In fact, however, this "objectively sufficient" proposal of the

---

both making easier our means of investigation, and developing in our minds greater demands than before. Cf. F. H. Lepargneur, *ibid.,* p. 292.

32. G. De Broglie, *Les signes de crédibilité de la révélation chrétienne,* p. 62: trans., *Revelation and Reason.*

---

33. Denzinger-Schönmetzer, n. 3014.
34. *Ibid.,* nn. 3009, 3539, 3876.

gospel—to speak in the terminology of the scholastics [35]—can be undermined by counter-signs. If for instance the preaching of the gospel in a country coincided with the spectacle of the habitual violation of the gospel among those who professed it (whether preachers or people) one could say that this spectacle would constitute a *counter-sign* or *witness against*. How can a religion which appeals to Christ, the Son of God, and which claims to transform the heart of man and make him a son of the Father, given life by the Spirit of God, offer at the same time the spectacle of division, hatred, cruelty, impiety and other immorality? If Christianity cannot show *in practice* this change in the human condition announced by the gospel, it confesses its failure. Christ and the Church are at this point so linked in the concrete economy of salvation that the presence of a counter-sign *today* can paralyze and even destroy the influence of the signs formerly posited by Christ. The sign of the gospel can be annulled by the counter-sign of a scandalous Christianity, even to the extent that among those who witness it the moral obligation to believe does not arise.

St. Augustine said long ago, "Those who approach me ready to believe . . . are turned aside by the bad lives of false or lukewarm Christians. How many do you suppose, brothers, would like to become Christians, but are offended by the bad morals of Christians?" [36] And in a letter of 14 January 1549, St. Francis Xavier wrote to St. Ignatius of Loyola, "As for the native pagans, they have a horror of Christianity, and the task of the moment is to protect against them those who have become Christians. No doubt many would be converted if the

---

35. Cf. Suarez, for example: "Statuendum est ad *sufficientem* objecti fidei propositionem non satis esse objectum utcumque proponi tamquam dictum seu revelatum a Deo, sed necessarium saltem esse cum talibus circumstantiis proponi ut prudenter appareat credibile, eo modo quo proponitur" (*De Fide,* disp. 4, sect. n. 3).

36. "Vicini mei nimium deterriti sunt mala vita malorum et falsorum christianorum. Quam multos enim putatis, fratres mei, velle esse christianos, sed offendi malis moribus christianorum?" (Augustinus, *Enarrationes in psalmos,* ps. 60, sermo II, 6: P. L., 36, col. 243).

neophytes were decently treated by the Portuguese, but seeing them despised no one wants to join them." [37] And in the sixteenth century again, Francis de Vitoria wrote in his *De Indis recenter inventis*:

"The Indians are not obliged to believe the moment they have heard the Christian faith preached, so that they would be sinning mortally against it by the mere fact that it had been announced to them as the true religion.... It does not even appear to me clearly that the Christian faith has yet been sufficiently announced and proposed to them, in such a way that they would be bound under pain of sin to accept it. They would be bound to believe only if the Christian faith were proposed to them with witness worthy of persuading them. And I do not hear that anyone has worked miracles among them, or shown them extraordinary examples of sanctity. On the contrary they have been shown the spectacle of manifold scandals, horrible crimes and innumerable impieties. It does not seem to me, therefore, that the Christian religion has been preached to them in such a holy and proportionate manner that they would be bound to adhere to it. And yet many religious and priests would have sufficed for this task, through their lives, their example and their apostolate, if they had not been prevented by men who have entirely different concerns." [38]

In the twentieth century the Second Vatican Council has stressed very strongly that division and lack of charity among Christians blots out the light of the Church. The decree on missions says, "Division among Christians damages the most holy cause of preaching the gospel to every creature, and for many shuts the door to faith." [39] And in the decree on ecu-

---

37. P.-L. J.-M. Cros, *Saint François de Xavier, sa vie et ses lettres* (2 vols., Paris, 1900), vol. 1, p. 424.

38. "Barbari non ad primum nuntium fidei christianae tenentur credere ipsum, ita quod peccent mortaliter non credentes solum per hoc quod simpliciter annuntiatur eis et proponitur quod vera religio est christiana et quod Christus est Salvator et Redemptor mundi, sine miraculis aut quacumque alia probatione aut suasione.... Non satis liquet mihi an fides christiana fuerit barbaris hactenus ita proposita et annuntiata ut teneantur

menism, the Council declares that discord among Christians "is a stumbling-block to the world, and an obstacle to the most holy of all causes, the preaching of the gospel to every creature." [40] Wherever the Church no longer offers the witness of unity and charity but that of division and hatred, she not only fails to draw men to her, but drives them from her in horror. The converts of the twentieth century confirm in their testimonies that the greatest obstacle to their entering the Church was, after their own past, the spectacle of unfaithful Christians.

In all these cases, *the lack of obviousness* which necessarily affects knowledge of a revelation made indirectly, through signs and historical witness, is increased by the fact that the gospel proposed as mankind's salvation avows itself incapable of producing the transformation it proclaims. For if it is true that Christ is the Sign *par excellence*, in whom there is no shadow, it is nonetheless true that the *total* sign of revelation is *Christ-and-his-work*, and that we have no access to the historical sign of Christ except through his present sign, the Church. It is through the Church that we know Christ, and it is by the

---

credere sub novo peccato. Hoc dico quia ... non tenentur credere nisi proponatur eis fides cum probabili persuasione. Sed miracula et signa nulla audio, nec exempla vitae adeo religiosa. Immo contra multa scandala et saeva facinora et multas impietates. Unde non videtur quod religio christiana satis commode et pie sit illis praedicata ut illi teneantur acquiescere: quamquam videntur multi religiosi et alii ecclesiastici viri, et vita et exemplis et diligenti praedicatione sufficienter operam et industriam adhibuisse in hoc negotio, nisi ab aliis, quibus alia cura est, impediti essent" (F. De Vitoria, *De Indis recenter inventis, relectio prior,* in: T. Urdanoz, ed., *Obras de Francisco de Vitoria* (BAC, Madrid, 1960), p. 692 and p. 695). On the same subject, see C. Journet, *L'Église du Verbe incarné,* II (Paris, 1951), pp. 852-859; *Ibid.,* "Les promulgations de la loi nouvelle ou manifestations de l'Église," *Nova et Vetera,* 40 (1965): 210-223.

39. "Divisio christianorum sanctissimae causae praedicandi Evangelium omni creaturae detrimentum affert et aditum ad fidem multis praecludit" (*Decretum de activitate missionali Ecclesiae,* n. 6).

---

40. "Quae sane divisio et aperte voluntati Christi contradicit et scandalo est mundo atque sanctissimae causae praedicandi Evangelium omni creaturae affert detrimentum" (*Decretum de oecumenismo,* n. 1).

Church that we measure the actual efficacy of the gospel. Hence if the life of the Church contradicts the gospel, it extinguishes or dims the brilliance of the total sign (Christ and his work), and renders it *ambiguous* to the point that in certain cases a man confronted with the gospel no longer feels himself bound in conscience to believe in a doctrine which, far from giving proof of what it says, clearly establishes the contrary. Life has refuted the gospel.

A particularly heavy responsibility rests, therefore, upon societies which profess to be Christian and Catholic. It is possible that whole nations have so obscured or distorted the gospel as to make it unrecognizable by sincere and upright minds. A nation, predominantly Catholic, which offered the spectacle of the habitual violation of the precepts of the natural law (respect for life, justice and truth), and which lived at the opposite pole from the evangelical law of brotherly love, or which appeared more given over to the pleasures of the flesh, more attached to the goods of this world than nations outside the Church, would constitute for our separated brethren or for pagans living in the midst of such a nation, a perpetual *counter-sign*, capable of annihilating the obligation to believe. The signs of revelation are so bound up together that the presence of a counter-sign can prevent the action of authentic signs, numerous and mutually coherent though these may be.

7. *The present age and eschatology*

Because they constitute an irruption of the beyond into our universe, of eternity into time, grace into nature, the signs of revelation arouse in man a sort of *tension*, between his attachment to earth—the sign of his present condition—and the reality of his future and definitive state. The signs are inserted into our world, elements of which they employ, but on the other hand they come to us as calls from a distant world, whose splendor they foreshadow. They therefore arouse in us a lively sense that though we live here, our home is there. This is a *salutary* tension, which prevents man from cleaving to the earth as if it were the definitive place of his existence, his home.

The signs keep him on the alert, waiting for the Bridegroom. This is true of miracle, of prophecy, of sanctity.

Because man is a child of the earth, he is tempted to establish himself there forever, and forget his condition as a pilgrim. He needs *security*, and he finds this security in understanding the world he lives in, in harnessing its forces and formulating its laws. And then, suddenly, a *miracle*, by its departure from known laws, excites his attention, but at the same time introduces insecurity into the texture of security: it upsets, and it is meant to upset.[41] Before the question posed by the miraculous event, man looks for a new security, trying to integrate this foreign element into a higher synthesis of the universe. He may stubbornly persist in seeking this integration at a scientific level, but in fact, miracle, by its structure as an anomaly, taking place in a religious context, is intended to help him to discover the principle of this integration in a higher order, an order of grace, dominated not by the determinism of laws alone, but by a *Person*, who uses the order of law for the sake of the order of person, that is, the order of salvation.[42]

The abnormality introduced into cosmic determinism thus becomes the expression of an interpersonal language, and the momentary disturbance caused in the network of laws serves to detach man from his earthly security in order to make him sensitive to the unpredictable designs of grace. He is invited to found his life, not on the security of laws, but on the love of a Person. Miracle reminds him that the real master of matter is not man, but the transcendent God. It reminds him also that the order of charity, into which he is called, incomparably surpasses the order of law, since God does not hesitate to break the latter in order to signify the existence of the former. And lastly it reminds him that we have already entered the final age, which is to culminate in the creation of a new heaven and a new earth.[43]

41. F. H. Lepargneur, "La nature fonctionelle du miracle," *Nouvelle Revue théologique*, 84 (1962): 284.

42. *Ibid.*, 284-286.

43. *Constitutio pastoralis de Ecclesia in mundo hujus temporis*, n. 39.

Miracle, said St. Augustine, strikes the senses in order to stir the spirit. It manifests itself to our eyes in order to lead us to wonder at the God we do not see, seeking to arouse in us the desire to contemplate in a spirit of faith and with purified eyes, the invisible God whom we have learnt to know through his visible works.[44] Because men do not pay attention to what they do not see, says Augustine, God makes use of temporal blessings (healing and resurrection from the dead) in order to establish their faith in the eternal blessings which they do not see.[45] Miracle both draws us to the sensible and at the same time detaches us from it. It moves the senses, but in order to direct the spirit; it makes use of our propensity to the material to raise us up to the spiritual: it is inserted into our world in order to introduce us to the world beyond.

While miracle introduces a tension between the order of law and the order of grace, *prophecy* introduces a tension between *human* history and *supernatural* history. Man instinctively wants to make himself the sole master and agent of human history. Whether the end is conceived as the advent of Absolute Spirit (as in Hegel) or as the advent of Humanity (as in Marxist conceptions) man claims to construct and direct this history himself. Then prophecy, by its presence, *makes us doubt* that human history is merely natural and in the hands of man alone. It proclaims that history has an end, and that its goal is a personal Life, intending to realize, in collaboration with man, a design of salvation, which is disclosed to man little by little. This design is the building up of the total Christ, and the construction of the heavenly city, the new Jerusalem, in the communion of the divine persons.

Lastly, *sanctity* introduces a tension between earthly man, subject to sin, and heavenly man, moved by the Spirit. The saint is one of us, living among us, and yet he disturbs us; for he gives the impression of living in another world. He lives among men, but he behaves already as the blessed do. He

---

44. S. Augustinus, *In Jo. Evang. tract.* 24: P.L., 35, col. 1592-1593.
45. S. Augustinus, *Sermones de Scripturis, sermo* LXXXVIII: P. L., 38, col. 539.

prefigures man's ultimate fulfillment, and anticipates our resurrection from the dead. His love, like that of God, is undivided,
and stoops to the dispossessed. In its purity it reminds us of
the transcendent action of resurrection upon flesh and blood.
In his detachment from earthly goods the saint shows those
of heaven already present in the world, filling to overflowing
the emptiness of the disinherited.[46] In his wholly filial way
of life, he recalls the freedom of Christ—totally free because
totally loving. The saint is the prophet of the age to come: by
his entire existence he witnesses to the new creation, *making
present* among men the future to which they are called.

In the tension which they sustain between time and eternity,
the signs of revelation are apt beyond an initial power to convert: they tend to develop in us our life of union with God.

8.   *The interconnection and convergence of the signs*

Just as the mysteries of Christianity form a coherent pattern, in which every part is consistent with every other part,
so too with the signs of revelation. If for purposes of analysis
we have to isolate each sign and submit it to a separate examination, we must never lose sight of the fact that in reality
the signs are never independent entities. They are bound up
with one another and cast light on one another; more than that,
they generally present themselves in constellations, acting by
means of convergence, just as our recognition of a person is
brought about not by one trait of his countenance, but by
the *tout ensemble* of his face.

So *miracle* and *message* sustain and illuminate each other.
"The miracles authenticate the doctrine, and the doctrine the
miracles," said Pascal.[47] On the one hand, the miracle as it

---

46. This is particularly true of the martyr, who sacrifices the present
life in order to witness to the reality and depth of the good which is to
come. On sanctity as an anticipation of the perfection of the life to
come, there are many conciliar texts. Cf. *Lumen gentium,* nn. 44 and 46;
Perfectae caritatis, n. 12.

47. Pascal, *Pensées,* fr. 803.

were recommends the prophet as the envoy of God, and seals
what he says as coming from God, since God would not lend
the support of his omnipotence to an objectively false doctrine.
But on the other hand it is from what he says that the miracle
derives its full significance; it is thanks to the message that its
meaning becomes rich and exact. The resurrection for instance,
torn out of the Christian synthesis, would no longer be anything but an unintelligible, unthinkable fact—a piece of pure
nonsense. And, lastly, the discernment of a miracle could
not be achieved without taking into account the context of
holiness in which it happens. The examination of the religious
context of a miracle implies ultimately an examination of the
moral value of the thaumaturge—his religious personality, his
faithfulness to God, his devotion to men, his spiritual and
intellectual courage.[48]

Holiness, *sanctity,* is, for its own part, closely connected with
message; for it is in holiness that the message takes on body
and life: it is from the lived gospel that the preached gospel
derives its force and demonstrates its truth. And on the other
hand, miracles are the quasi-normal accompaniment of the
presence of holiness in our world: they arise spontaneously, as
ordinary signs of the love with which God surrounds his saints,
as sparks of the operative presence of grace in them, of their
sharing in the glory of the risen Christ.[49]

It is in the life of Christ that this interconnection of the
signs is most clearly seen. What confirms the truth of his
testimony is not simply the appearance of miracles and prophecies, but even more the fact that his testimony and the signs
he gave form a coherent whole, whose elements are all at
the same depth, and interwoven like the threads of a seamless
fabric. Christ presents himself as the Father's Son and the
Father's equal, sharing the Father's secrets and his power,
as the Savior from sin and the vanquisher of death. Correspondingly he appears among men in the glory of Yahweh, exercising

48. R. W. Gleason, "Miracles and Contemporary Theology," *Thought,*
37 (Spring 1962), p. 21.
49. L. Monden, *Le Miracle, signe de salut,* pp. 68-69.

power over the cosmos, over sickness and death; he is the object of a miracle unique in history, a spontaneous and glorious resurrection; he is "holy before God, terrible to demons, totally without sin" (Pascal); finally his teaching is such that even his enemies confess that "never man spoke like this man." His witness to himself, his miracles, his wisdom, his holiness, his resurrection—all this holds together, all this is on the same plane. More than this, Christ is the source of a society in which its founder's signs of power and sanctity are prolonged. Bound to one another, bound to the testimony and work of Christ, the signs form an indivisible cluster of light.

The *presentation* of signs must, then, like their economy itself, be synthetizing, "catholic." The proof of Christianity emerges from the Christian synthesis of the signs, that is from the totality of signs in Christ and the Church. The signs flow from Christ and the Church like rays of light from a single flame, and in the design of God they are intended to act by the convergence of their rays. By their multiplicity, their diversity and their unity, they show that the salvation preached and proclaimed has really taken place. It is only, then, from pedagogical necessity, that we separate what in reality is one.

This Christian synthesis of the signs is in the first place a *collective possession* of the Church as a social body; for no individual Christian could claim to know, still less to exhaust the intelligibility of, each and all of the signs of revelation. Individual believers, in various degrees, according to their intelligence, cultivation and grace, share in the knowledge of the Church. This participation in the collective knowledge and certainty of the Church has its importance, especially in the case of signs—such as that for instance which is drawn from the fulfillment of messianic prophecy—which are rich in intelligibility but very complex, and consequently difficult to interpret.

At the individual level, it needs to be remembered, there is from one person to another, an "irreducible originality in the synthesis of signs." [50] Such diversity is not remarkable; for

---

50. G. De Broglie, *Les signes de crédibilité de la révélation chrétienne*, pp. 154-155: trans., *Revelation and Reason*.

it is often a matter of appreciating values of the spiritual order
(in the case of holiness), or of recognizing correspondences with
one's own concrete aspirations (in the case of message). Judgments of this sort are always founded to a certain extent on
subjective elements; for each one assesses values according to
his own inclinations, whether these are native, acquired or infused. This law of variability was already at work among the
first auditors of Christ, the apostles, the scribes and Pharisees,
and the common people. Not only did the experience which
constituted the point of departure for a judgment differ from
one individual to another, but also the action of the signs which
each perceived depended to a large extent on his previous
knowledge, his culture, his temperament, his center of interest,
his prejudices; his intellectual and moral dispositions.[51] It was
all these variable factors which diversified the synthesis which
each one made from that of his neighbor.

If this was true of the complex sign of Christ, it is no
less true of the complex sign of the Church. No individual
can have anything more than a limited perception of the
Church and her manifestations, a perception commensurate
with his own experience, study and chance encounters. There
are no two Christians whose faith is founded on precisely the
same motives of credibility; nor are there any two persons whose
synthesis of the signs, made on the basis of one and the same
apologetical demonstration, would be identical. The synthesis
presented would affect each in his own way.

Let us notice finally that the synthesis of the signs on
which Christian faith is founded is never made once for all.
It can always be enriched and strengthened by study and experience. For his intellectual and spiritual health every Christian
should constantly nourish his own personal synthesis of the
signs of Christian credibility. A deeper study of the signs will
perhaps reveal their cogency in a way scarcely glimpsed before.

---

51. *Ibid.*, p. 155.

9. The unity of the signs in Christ and the Church

The more we study the signs, and the more we seek to understand their economy, the more we realize that their center of unity and gravity is to be found in Christ and in the Church, which, century after century, is the sacrament of Christ.

All the signs emanate from Christ, and it is in him that their synthesis is complete. He is in Person the Sign of revelation *par excellence*, the absolutely sure sign, adapted to the intelligence of us all. If the signs form a unified and coherent synthesis, it is because the center from which they radiate is a Person. Christ is the goal and bond of the totality of signs.

Christ is at once the Fullness and the Sign of revelation. He reveals the Father in his words and in his works, in his death and resurrection, in his whole presence and the manifestation which he makes of himself." [52] But because Christ is present among men as the Father's Son, there is in his message, in his actions and his behavior as the incarnate Word, a radiance which is properly speaking his glory, and which designates him as the Father's Son. In him, the same realities which serve to communicate revelation serve also to *authenticate* it. The sublimity of his doctrine, the holiness of his life, the power deployed in his miracles and in his resurrection, the excess of charity manifested by his death, all this radiance of the being and action of Christ is, as the constitution *Dei verbum* tells us, a witness which confirms the truth of his words, that in him God is present among us to save us and bring us to everlasting life. [53] The signs of revelation are not therefore external to Christ; they

---

52. *Constitutio dogmatica de divina revelatione*, c. 1, n. 4.

53. "Quapropter Ipse, quem qui videt, videt et Patrem (cf. Jn 14, 9), tota suiipsius praesentia ac manifestatione, verbis et operibus, signis et miraculis, praesertim autem morte sua et gloriosa ex mortuis resurrectione, misso tandem Spiritu veritatis, revelationem complendo perficit ac testimonio divino confirmat, Deum nempe nobiscum esse ad nos ex peccati mortisque tenebris liberandos et in aeternam vitam resuscitandos" (*Constitutio dogmatica de divina revelatione*, c. 1, n. 4).

are the shining among men of his power and wisdom and holiness as the Father's Son. And we pass directly from the reflection of light to its source; we conclude from the splendor we see to the truth of the testimony.

All the particular signs have value and consistency only in so far as they carry us back to Christ, their center and their synthesis. *Miracle* is the shining of salvation through the supernaturalized and transformed cosmos. But this supernaturalization implies at its root the Person of Christ, on whom this influx of divine light and life into our world depends.[54] The transformation of the cosmos, in particular, is closely linked with the glory of the risen Christ, whose body is a perpetual miracle. In the risen Christ, the work of salvation is accomplished, the new creation is complete, and even the cosmos is affected by it. In the risen Christ, the two realities of invisible salvation and visible transformation of the world coincide. In this context of salvation, miracle appears as the gesture of the risen Christ. It is the visible sign of the profound mutation which, in him, affects man and the whole universe inhabited by man. Henceforth every miracle proceeds from the risen Christ.[55]

As in the case of miracle so in the case of history: Christ is the end and object of history, who illumines the whole past by anticipation. *Prophecy* is a fact of eschatology, which has no meaning except in the culmination of all times and ages in the Person of Christ. Any and every point in history is explicable only through this end for which it prepares. "It is because Christ is eternity in time that the definitive totalization of time is a reality."[56] Christ announced, Christ promised, is the principle of intelligibility of all prophecy: it was thus that Christ presented himself to the disciples on the way to Emmaus; it was thus that Peter on the morning of Pentecost, and Stephen, before the Sanhedrin, presented Christ.

---

54. C. Dumont, "Unité et diversité des signes de la Révélation," *Nouvelle Revue théologique*, 80 (1958): 154.

55. *Ibid.*, pp. 139-140.

56. *Ibid.*, p. 154.

Christ is the unitary principle which dominates everything. From whatever angle one looks at revelation and its signs, one's eyes are drawn in the end to him. Most of all is this evident in the case of *sanctity*. Holiness indeed has no meaning except in reference to Christ, the source and exemplar of all holiness. Through his resurrection and the sending of the Spirit, Christ becomes the principle of all sanctification and of all filial life. The Spirit who moves the saints to do always the will of the Father is the Spirit of Christ himself; he is a filial Spirit, a Spirit of love.

In the Incarnation, the human body has its capacity for expression raised to the infinite: it expresses God. It is in fact by means of his Body that Christ makes God present among men. He manifests God through all the resources, all the virtualities of human nature. Miracle and sanctity are rays of his glory, that is of his divine being, which are visible through his human Body. The risen Christ prolongs his action in another Body, which is also truly his Body and his permanent means of expression in history, that is, in the Church.[57] And just as Christ was at once the Revealer and the Sign of revelation, so the Church is at once the presence of revelation through the centuries and the sign of that revelation.[58] The relationship between the signs of the Church and the signs of Christ is the same as that between the mystical Body of Christ and his glorious risen Body. Because the Church is the Bride and the very Body of Christ, the traits of the Bridegroom are visible in her. The characteristics which revealed God in Christ continue to reveal him in the Church. The glory which shone in the face of Christ shines now in the face of the Church. Throughout the centuries the Church is the sacrament of Christ [59]; she is "the great power of signs set up among the nations, even as Christ was in his

---

57. J. Mouroux, *Sens chrétien de l'homme* (Paris, 1945), p. 79: trans., *The Meaning of Man* (New York, no date).

58. Martin declared to the First Vatican Council: "Ecclesia, quae quasi concreta est divina revelatio exhibens nobis cum veritatibus credendis etiam motiva credibilitatis" (Coll. Lac., VII: col. 167).

59. *Constitutio dogmatica de Ecclesia*, c. 1, n. 1.

own person." [60] But whereas the signs in Christ are concentrated in a single point of space and time, in the Church they are spread out through the dimensions of history and geography. In the Church as in Christ there are found signs in nature ("admirable propagation" for instance and miracles), in history (unity, stability, durability), and in man (sanctity, martyrdom, fruitfulness in good works). But unlike Christ, the Church, because she is composed of sinners, shows signs of weakness as well as signs of glory. Yet she remains nonetheless a sign; for it is through her weaknesses, and in spite of them, that the power of God manifests itself and triumphs in her.

10. *The total Sign: Christ in the Church*

Christ and the Church are then the two great signs of revelation, and in fact the only two signs. All the historical signs of revelation come back to Christ, and all the signs from Pentecost to the parousia come back to Christ's Church, as his Bride and the mystical Body of his risen life. The signs are the radiance of his glory and the glory of his Bride.

But we can carry this synthetic view of the signs still further, and say that in the last analysis there is only *one* sign of the truth of Christianity and that is *Christ-in-the-Church*. The *total* sign is the Sign of Christ perceived through the Church, the sacrament of Christ, or the sign of the Sign of God.

In the economy of salvation, the sign of Christ and the sign of the Church are so inseparable that every darkening of the sign of the Church affects at the same time the action of the sign of Christ—not that Christ in himself can become less luminous, but that his light like that of the sun screened by clouds no longer reaches mankind. Just as it is the Church's mission to offer Christ and his word of salvation to the men of every age, so it is her mission also to manifest to them the

---

60. J. Mouroux, *Sens chrétien de l'homme*, p. 79: trans., *The Meaning of Man.*

efficacy of that word. She must then present herself to the men of each generation in the visible likeness of the salvation accomplished and proclaimed by the gospel, so that the sight of men gathered together in charity may witness more loudly than the voices of preachers that Charity has come among us. In the time of Pilate and Caesar men encountered salvation in Christ. Now it is in the Church and through the Church that men normally encounter Christ and salvation. If the word of the Church ceases to make itself heard, the world dies in ignorance of the salvation which is offered to it. But if the Church ceases to live by the word of salvation, this word itself becomes a vain word, a lie, incapable of keeping its promises and therefore without efficacy. The Church must be the transparent sign of Christ whom she announces, so that she may diffuse, without reducing or corrupting it, the plenitude of his light and his glory. The total sign is Christ in the Church and through the Church.*

---

* Translator's note: I was very grateful indeed to be able to check my translation of Chapter II with the text of Fr. Avery Dulles, S.J., of Woodstock, who had translated this chapter for his students.

CHAPTER III

Christ, the Sign of Revelation

ACCORDING TO THE CONSTITUTION DEI VERBUM

The first chapter of the constitution *Dei verbum* presents Christ as at the same time the Fullness and the Sign of revelation. The paragraph which situates him in the history of the world and in the economy of revelation, and which proposes him as the climax and perfection of this history and this economy is probably the high point of the constitution's achievement. After speaking to us through the prophets, says the text, God has spoken to us in his Son (Heb 1:1-2). He has sent the Son, who is his eternal Word, to live among men to tell us the secrets of that divine life into which he invites and desires us to be introduced. Jesus Christ is, then, the Word of God made flesh, become one of us, that is, become man, and sent to us in order to meet and understand us at our own level. Jesus Christ is the Word of God who literally "speaks the words of God, and accomplishes the work of salvation which the Father has given him to do" (Jn 5:36; 17:4). Christ is at once the supreme Revealer and the supreme Revelation, the God who reveals and the Mystery which is revealed. "It is, then, he," the text of the constitution continues "—to see him is to see the Father (Jn 14:9)—who, through his whole presence and the manifestation which he makes of himself, through his

words and his works, through his signs and his miracles, and
most of all through his death and glorious resurrection from
the dead and through the sending of the Spirit of truth, gives
to revelation its complete fulfillment and the confirmation of
divine witness that God himself is with us to save us from
the darkness of sin and death and bring us to everlasting life." [1]
So, by means of the same reality of his presence and manifestation in the world, Christ is both the Revelation of the Father
and the Sign of the authenticity of this revelation: *he is in
himself the Sign of revelation.*

1. *Literary and doctrinal antecedents*

This statement of the Second Vatican Council suggests in
its literary structure and doctrinal content two comparisons,
which both throw a good deal of light on the text of the constitution itself.

1. The first, of a doctrinal sort, is suggested by the text of
Pius IX's encyclical *Qui pluribus* (9 November 1846). Enumerat-
ing and assembling in a vast synthesis all the signs which allow
us to establish with certainty the divine origin of Christianity,
the encyclical brings back all the signs of revelation to Christ
and his message. The Christian faith, says the text, "was confirmed by the birth of its author, Jesus Christ, who led it to
perfection through his life, his death, his resurrection, his wisdom, his miracles, his prophecies." [2] The likeness of this to the
text of the Second Vatican Council is striking, both in form
and in content:

---

1. "Quapropter Ipse, quem qui videt, videt et Patrem (cf. Jn 14,
9), tota suiipsius praesentia ac manifestatione, verbis et operibus, signis
et miraculis, praesertim autem morte sua et gloriosa ex mortuis resurrectione, misso tandem Spiritu veritatis, revelationem complendo perficit ac testimonio divino confirmat, Deum nempe nobiscum esse ad nos
ex peccati mortisque tenebris liberandos et in aeternam vitam resuscitandos"
(*De divina revelatione*, c. 1, n. 4).
2. Denzinger-Schönmetzer, n. 2779.

Qui pluribus	*The Second Vatican Council*
HAEC FIDES	JESUS CHRISTUS
	tota suiipsius praesentia
	ac manifestatione,
nativitate, vita,	verbis et operibus,
morte, resurrectione,	signis et miraculis,
sapientia, prodigiis,	praesertim autem morte sua
vaticinationibus	et gloriosa ex mortuis resurrectione
	misso tandem Spiritu veritatis
JESU CHRISTI	REVELATIONEM
divini sui AUCTORIS	COMPLENDO PERFICIT
et CONSUMMATORIS	ac divino testimonio
CONFIRMATA	CONFIRMAT

These two texts are at the same time like and unlike. In both cases they deal with the signs constituted by the life and works of Christ; in both cases also, Christ is presented as the author and the consummation of revelation (Heb 1:1-2); finally in both cases it is stated that Christ's life and works *confirm* revelation. It is noticeable, nevertheless, that there are important differences in the respective orientation of the texts. In the encyclical, attention is directed first and foremost upon *the object of faith* itself, that is to say the doctrine of salvation of which Christ is the author; in *Dei verbum,* Christ, the Son of the Father and the Word of the Father, is first of all in evidence. In the encyclical, the signs are brought back to Christ, but not in that relationship in depth which makes the Person of the Word incarnate the focus from which the signs radiate. The point of the text turns upon the fact that the *Christian faith* (in the objective sense) is *confirmed* by the life, words and works of Christ, who is both its author and its fulfillment. But the encyclical does not express as pregnantly as the constitution *Dei verbum* the fact that Christ, *in and by the whole of himself,* and in and by the same realities, at once *consummates* and *confirms* revelation. Nevertheless, the text of the encyclical, by the synthetizing way in which it presents the signs, and brings them all back to Christ, anticipates both the doctrine and the literary structure of the Second Vatican Council.

2. A second parallel, this time rather of a literary sort, is suggested by a text of the First Vatican Council on the Church, *in and by herself* a motive of credibility, in the same way as Christ, *in and by himself*, is the Sign of revelation. Although nothing, either in the expositions of Christ as the Evidence of faith, or in the illustrative notes which accompany the diverse redactions of *Dei verbum*, leaves room for believing that there was any conscious and deliberate connection between the declarations of the Second Vatican Council and those of the First, it is impossible not to be struck by the parallelism between the two texts which propose the fundamental signs of revelation, Christ and the Church.

Of the *Church,* the First Vatican Council says that she is "the guardian and governor of the word revealed." [3] Of *Christ,* the Second Vatican Council says that he gives to revelation "its complete fulfillment"; for he is in person the very Word of God made flesh. The *Church* is *"in and by herself,"* that is, by her presence and manifestation in the world, the sign of her divine mission. *Christ,* in the same way, confirms revelation "in and through his whole presence and the manifestation which he makes of himself" in the world. These general statements are followed in each case by a more detailed treatment. The *Church* is a sign "by reason of her marvelous expansion, her eminent sanctity, her inexhaustible fruitfulness in every good, by reason of her Catholic unity and her invincible stability." *Christ* is the sign of revelation "through his words and his works, by his signs and his miracles, and above all through his death and glorious resurrection from the dead, and through the sending of the Spirit of truth." *The Church,* concludes the First Vatican Council, is thus "a great and perpetual motive of credibility, and an undeniable witness to her divine mission." *Christ,* says the Second Vatican Council, gives to revelation "the confirmation of divine witness that God is among us to save us from the darkness of sin and death and bring us to everlasting life."

---

3. *Ibid.,* n. 3012.

Vatican I	Vatican II
(a) ECCLESIA	(a) CHRISTUS, Filius Dei Verbum caro factum
(b) custos et magistra verbi revelati . . .	(b) revelationem complendo perficit
(c) per seipsa	(c) tota suiipsius praesentia ac manifestatione,
(d) ob suam admirabilem propagationem, eximiam sanctitatem et inexhaustam in omnibus bonis foecunditatem, ob catholicam unitatem invictamque stabilitatem	(d) verbis et operibus, signis et miraculis, morte sua et gloriosa ex mortuis resurrectione, misso tandem Spiritu veritatis,
(e) magnum quoddam et perpetuum est motivum credibilitatis et divinae suae legationis testimonium irrefragabile.	(e) et testimonio divino confirmat Deum nempe nobiscum esse ad nos ex peccati mortisque tenebris liberandos et in aeternam vitam resuscitandos.

Since he is among us as the Father's Son, as the Word of the Father, Christ occupies a unique and privileged position in revelation: he is at once revelation's *Plenitude* and, *par excellence,* its *Sign*—the Sign which *manifests God* and manifests itself *as God.* But we must never separate from Christ his substantial prolongation through the centuries, that is to say the Church. The Church refers us to Christ, whose sign she is: she is the sign of the Sign of God. So the Second Vatican Council, which declares in *Dei verbum* that Christ is in himself the Sign of revelation, declares also in *Lumen gentium* that "the Church is, in Christ, as it were the sacrament, that is to say, at once the sign and the means, of the deep union between God and the human race as a whole."[4] From a dogmatic point of view, the mystery of Christ is of course primary, and it is by reference to Christ that the Church is to be defined, the mystery of the Church being subordinate to the mystery of Christ.

Hence one may ask oneself with a certain astonishment how it has come about that the magisterium declared first of the Church—at the First Vatican Council—that she is a sign in herself, and then, only after another century—at the Second

---

4. *Constitutio dogmatica de Ecclesia,* c. 1, n. 1.

Vatican Council—that Christ in himself is the Sign of revelation? The encyclical *Qui Pluribus*, it is true, gave prominence to the signs of the gospel, the life and the works of Christ, and the First Vatican Council declared in a general way, that "Moses and the prophets and above all Christ our Lord performed a great many miracles, and made prophecies of a very striking sort,"[5] but the magisterium had not yet discovered that happy way of expressing the matter discovered by the Second Vatican Council, which in one and the same phrase presents Christ as at once the supreme Revealer and the primordial, unequivocal Sign of revelation, and both of these through the same realities of his life.

The dialectical movement through which the emphasis has passed from the sign of the Church to the sign of Christ seems to have been this. The Second Vatican Council was characterized by a more lively awareness of the mystery of the Church—to which the constitution *Lumen gentium* is witness enough. Now it is precisely, it would seem, because the Church has been at pains to define her essence more exactly, that she has, as it were, *ceased to be centered on herself*, in order to be centered more wholly upon Christ.[6] It is in living more deeply the mystery of her own being that she is able to see more clearly her relation to Christ and his word. That is why the Second Vatican Council, which is so ecclesiocentric, is at the same time so Christocentric. While the constitution *Dei verbum* presents Christ as the Sign of God, the constitution *Lumen gentium* presents the Church as sign or sacrament "in Christ," and the magisterium does not place itself "over the word of God" but "at the service of the word of God."[7]

If we now examine the text of the Second Vatican Council in detail, we can group its elements either by setting out from the general structure of revelation as described in section two of the constitution (*gesta et verba intrinsece inter se connexa*),

---

5. Denzinger-Schönmetzer, n. 3009.

6. G. Martelet, "Horizon théologique de la deuxième session du Concile," *Nouvelle Revue théologique*, 86 (1964): 452-453.

7. *Constitutio dogmatica de divina revelatione*, c. 2, n. 10.

and applying this structure to the case of Christ, or by taking as our point of departure the first statement of the text we are studying, that is, that Christ is both Revealer and Sign of revelation through "his whole presence and through the manifestation which he makes of himself."

Looking at the matter from the first point of view we can distinguish, so to speak, the watershed of *facere* and *docere*. On one side, the side of words, we shall be able to locate the sign of "message," or the gospel (the sublimity and wisdom of this message); on the other, the side of deeds, we can place Christ's acts of mercy and forgiveness, his miracles and his resurrection, the superabundance of charity manifested by his passion and death, and finally the sending of the Spirit, with all the charisms with which he came.

In the second perspective, the signs appear as rays of light emanating from the same focal point. It seems to have been the intention of the Council to present the Incarnation of the Son, taken in the concrete, as the epiphany of God and also as *the veiled epiphany of his own glory*. Christ reveals through his works, but at the same time there is, in his works, especially in his miracles and his resurrection, a deployment of power which witnesses to the fact that in Christ the very power of Yahweh is in operation. Christ reveals through his words, but there is, in his teaching, such wisdom, such sublimity, that this teaching seems indeed to be the doctrine of the Father, as Christ himself affirms. Christ reveals the love of the Father, but there is, in his acts of mercy and forgiveness, in his attitude towards sinners, in the giving of himself even to the sacrifice of his life, the expression of a charity which is its own witness that, in the charity of Christ, we have known the charity of God.

2. *The signs and Christ's witness*

The signs of revelation are closely bound up with Christ's witness to himself and to his mission as Savior. This is what the Council is indicating when it says that Christ through his words and his works, through his miracles, his death and his resurrection, gives to revelation "the confirmation of divine witness that God himself is with us to save us from the darkness of sin and death and bring us to everlasting life." This is, indeed, the substance of Christ's witness: he presents himself, not only as the Messiah, the son of David, but as the equivalent of God among us, as Emmanuel. All his statements amount to this. Not that he declared himself God with the precision of terms of the Council of Nicea: [8] the scandal of God in the flesh was too great to be announced as bluntly as that.[9] He made use of titles already current in the tradition of the Old Testament, charging them with a meaning and orientation himself, in order to unveil gradually the mystery of his Person. By his words, as well as by his actions and his attitudes, he gave men to understand that he was more than human, beyond the prophets, and beyond the angels.

On the plane of verbal declarations, Christ, as we know, made use above all of that profound and mysterious figure with its manifold resonances, Daniel's Son of man. He presented himself as him who gives his life for the salvation of all (Mk 8: 31; Lk 9:22; Mt 17:12 and Mk 9:12; 9:31; 10:32-34), as he who "is to come to seek and save that which was lost" (Lk 19:10). "The Son of man came not to be served but to serve, and to give his life as a ransom for many" (Mk 10:45; cf. Jn 10, 10). The title, the Son of man, is, besides, associated with transcendent conceptions and a glorious destiny. At the most solemn moment of his earthly ministry, summoned to explain himself before the Sanhedrin, Christ declared himself "Christ, the Son of the Blessed." And then he added, "And you shall see the Son of man sitting at the right hand of power, and coming with the clouds of heaven" (Mk 14:62; Mt 26:64). In combining thus in one statement, the given images of psalm 110 and the vision of Daniel (Dn 7:13), Christ elevated himself to the plane of divinity. The members of the Sanhedrin understood so well that they cried out at the blasphemy. Not only did Christ attribute

---

8. Denzinger-Schönmetzer, n. 125.

9. R. E. Brown, "Does the New Testament call Jesus God?" *Theological Studies*, 26 (1965): 545-573.

to himself the future role of universal Judge at the end of time, but he declared that he was even *now* this celestial person, endowed with the prerogatives of God: even now, he had power "to remit sins" (Mk 2:7), and even now, he was the Lord of the sabbath (Mk 2:23-28). In fact, in other texts, Christ presented himself as the Son of the Father, sharing the inmost depths of the Father, the one and only person who enjoyed the Father's confidence and revealed his secrets (Mt 11:25-27). He was the Son and heir, sent after all the prophets had been sent, and put to death by the murderous vine-dressers (Mk 12:1-12).

These declarations of Christ during his ministry, although made in the context of the discretion imposed by the too "earthly" hopes of the Jews of his time, are nonetheless enough in themselves, in their number and convergence, to assure us that Christ himself proposed himself as the long-awaited Messiah, as the Savior who atones through his suffering and death for the sins of the world, as the pre-existent and eschatological Son of man, as the Son of the Father, who is the Good Shepherd, giving his life for the sheep. The Resurrection and Pentecost finally convinced the apostles that Christ *really* belonged to the world of the divine, and that he was *really* the Son of God come to give us life.[10] This awareness, already present during the lifetime of Christ, matured gradually, and continued to do so throughout the first century. St. John represents the furthest point in this reflection of the early Church on the divinity of the Christ of history. St. John, in fact, describes Christ as the eternal Word of God, distinct from him, but God as he is God. This Word, incarnate among men, is the Son of the Father, his only-begotten Son, come into the world to reveal the Father, and to make us his children (Jn 1:1-18). Christ is the Son sent in order that "whoever believes in him should not perish, but have everlasting life" (Jn 3:16; 10:10). He is the Resurrection and the Life (Jn 11:25-26). The inner life of the Father and the Son is a life of mutual presence and mutual immanence

---

10. P. Benoit, "La divinité de Jésus dans les Évangiles synoptiques," *Lumière et Vie*, n. 9 (April 1953), pp. 43-74; P.-E. Langevin, *Jésus Seigneur et l'eschatologie* (Bruges and Paris, 1967).

(Jn 10:38; 12:44; 14:9). St. John enunciates the primordial truth of Christianity: Jesus Christ is God and Savior. This also is what the Second Vatican Council has declared: Christ is *God-with-us* to save us from the darkness of sin and death and bring us to everlasting life.

All the signs of Christ's life are closely bound up with his witness to his mission as Savior, and have no meaning except in relation to this witness. Let me illustrate this by a few examples. Christ comes to destroy the power of sin and death, the empire of Satan. And his miracles appear precisely as acts of power, which demonstrate on a material plane, the *reality* of the spiritual liberation he has accomplished. Cures and exorcisms are only *figures* or *symbols* of the annihilation of Satan's power: they show that his kingdom is demonstrably crumbling and that the kingdom of God has come.[11] The healing of the paralytic establishes the fact that Christ has, as he declares, the power to remit sins (Mk 2:10). The setting free of those who are possessed is proof of the coming of the kingdom of God (Mt 12:28) and of Christ's victory over the Adversary (Lk 11:22; Acts 10:38). "The miracles of Jesus," says the constitution *Lumen gentium*, "prove that the kingdom of God has already come among us: 'if I by the finger of God cast out devils, no doubt the kingdom of God is come upon you.'"[12] In the raising of Lazarus Christ showed his sovereignty over life and death (Jn 11:1-44). And the miracles performed for pagans, whether by Christ (Mt 8:5-13), or in the past by Elijah and Elisha (for the widow of Sidon and Naaman the Syrian: Lk 4:25-28), emphasize the fact that salvation has come not only to the Jews, but also to the pagans.[13] All Christ's miracles are thus in intimate

---

11. J. Kallas, *The Significance of the Synoptic Miracles*, (London, 1961), pp. 77-79; Ph. H. Menoud, "La signification du miracle dans le Nouveau Testament," *Revue d'histoire et de philosophie religieuses*, 1948-1949, n. 3, p. 180.

12. "Miracula etiam Jesu Regnum jam in terris pervenisse comprobant: si in digito Dei ejicio daemonia, profecto pervenit in vos Regnum Dei" (Lk 11, 20; Mt 12, 28). Cf. *Constitutio dogmatica de Ecclesia*, c. 1, n. 5.

13. A. Feuillet, "La signification fondamentale du premier miracle de Cana," *Revue thomiste*, 65 (1965), p. 534; A. Richardson, *The Miracle*

relation to the salvation which he declares that he brings. They witness that Christ comes into the world as Savior, to save from destruction and communicate life.[14]

This bond between the witness of Christ as God the Savior and the signs he gave is still more apparent in the case of the resurrection. Indeed, neither Christ's witness to his close relationship to the Father and to his *rôle* as Judge of the world nor the divine prerogatives he attributes to himself and the central place he claims in the religion he founded would be acceptable, not even his holiness would be acceptable, if his whole life and work had ended in the corruption of the tomb. How could God have permitted the ignominy of corruption to overtake the well-beloved Son with whom he shared in an absolute way his own inner life? And how can Christ say that he is the Savior of all men, the conqueror of death and sin, the vanquisher of Satan, if he himself succumbs finally in death? On the other hand if Christ really rose from the dead, his witness immediately appears intelligible and valid; while his resurrection itself is unintelligible without the light thrown on it by his witness. Indeed what meaning can there be to Christ's glorious resurrection if he is only one prophet among all the rest? To give such glory to a merely human representative would lack a sense of proportion.[15] The resurrection becomes intelligible and acceptable only if Christ assumes in the religious order a really *unique dimension,* a dimension such that a miracle *unique* in the religious history of humanity finds its justification in the *unique* mission which Christ claims for himself and in the mystery of holiness which shines in him. Each illuminated by the other, Christ's witness and his resurrection form a con-

---

Stories of the Gospels (London, 1956), pp. 132-133.

14. R. Latourelle, *Théologie de la Révélation* (third edition, Bruges-Paris, 1969), pp. 471-472: trans., *Theology of Revelation* (New York, 1966), pp. 390-391.

15. Bultmann is consistent with himself when on the one hand he sees in Christ only one prophet among the rest, and, on the other hand, refuses to admit the Incarnation and the Resurrection in the Catholic sense.

sistent whole. An admirable proportion exists between his resurrection and his witness to himself (as Messiah, as Son of the Father, as Savior of the world and universal Judge). If Christ is really the Father's Son sent among men in order to save them from sin and death by his obedience, even to death on the cross, then the resurrection signifies that he has fulfilled his mission. His obedience has saved rebellious man; his sacrifice has destroyed death at its root. In him, the first-born among the dead (Col 1:18), the whole of mankind rises again (Rm 6:3-4). "If the spirit of him who raised up Jesus from the dead dwells in you, he who raised Christ from the dead will give life also to your mortal bodies through his Spirit who dwells in you" (Rm 8:11).

3.   The signs and Christ's Person

The text of the constitution *Dei verbum* says that Christ *confirms* revelation "through his whole presence and through the manifestation which he makes of himself." The schema had said, "through his whole person," but this expression was abandoned to avoid the ambiguity it carries, since it is through the person of the incarnate Word (not only through the Person of the Word), that is to say through all the significative and expressive virtualities of his human nature, that Christ manifests the glory of the Son. The Council's meaning is, in any case, clear: the signs of revelation are not foreign or exterior to Christ. They are Christ himself in the radiance of his presence and his manifestation in the world.

The First Vatican Council said of historical revelation, that God had given us, as well as revelation itself and the help of the Spirit, sure signs that this revelation was true. This was a general statement which applied to the economy of both Testaments. The Second Vatican Council took up this statement, but in a context distinctly Trinitarian and therefore more personalist. Christ, who is the Father's Son and his substantial Word in the visibility of flesh, is the Father's gift to men (*misit*

enim Filium suum, aeternum scilicet Verbum). Through his
presence and through his manifestation as the incarnate Word,
he is at once the Revealer of the Father and the Sign of the
divine authenticity of this revelation which he constitutes and
which he brings into the world. But man could not receive the
Father's revelation in Jesus Christ without the action of the
Spirit of truth, sent by Christ, who transforms the human intelligence and heart.[16] The personalist point of view of the
Second Vatican Council appears again in the fact that the
Council reattaches all the signs to this personal center which
is Christ. All the signs emanate from him and lead back to him:
they are in reality only the refracted light of his epiphany among
men.

In this way, just as it personalized revelation, the Council
has personalized signs. This rectification of perspective would
seem to be of very considerable importance for ecumenical
dialogue. If, in the past, this vision of the signs as inseparable
from the Person of Jesus Christ was sometimes forgotten, and
the signs too often made to appear as *detached* pieces of evidence
guaranteeing from outside a revelation with which they seemed
to have little to do, might not this be because theology had
unconsciously cut its biblical connections? For this way of
presenting the signs, as unified in Jesus Christ, is that of
scripture itself.

In scripture in fact—and this is especially so in St. John,
to whom the Council refers itself—*Christ in his entirety* is the
enigmatic sign which demands to be deciphered. If the total
sign is not read none of the partial signs (miracles and prophecies) will be read; for these cannot be understood correctly
except in relation to Christ who gives them. And on the other
hand, if we close our eyes against the light of the partial signs,
we shall no longer be able to decipher the Person to whom
they lead back. Those who steel themselves against the partial
signs are equally steeled against the total sign, the Sign of

---

16. *Constitutio dogmatica de divina revelatione,* c. 1, n. 5.

God who is Christ. If we accept the signs, we accept the person of Christ; if we refuse them, we refuse him. There is a necessary relation between the two attitudes, precisely because the signs, being manifestations of Christ's divine action, proclaim his divine being. If, therefore, one refuses to recognize Christ's divine action, one refuses also to recognize his Person as the Son. Accepting Christ's signs is, in practice, equivalent to accepting Christ.

What is at stake then, in the signs, is the mystery of Christ's Person. In John 2:18, the Jews ask for a sign: Christ refers them immediately to his own Person. The sickness of Lazarus is "that the Son of God might be glorified thereby" (Jn 11:4). Christ raises Lazarus because he is "the Resurrection" (11, 25). If he gives sight to the man blind from birth, it is because he is the Light of the world (8, 12). If he gives bread in superabundance, it is because he is the "Bread of God . . . who gives life to the world" (6:33). In Christ's cures on the sabbath, in his discussions with the Pharisees on the subject of Beelzebub, the argument always centers in the mystery of his Person. The reality denoted by the miracles is the Person of the Father's Son. The glory shed by the signs (2:11; 11:40), the witness given by the works (5:36; 10:25), the light and the life which they bring (6:35; 11:25), the judgment which they make between those who believe and those who do not (2:11; 4:53; 6: 66, 69), all this is centered in him who declares *I am* (8:24, 28, 58; 13:19). All the miracles are tied to the Person of Jesus, and oriented towards it. The Jews refused to accept the signs because the signs pointed towards Christ, and revealed in him the sovereign power of the living God.

The same thing is true of the gospel of Christ. To accept his words and his witness (3:11, 32; 12:48) is to accept Christ himself (5:43; 6:68). To recognize the truth of his words (17: 17) is to recognize him as the truth (14:6). To recognize that his word is life (6:63) is to recognize him as the life (14:6; 11:25). To accept the good news, is to recognize that Christ, and he alone, is Light and Life, and to admit that without him

man is only fragility, shadow and deceit. It is to recognize
that man needs to be saved. The character of this situation
is unique, unique to him who is in Person, the Way, the Truth
and the Life (14:6).[17]

4. *Christ's glory and the Father's witness*

The constitution *Dei verbum* does not say explicitly by what
dialectic we pass from the signifier to the signified, that is to
say from Christ as an observable phenomenon to Christ identified as the Son of God. It simply declares that there is, in his
whole presence and manifestation of himself in the world, a
divine witness attesting that in Christ God is-with-us. Nevertheless we can draw from the Council's manner of speaking and
the terminology it employs certain indications which may help
us to discover what this dialectic of the mind is.

As we have already noticed, the point of view adopted by
the Council is St. John's. Similarly the words it uses are his.
Among nouns, we find, Word, words, manifestation, signs, work,
works, glory, Spirit of truth, witness, darkness, eternal life; and
among verbs, to speak words, to do and finish work or works, to
send, to see, to make known, to dwell, to give light. In thus
presenting the whole life and action of Christ as an *epiphany*
of God in the flesh, the Council reminds us of the words of St.
John quoted at the outset of the constitution: "We proclaim
to you that eternal life which was with the Father and which
was *manifested* to us" (1 Jn 1:2). The Life, which was in God
with the Father, was manifested to us. God emerged from his
mystery and thanks to the sign of Christ's humanity John
was able to see and hear the Word of God. The text which we
are studying says in its turn that Christ consummates and
confirms revelation through "his whole *presence* and the *manifestation* which he makes of himself." It is then through the
manifestation or *epiphany* of himself that Christ is at once
Revelation and Sign of revelation.

17. A. Decourtray, "La conception johannique de la foi," *Nouvelle Revue théologique,* 81 (1959): 563.

His humanity is the visible sign of an invisible and holy reality. It is the visible sign (that which we have seen with our eyes and heard with our ears and touched with our hands) of the living God whom no man has ever seen (Jn 1:18). It was in manifesting himself in the visibility of the flesh that Christ revealed to us the invisible reality of God. He is the epiphany in the flesh and through the flesh of the invisible Word, the manifested utterance, the corporeal expression of God. Just as the body is the ex-pression of the soul, so Christ's humanity is the ex-pression of God. His love is the human form of the redeeming love of God, "God's love becoming visible." [18] In Christ "the kindness and love of God our Savior towards man appeared" to us (Tt 3:4). In its deepest sense, its deepest reality, the Christian economy is a *sacramental* economy, since it is the manifestation and communication of the invisible by means of the visible. The humanity of Christ is the Sacrament or the Sign of God *par excellence*.

But this epiphany is also a *glorious* epiphany, the supreme theophany of God. St. John, who said, "The Life was manifested and we have seen it" (1 Jn 1:2), said also, "The Word was made flesh and dwelt among us and we beheld his glory" (Jn 1:14). At Cana, Christ did his first miracle and thus "manifested forth his glory" (2:11). As it is through his humanity that Christ reveals God, it is also through his humanity that he reveals himself as God. The Incarnation is both the foundation and the instrument of revelation, as well as of the manifestation of Christ in his glory as the Son. For St. John, Christ's miracles, especially, are manifestations of his glory as the incarnate Word. They are the *gestes*, the deeds which are gestures, the *significant acts* of the Word made flesh, in the same way as those of Yahweh at the time of the Exodus. Since Christ is the irruption of God into the world, he is the permanent miracle (Acts 2:22), and his miracles are the *significant acts* or *works* of the Son

---

18. R. Latourelle, *Théologie de la Révélation*, pp. 438-440: trans., *Theology of Revelation*, pp. 360-361. E. H. Schillebeeckx, *Le Christ Sacrement de la Rencontre de Dieu* (Paris, 1960), p. 39: trans., *Christ: the Sacrament of the Encounter with God* (London and New York, 1963).

of the Father, who exercises in his own right the power of God. Glory, which defined Yahweh, also defines Christ.

Nevertheless, during Christ's earthly life, this glory manifests itself in alternations of light and shadow. Now it is hidden in the night of the agony; now it appears in the splendor of the Transfiguration (2 P 1:17-18; Mk 9:2-8) or in acts of power. At Cana, the disciples suspected that God was there, present in Person. They had an incipient intuition, confused but exact, of Christ's divine glory revealed through his humanity.[19] In the same way, in the cures of the sick or the possessed, in the raising of the dead, in the control of cosmic forces, what happens is the epiphany of Christ's *Lordship*. In showing his sovereignty over the cosmos, over the powers of evil, over sickness and death, Christ appears in the world with the attribute of power, of Δύναμις τοῦ Θεοῦ which belongs to the Lord God, to the Κύριος.

Another indication which throws light on the dialectic of the sign constituted by Christ's presence and manifestation in the world is given us by the use, in the text of the constitution, of the word *witness*, a specifically Johannine term.[20] Christ through his words and his works, by his signs and his miracles, through his death and his resurrection, brings to revelation the confirmation of a *divine witness*. In the context of St. John's gospel, the word has a juridical ring. It suggests a public deposition by Christ in the course of a vast trial in which he is opposed to the world. Christ witnesses to what he has seen

---

19. D. Mollat, *Initiation à la lecture spirituelle de saint Jean* (Paris, 1964), p. 16.

20. On this theme of witness in St. John, the following are relevant: N. Brox, *Zuege und Märtyrer* (München, 1961), pp. 70-106; I. de la Potterie, "La notion de témoignage dans S. Jean," in: *Sacra Pagina* (2 vols., Paris-Gembloux, 1959), 2: 192-208; B. Trépanier, "L'idée de témoin dans les écrits johanniques," *Revue de l'Université d'Ottawa*, 15 (1945): 27° - 63°; A. Vanhoye, "Témoignage et vie en Dieu selon le quatrième Evangile," *Christus*, n. 6 (April 1955), pp. 150-171; D. Mollat, "Le Semeion johannique," in: *Sacra Pagina*, 2: 219-228; R. Latourelle, *Théologie de la Révélation*, pp. 75-84: trans., *Theology of Revelation*, pp. 73-78.

and heard in his life with the Father, but men are unwilling to accept his testimony. "We speak of what we know and bear witness to what we have seen; but you do not receive our testimony" (Jn 3:11). "I have come in my Father's name and you do not receive me" (5:43). There is the evidence for Christ of John the Baptist (1:17), of the apostle himself (19:35; 21: 24), of scripture (5:39), of the Spirit of Truth (15:26), and finally of the Father, through the works which he grants the Son to do. The Father indeed "loves the Son and has given all things into his hands" (3:35); in particular, he has granted to the Son his own power, so that the Son may do the works that the Father does, and so be recognized as sent by the Father: "the works that the Father has *granted* me to finish, the same works that *I do,* bear witness of me, that the Father has sent me" (5:36; 10:25). Christ's *works* are at the same time *his* works (5:36; 7:21; 10:25) and the works of the Father; for the Father is in him and he in the Father (10:38; 14:10-11), and what belongs to the Father belongs equally to the Son (17: 10). The Son, like the Father, disposes; he judges and raises· the dead (5:25-30).

The fact that the Father thus *grants* to Christ, who presents himself to the world as the Father's Son, *both* his power *and* his works, reveals between the Father and the Son a perfect union of will, and this constitutes the Father's witness to the Son. Christ's works *witness* that he is really the Son sent by the Father, since he has at his disposition the Father's power over life and death. It is because of this witness to Christ by the Father, that Christ appears as the authentic and authorized *exegete* of the Father (1:18). Christ's works witness that his verbal testimony is true; for they constitute upon his life and mission, the seal of the omnipotence of God.

This witness to Christ by the Father, through works of power, takes away from the Jews all excuse. Their opposition becomes culpable: "If I had not done among them works which no other man did, they would not have had sin, but now they have seen and hated both me and my Father" (15:24; 9:41). It was in vain that Christ tried to lead the Jews to an understanding of his divine Sonship through the works which he did among them. The Father's witness through these works was designed to make known in Christ the glory of the only-begotten Son, present in the world with the power of Yahweh. But this witness, like other witnesses, was rejected.

5. *The dialectic of the sign*

In this way, according to the Council, the whole life and activity of Christ (words, works, death, resurrection) present themselves as an epiphany of the Son in the flesh. The radiance of this epiphany constitutes a *divine witness* that Christ is really what he declares himself to be, *God-with-us*. But by what mental process do we pass from what we observe to the truth of what is? How does this *unique sign* which is Christ operate on the mind?

What we begin by observing is a *radiance,* a splendor (or casting back of light), emanating from a personal center. This radiance is not simple, but complex. It is a radiance of *power,* manifesting itself in Christ's sovereignty, over the cosmos, over sickness and over death itself. It is a radiance of *truth,* manifesting itself in the gospel which Christ brings to the world, a message which has illumined and sanctified millions of human beings to whom it has been the inspiration of their lives. It is a radiance of *holiness,* manifesting itself in Christ's acts of charity and forgiveness and consummated in the silent giving of his life for the salvation of all men. It is a radiance which reaches its zenith in the miracle, unique in history, of a spontaneous and *glorious resurrection.* And yet this radiance is not confined to the past; for Christ is prolonged in time in his *Church,* marked century after century by the charisms which are his work.

This radiance is the sign of Fullness, of Wholeness. Christ's presence in the world is the presence of a Plenitude, of an unparalleled order of values, a completeness of meaning, a fullness of love.

I have said "a completeness of *meaning.*" In a world desperately given over to technology and bureaucracy, where man is delivered into the hands of anonymous powers; in a world which prides itself on its progress but is debased by war, racial conflict, strife and violence; in a world apparently provided with everything and yet incapable of forgiveness or real love, life seems to have lost its meaning, its *sense*. And men are waiting hopelessly for something which would give everything meaning, which would give sense to life, to work, to suffering, to solitude, to death. The speed and noise of our world do not contrive to stifle the fundamental questions: where are we going? who are we? why do we exist? Men are waiting for truth. They look for it where they can and as they can: in nation, in class, in politics, in the human sciences, in artificial paradises, in terrorism. And in this chaos and darkness, the tenuous figure of Christ, lost in space and time, appears as the *Mediator of meaning*. When a man listens to Christ he learns something of the reason why he feels alienated, disorientated, anxious, and in despair. A pathway of light opens before him, which illuminates life and suffering and death: Christ's message is mysterious but sublime, a source of inexhaustible meaning.[21]

The substance of this message is that man, left to himself, can be reduced to hatred and sin, egoism and death, but that through grace the absolute love of God has entered his heart to give him, if he will accept it, God's own life and God's own love. It is in and through Christ that this Gift is given to us. The Father's Son in the inner life of the Trinity, God in the flesh among men, Christ makes us the Father's children, with the Spirit of the Father and the Son, who is the Spirit of love, within us, and he binds all men together in this love. In Christ, the mystery of "others" is resolved at depth. "Others" are Christ, the Father's call to the love of all men. "Others" are the Son of man, the suffering servant, who is hungry and thirsty, naked and sick and abandoned, but destined to the glory of the well-beloved Son. In Christ, no one is any longer "foreign," but all the children of the same Father, with the same brother in

21. A. Manaranche, *Je crois en Jésus-Christ aujourd'hui* (Paris, 1968), p. 39; *Ibid., Quel salut?* (Paris, 1969), pp. 223-224.

Christ. There is now only the love of the Father and of the Son, and the love of men united to each other by the same Spirit. It is in this that *salvation* consists.

Christ's presence in the world thus appears as a *plenitude of love*. That is its *meaning*. If God is Love (1 Jn 4:8-10), no love has ever looked so like this love as the love of God in Christ; no love has ever suggested it in a more astonishing way. In him, "the kindness of God our Savior and his love for men" has "appeared" to us (Tt 3:4). He is the epiphany of love. Man has never felt himself more truly or more deeply loved than by Christ, whose life was a total consecration of himself to God and to men. In a world of self-interest, egoism and hatred, Christ appears as sheer Love, unshadowed, eager and faithful, *given* and *given up*, to the point of sacrificing his life for the salvation of all: *dilexit . . . tradidit seipsum*. The "little people," the poor, the humble, the unfortunate, those whom men ignore, despise or reject, those who sin, have never been aware of a look turned on them which was so penetrating and yet at the same time so accessible, so full of love and compassion without any shadow of revulsion. In Christ, men—the apostles, the publicans, the Samaritan woman, Mary Magdalene, the good thief— discover the existence of a love which is absolute, loving man in himself and for himself, and the possibility of a dialogue and communion with this love. They have suddenly revealed to them a new world, which transcends ours.

The presence of a plenitude of love such as this acts as a magnet. It draws men towards it. With the tacit encouragement of grace, which operates in every man and invites him to a communion of life with God, man secretly aspires to this fullness of love whose existence he has, through Christ, come dimly to perceive. From the deepest recesses of his being a challenge rises and gathers force. If salvation exists, would it not lie in this Plenitude, in this *personal Presence* who says that he is the Father's Son, sent to dwell among men as the Way, the Truth and the Life? If God has a face and a name, would not this face and name be Jesus? If God is Love and Truth, would not Christ be this Truth and Love?

In this intuitive grasp which is already a total grasp, Christ's radiance appears as a *Sign of Presence*: the light of Christ suggests the presence of salvation, and designates Christ's person as the *locus* of this presence. If God does save us, where is salvation to be found if not in this focus of holiness and wisdom and power? It may happen that the sign will still be only imperfectly identified, and not yield its secret until later, but its light will draw men to it, as light does in darkness, and they will not be able to withdraw their eyes, speculating upon the nature of the light. But it may happen also that, in this first *spontaneous discerning* of the sign, drawn by Christ's radiance and struck by the intensity of light which emanates from the focal point from which the radiance seems to proceed, men pass directly from the light observed to the source of light, and under the influence of grace, which illumines and moves them within, conclude "God is there. Christ is the Sign of God. We have seen his glory."

For the Jews in particular this three-fold radiance of holiness, wisdom and power was singularly evocative. The God of the Old Testament had in effect manifested himself to them as an omnipotent God, a true God, a God thrice holy. And in Jesus Christ the splendor of power and wisdom and holiness shone with a brilliance never attained by any of God's messengers. The mere co-existence in him of this three-fold light was already enough, by itself, to raise the question of his identity. It is indeed this reaction which is enshrined in the comments, "What manner of man is this that even the wind and the sea obey him?" (Mk 4:41), "What thing is this? ... he commands even the unclean spirits and they obey him" (Mk 1:27), "Never man spoke like this man" (Jn 7:46) and after the cure of the paralytic whose sins Christ forgave: "We never saw anything like this" (Mk 2:12).

If, now, we try to express more explicitly what takes place in the course of this spontaneous discerning of Christ as Sign, if we try to take to pieces the process which leads the mind from the Sign to the Reality, it seems that what happens is something like this.

We are struck at first by an *admirable proportion* between Christ's witness and the signs which accompany it. Remember that Christ's witness, in substance, concerns himself. He presented himself to the world not only as the Messiah, but also as the Servant of Yahweh, the voluntary victim who offered himself for the sins of all men, as the Son of man, who was to reign over all nations and judge them at the end of time, as the Son of the Father, sharing an inner life with the Father, which placed him beyond the prophets and angels. By his statements and his way of acting Christ elevated himself to the plane of divinity. And answering to this, there is in the authority and sublimity of his message, in the power of his actions, in the fact of his resurrection, in the foundation of his Church a splendor more like the divine than the human. Christ's testimony and his personal radiance correspond to each other, as sublimities of the same order. As Bossuet put it, very exactly, "Everything holds together in his person: his life, his doctrine, his miracles. The same truth is reflected everywhere: everything converges, to manifest man's Master and the model of perfection." [22]

This correspondence between Christ's *testimony* and the *radiance* of his person is a complex phenomenon which demands a *sufficient explanation*. How are we to explain in Christ his towering claim to be the Savior of mankind, the conqueror of sin and death, the universal, eschatological Judge, the Son sharing with the Father both knowledge and power? And how, on the other hand, are we to explain his power over the cosmos, over spiritual entities, over sickness and death, the sublimity of his words and the dazzling holiness of his life? What is the key to this *harmony in transcendence?* Would not the truth of Christ's witness to himself explain the phenomenon observed? If we recognize as true the explanation he offered of the Mystery of his person, everything lights up and becomes intelligible: the synthesis which he makes of apparently contradictory figures (especially those of the suffering servant and

---

22. Bossuet, *Discours sur l'histoire universelle,* II, 19.

the glorious Son of man), *and* the paradoxes of his own personality (its combination of simplicity and authority, humility
and unheard of claims, a sense of sin in others and of absolute
purity in himself), *and* the complex radiance of power and
wisdom and holiness which is manifest in him, *and* the presence
in the Church of the same paradoxes and the same charisms.
If Christ spoke the truth, everything falls into place: the radiance
of his action witnesses to the glory of his divine being. This is
equivalent to what the Council said when it declared that the
glory manifested in Christ constitutes a divine testimony to
the fact that he is really *God-with-us*, to save us from sin and
death and bring us to everlasting life. If, on the contrary, Christ
is not the Person he claims to be, he constitutes the greatest
riddle of all time, a pure, unintelligible, subsisting riddle. And
yet we have to recognize that this riddle has been the pivot
on which the history of the world has turned for two thousand
years.

Thus Christ is in himself Sign, in a double sense. First of all
he is Sign in the sense that through his words and his works,
through his life, his death and his resurrection, and in short
through all the expressive resources of his human nature, he
expresses God and God's design for salvation. He is Sign also
in the sense that there is, in all these same realities of his life
and activity among men, a radiance which is *expressive* of the
glory of the Son of God. Christ expresses the Father, but
this expression has in itself a splendor which is reflected from
its source and allows us to identify it. It is through his Incarnation that Christ tells men of the Father's saving design, and it
is through his Incarnation that men identify Christ as the Son
of God. In this movement in which our minds return towards
Christ, we are aware first of an unaccustomed radiance, an indication of Plenitude; then we are conscious of a harmony, a
singular correspondence between this radiance and Christ's testimony to himself. And we infer that the truth of this testimony
is the explanation of the phenomenon observed. We conclude
from Christ's *doing* to his *being*, on the basis of his *saying*.
His being and his action are what his words indicate they are,

that is, divine. Christ *is* what he *says* and what he *manifests*. We conclude from the splendor (the "light cast back") which we have observed, to the truth of his being, on the basis of his testimony. The three realities are coherent in themselves and of the same order of magnitude. The *key* or sufficient explanation of the whole is the reality of the Son of God present among us. The signs, it is obvious, are inseparable from the Person who has to be identified from the characteristics observed: they are the signs of an enigma, a personal *Mystery*.

6. Men confronted by the Sign

The fundamental Sign which Christ constitutes, through his presence and activity in the world, represents, in man's religious history, a case which is absolutely unique. Christ's work and teaching and resurrection have the function of authenticating his mission as one sent by God, not sent however in the mere capacity of prophet or human Messiah, but in virtue of being the Father's Son, sharing the Father's knowledge (Mt 11:27) and omnipotence (Mt 28:18; Jn 3:35). Seen in relation to his testimony to himself, the signs Christ "did" confirm the central affirmation of this testimony, that he is the Son of the living God. Christ's signs point towards the mystery of his Person. All the manifestations of glory in his life are aimed at making him known as the Father's Son, sent to save mankind: "Now Jesus did many other signs in the presence of the disciples which are not written in this book; but these are written that you may believe that Jesus is the Christ, the Son of God, and that believing you may have life through his name" (Jn 20:30-31).

It is important to remember this unique situation if we are to understand the attitude of a man confronted by the sign of Christ, whether directly, as in the case of Jesus' contemporaries, or indirectly through history or the witness of the Church, as is the case with men today. To acknowledge Christ's signs and see their meaning is in fact to run the risk of meeting God; for the end of all Christ's signs is to make manifest his real identity as the Son of God. One has an immediate presentiment of the drama of conscience, which is played out in all its complexity around the Person of Christ. As soon as a man discovers in what directions the signs are leading him, he realizes that he cannot acknowledge them without a conflict which will involve the whole of his life.[23] He finds himself on trial, as the Jews did when confronted by the signs of the Exodus. In both cases, man is introduced by the signs into the presence of God, and has to make a choice.[24] The works of Christ, like those of Yahweh in the desert, put man in a position from which there is no escape without a decision: for light or darkness, faith or incredulity, life or death.[25]

It is this drama of conscience which is illustrated in the gospel of St. John. When Jesus appears, parties are formed; men are divided into two categories (Jn 6:53, 60-71). They opt for or against Christ. Some believe: thanks to the signs and their own inner availability, they acknowledge Christ as a great prophet, as the Messiah, and sometimes they even recognize the living mystery of his divine glory. "Lord, I believe," said the blind man whose eyes were opened (9:38). "To whom shall we go?" said Peter. "You have the words of eternal life" (6:68). Christ's contemporaries had not, to be sure, as men have today, the additional light provided by the fact of the resurrection and the spectacle of the Church's life from age to age: yet there were nevertheless those among them who saw something of the glory of Christ (2:11). Others, on the contrary, swerved away from the operation of the signs and refused to believe in Jesus' mission: "You do not receive our witness" (3:11; 3:32; 5:38). "I have come in my Father's name and you do not receive me" (5:43; 6:36; 8:19; 8:46; 15:24).

The unique situation constituted by Christ's presence in the world and by the seriousness of the choice which it brings about explains men's resistance to the signs of his glory, and even their reacting against them with violence or a rabid deter-

---

23. J. Alfaro, *Fides, Spes, Caritas* (ad usum auditorum, Romae, 1963), p. 409.

24. A. Lefèvre, art. "Miracle," DBS 5: 1307.

25. D. Mollat, "Le Semeion johannique," in: *Sacra Pagina*, 2: 216-217.

mination not to see. For to acknowledge Christ's signs is, it needs to be stressed, to expose oneself to the light of God, to recognize the deceit and darkness in oneself; it is to accept the risk of conversion, of having to live according to the truth acknowledged and accepted; it is to prefer Someone to something. This is a difficult thing for sensual and rebellious man to do. In certain cases described by the gospel it would seem even that there is more to the matter than that. Behind the human refusal one divines a deeper resistance and a more obscure drama, the action of the Adversary, who opposes himself to the One who is stronger than he (Lk 11:21-22). This mystery of the presence of the Adversary appears especially in the rage of the Pharisees against Christ. They declare that he "deceives the people" (Jn 7:12), that he "is not of God because he does not keep the sabbath" (Jn 9:16; Mk 3:1-6; Lk 13, 10-16), that he casts out devils by the help of Beelzebub (Mk 3:22; Lk 11:15; Mt 12:24-28). After the healing of the man born blind, they persist in their refusal to see: "*We know* that this man is a sinner" (Jn 9:24). And yet Christ has said, "Which of you convicts me of sin?" (8:46). In his mission as sent by the Father, Christ does not deceive men. There is in him neither imposture nor lack of faithfulness to the truth. "His innocence is the unmixed purity of the Son, reflecting without distortion or shortcoming the Father's mind." [26] Christ's holiness provokes his adversaries; for sin has darkened them. "If you were blind," Christ says to them, "you would have no sin, but you say, 'we see,' and so your sin remains" (9:41). The light of Christ had come, but "they loved darkness rather than light because their deeds were evil." "Everyone who does evil hates the light...lest his deeds should be exposed" (3:19-20). The raising of Lazarus sums up this dramatic aspect of Christ's signs. Christ has just revealed himself as the Master of life and death. He is in Person "the resurrection and the life" (11:25). The chief priests and the Pharisees have seen his work, but they understand that his power is a menace to their own (11:

---

26. D. Mollat, *Initiation à la lecture spirituelle de saint Jean,* p. 49.

47-48). Light does not illumine them, but darkens and hardens them instead. "From that day on they took counsel how to put him to death" (11:53). They wished also to remove Lazarus, as a living witness to the sign done (12:10-11). This hatred of the Pharisees and the doctors of the law masks a still deeper hatred, that of the "Prince of this world," the "father of lies" and a "murderer from the beginning," who feels his power over men slipping away from him and kindles their passions to accomplish his work of death. Cures and exorcisms are signs that Christ is invested with the power of God, and the kingdom of God has come.

Since the signs, in Christ's case, manifest the *presence* and *action* of God among us, they presuppose on man's part a minimum of the dispositions necessary to see and follow them, and on God's part the operation of grace, helping us to allow ourselves to be guided to the end to which they lead.

We have already seen, in St. John's gospel, the importance of human dispositions. There are indeed dispositions which paralyze the action of the signs, even of the most striking of them. This is particularly so in the case of a lack of disinterestedness, which often goes with self-sufficiency. Lack of disinterestedness is betrayed by constant self-seeking in all its forms, a seeking for influence, power, and pleasure, and also by a rigidness of routine and by laziness and so on. Self-sufficiency is the pretention to have no need of anyone else. Whatever form it may take self-sufficiency engenders contempt, and closes the mind against the action of anything outside. When a man shuts himself up in himself, he is immunized against both God and men. How then could he recognize in Christ this Other *par excellence* who is God, and who asks him to confess his own poverty and sin? Christ appears to him to menace his autonomy. Like the Pharisees, greedy for influence and authority, menaced in their power and enclosed in their self-sufficiency, he is impermeable to the action of the signs. Far from surrendering himself to the light which is offered, he rages against it. He wishes to obliterate the Sign and every trace of the Sign.[27] Human dispositions would not however be enough when it is a question of the Sign of Christ. In the case of Christ, the operation which consists in perceiving the meaning of the signs is the same as that which consists in recognizing in Jesus of Nazareth the glory of the Father's Son. The signs which Christ offers are signs of his personal Mystery, and their end is to lead man to this Mystery. In fact *that* is where Christ wished in the course of his earthly life to lead the Jews of his time. Just as he tried to lead them to an understanding of his divine Sonship, so he tried to lead them to recognize in his miracles, not merely prodigies, but the works of the Father's Son, present and acting in their midst.

This unique position as far as Christ is concerned has an important consequence. If the signs which he does are signs of his personal Mystery, man's discernment of this, in a living commitment to the way of salvation, needs, united to, and inseparably from, interior dispositions, the operation of grace. The signs are given; they are, in themselves, sufficient, but man is separated from God by an abyss, even after the Incarnation. How could man, without special help, grasp that Christ's acts are God's acts and that Christ's words are God's words? How could he understand that it is God himself in person who is speaking to him and giving him a sign? In order to follow the signs through to their *end in God,* and to identify them aright, we need illumination from "the Father of lights." However great the power of Christ's works, the sublimity of his doctrine or the impact of his holiness, encountering the signs could not bring about the recognition in Jesus of the living God unless the Father drew us (6:44) and the Spirit gave us grace (2 Cor 1:21-22). Because discerning the signs of Christ coincides with identifying Christ as the Son of the Father, it presupposes the operation of grace, not only in the confession of faith itself, but all along the way which leads man through the signs to recognize in Jesus of Nazareth the Son of God,

---

27. A. Vanhoye, "Notre foi, oeuvre divine d'après le quatrième Évangile," *Nouvelle Revue théologique,* 86 (1964): 347-349.

and in his words the very words of God.[28] In short, since the
end to which the signs are directed is the personal Mystery
of Christ, and the signs are an invitation to have faith in this
Mystery, there needs to be in man from the outset an *attitude*
of faith, that is a grace of openness to the supernatural.

After what has just been said of the unique position of
Christ, it is easy to understand that we cannot have factual evidence of revelation. Revelation is indeed known to us only
through the double mediation of *signs* and the *historical testimony*
which reports them to us. In the present case, moreover,
the signs are signs of the personal mystery of the incarnate
Word, a mystery enveloped for us in a radical obscurity. When
the mind moves on the plane of mystery, signs and testimony,
it cannot obtain evidence, but only moral certainty. This is
not an inferior certainty, but it is the only kind possible. It is
also, in some cases, a very high form of certainty, as, for instance, in the spontaneous discernment of the apostles or in
the scientific discernment of theological research. It follows
also that the signs given by Christ, although striking, leave room
for freedom and merit. They do not act by compulsion but by
invitation, an invitation added and wedded to the help of grace
and the appeal of the gospel.[29]

---

28. *Ibid.*, pp. 341-342.

29. On this point the encyclical *Ecclesiam suam* is emphatic: "Quin
immo Christus sive miraculorum numerum (Mt 12:38f), sive eorumdem
vim probativam cum ad condiciones tum ad voluntatem audientium ap-
tavit (Mt 12:13f); eo nimirum consilio, ut iidem juverentur ad libere
assentiendum divinae revelationi, neque exinde suae assensionis praemio
carerent" (AAS 56 [1964] 642-643). The Second Vatican Council, in
the decree on religious liberty, says in the same sense: "Miraculis utique
praedicationem suam suffulsit et confirmavit, ut fidem auditorum excitaret
atque comprobaret, non ut in eos coercitionem exerceret," n. 11.

CHAPTER IV

The Church, The Sign of the Coming of Salvation In Jesus Christ

Let me explain at once what I mean by this title. By *salvation* I understand the union of man with God, who divinizes man by a communication of himself which is wholly gratuitous and wholly new. This union or covenant between man and God is the root and source of the communion of men with one another. Begun here in this world, it will be consummated in the life to come.

One can say in a general way that the Church is the sign of salvation; for she represents and communicates the invisible grace of salvation. She is the sign, and the effective sign, of a spiritual reality, that is, the union of men with God, and through this union, the union of men with one another. She is the *sacrament of salvation.* This general sense in which the Church is a sign can then be analyzed, and one can recognize in it a three-fold meaning.

(1) The Church is the sign of salvation, first of all, in the sense that through faith in the gospel, through baptism and the Eucharist, she *realizes* salvation. She is the place where Christ the Savior acts, through the operation of the Spirit. She is an institution for salvation; much more than that she is the only institution with a mandate from Christ to reunite all men and form the one People of God, the Body of Christ.

(2) Secondly, the Church is the manifest sign of salvation; for she both *represents* and *images,* in man's world, the union of men with God and the union of men with one another. The Church is the real presence of this union, already accomplished but always to be perfected, in which men are united to one another through their union with God in Christ. In this sense the Church is already, explicitly, the presence of salvation among us, with the plenitude of good which this salvation brings. She is the visible prototype of this communion which is destined to incorporate the whole of mankind, and which is already realized inchoatively, at least in an obscure, implicit, anonymous way, through the action of saving grace, which penetrates mankind and draws men to God. The Church is already, in this world, the fulfillment of God's saving will; for she is already the mystery of communion in practice, communion with God (the People of God) and communion with men (the union of men with one another). In Pauline terms, she is the Mystery, or God's saving design in the phase of its fulfillment and its visible manifestation.[1]

(3) Thirdly, to the extent to which this mystery of salvation or communion (communion with God and communion with one another) *radiates* an intense light among men, it becomes, even for non-believers, a perceptible sign of the coming of salvation into the world. One can then speak of the Church as a motive of credibility. That is, when the People of God, gathered together in unity, is faithful to its vocation to holiness and lives fully its life of union with God and union with men, it *witnesses,* by its very presence, to the fact that the salvation proclaimed and preached by the Church has really come to mankind to transform and sanctify it. The kingdom of God is here, since men live in unity and charity. When individual members of the Church and local communities live in this way the life of Christ and of his Spirit, then the Church

---

1. R. Latourelle, *Théologie de la Révélation* (third edition, Bruges and Paris, 1969), p. 65: trans., *Theology of Revelation* (Alba House, New York, 1966), p. 63.

becomes the transparent sign of her divine origin. We see in
her something of the glory which shone in the face of Christ.

The Church not only is, but has to be, the sign of salvation
for men. God's saving design existed to be sure before the
Incarnation, but the object of the Incarnation was to manifest
this will to save all men in the visibility of the flesh. The Incarnation is the epiphany of salvation as compared with the
history of salvation. And in the same way as Christ is the revealing and operative Sign of God's saving will, so the Church,
in her turn, through the profession of faith and the life in unity
and charity of Christian people, must be the revealing and
operative sign of this saving will. She must be the epiphany,
historically observable, of the coming of salvation in Jesus
Christ; she must make visible the mystery of salvation which
is already at work, silent and hidden within mankind; she
must make visible among men God's love for men, which appeared and was made manifest in Jesus Christ.

When the following chapters, then, speak of the Church as
the sign of the coming of salvation, they mean this: the more
the Church lives in full her reality as a sacramental sign, that
is to say, the more she both *expresses and realizes* what she *is,*
the more she will be a sign or motive of credibility. The
Church *gives-a-sign* (in the third sense) in the measure in
which she is a sign in the first two senses (a sign which realizes
salvation). In other words, when the life of the members of
Christ in unity and charity is in accord with the gospel, and
when this accord is deeply lived, this life becomes a sign, not
merely an allusive but an *expressive* sign, of the reality signified:
it manifests visibly, even to the eyes of non-believers, that the
Church is really the *locus* of salvation in Jesus Christ as she
proclaims, and that the Spirit of Christ, which is the Spirit
of love, really does live among men. The Church then becomes
the visible and historical sign of the Spirit of Christ, who is
the invisible source and principle of unity in the Church.[2]

---

2. On this theme of the Church as sign, see: E. Schillebeeckx, "Ecclesia in mundo hujus temporis," *Angelicum,* 43 (1966), 340-352; *Ibid.,*
"La condizione del cristiano nella civiltà secolare," in: *La Chiesa provocata*

Seen in this perspective, the economy of sacramental signs and the economy of the signs of revelation are obviously not parallel and independent economies. On the contrary, they are reunited, and each articulates the other. For it is in so far as the ecclesial community draws its life from the source in which the sacraments arise, that it becomes a "sign lifted up before the nations." [3]

1. From the First Vatican Council to the Second

The idea that the presence of the Church in the world through the centuries, with all the manifold good which she represents, constitutes a sign of her divine origin, a sign capable of providing justification for Christian faith, was not a discovery of the First Vatican Council. The argument is, to tell the truth, a traditional one in the Church. It has its roots in Acts, where the life of the early ecclesial community is described (2:44-45), and it would seem that a prefiguration of it might be found in the Old Testament, in the presence of the People of God, the sign lifted up before the nations.[4] From the first, the Fathers, especially Irenaeus, Tertullian, Origen and Augustine, invoke, in order to defend Christianity, the miraculous way in which it spread, the constancy of its martyrs, the astonishing brilliance of its holiness. The argument was in due course developed by Savonarola in the fifteenth century, by Bossuet and Pascal in

---

dal mondo (Brescia, 1969), pp. 34-57; P. Smulders, "L'Église, sacrement du salut," in G. Baraúna, ed., *L'Église de Vatican II* (3 vols., Paris, 1966), vol. 2: 313-338; J. L. Witte, "L'Église, *sacramentum unitatis* du cosmos et du genre humain," *Ibid.*, pp. 457-491; Y. Congar, "L'Église, sacrement universel du salut," *Église vivante*, 17 (1965): 339-355; H. Mühlen, *Una Mystica Persona* (Paderborn, 1967²); A. Manaranche, *Quel salut?* (Paris, 1969), pp. 189-223; W. J. Richardson, ed., *The Church as Sign* (New York, 1968).

---

3. Chapter IX returns to this connection between the two economies.
4. W. Bulst, "Israel als signum levatum in Nationes, Die Idee vom Zeichencharakter Israels in den Schriften des Alten Testamentes in Analogie zum Zeichencharakter der Kirche," *Zeitschrift für Katholische Theologie,* 74 (1952): 167-204.

the sixteenth, by Fénelon in the seventeenth, by Balmes, Lacordaire, Bautain and Dechamps in the nineteenth, and, immediately
before the First Vatican Council, by J. Kleutgen and J. B. Franzelin. The First Vatican Council sanctioned with its authority
the value of this sign and gave the argument, if not its definitive formulation, at least its most important one.[5] The argument itself has been taken up many times since, by popes Leo
XIII, Pius X, Pius XI, Pius XII and John XXIII.

"It is to the Catholic Church," says the Council, "that we
must relate all these numerous signs, so admirably disposed by
God to manifest the credibility of the Christian faith. The Church,
moreover, because of her marvelous expansion, her eminent
holiness, her inexhaustible fruitfulness in all good, because of
her Catholic unity and her unshakable stability, is *of herself*
a great and perpetual motive of credibility and an undeniable
witness to her divine message." [6] Let us detach from this text
its explicit statements, as also what it suggests to the mind.

Not only does the Church receive as her legitimate heritage
and offer to men the historical signs of revelation in Jesus
Christ, but beyond that, of *herself*, that is to say through her
whole presence and manifestation in the world, she signifies
that her mission is from God. Not only does she possess as,
so to speak, a family fortune, the historical grounds on which
we believe the Christian faith to be divinely revealed, but she
is in herself and through herself a motive of credibility. In the
same way as Christ *gave-a-sign* to the men of his time through
the radiance of his whole being (through his teaching, his
wisdom, his holiness, his miracles, his passion and death and
resurrection), so the Church also, through the radiance of her
whole being (through her expansion, her unity, her stability,
her holiness, her fruitfulness) *gives-a-sign* to men of all times
that she has her message and her mission from God. She shares
in the glory of Christ.

---

5. R. Latourelle, *Théologie de la Révélation,* pp. 499-500: trans.,
Theology of Revelation, pp. 417-418.
6. DS 3013-3014.

The process by which we pass directly from the Church to her divine origin takes its bearings from phenomenology rather than history. The movement of the mind is this. On the one hand the Church proclaims that she has a saving mission and that this mission is divine. On the other hand the *tout-ensemble* of astonishing characteristics which she exhibits leads us legitimately to think that this claim is well-founded. If then the Church is of God, and if she bears witness to the fact that she was founded by Christ, the Son of the living God, in order to offer men the good news of salvation, we are bound to receive her witness as true and give credence to it. By this procedure we recognize the Church directly as the Church of God and therefore to be believed. Not only does she present herself to us as the heir and depository of the signs which accompanied the historical promulgation of the gospel, but she herself, through her epiphany in the course of the centuries, attests that her mission is from God.

In its original form the conciliar text proposed the argument more concisely, simply stating, "The Church, moreover, is of herself a great and perpetual motive of credibility and an undeniable witness to her divine mission."[7] It was the bishops Dupanloup and Ballerini who insisted that the reasons why the Church is a great and perpetual motive of credibility should be made explicit, and it was Dupanloup who elaborated and illustrated the general statement in terms which the Council fathers accepted, "*ut pulchram expositionem motivi credibilitatis quod in Ecclesia continetur.*"[8]

The mental process suggested by the Council is then different from the *historical* procedure by which we establish the foundation of the Church by Christ and the continuity of this Church with the Catholic Church today. In other words, it is not a question here of the argument known as the "notes" of the Church, which consists in recognizing in the Church of

---

7. "Quin etiam Ecclesia per seipsa magnum quoddam et perpetuum est motivum credibilitatis suae et divinae suae legationis testimonium irrefragabile" (Mansi 53: 167A).

8. Mansi 51: 326 BC.

today the essential and exclusive properties given by Christ to the institution which he founded. It is a matter rather of an empirical process which takes its point of departure in the Church as an observable and unusual spatio-temporal phenomenon. In the argument from the "notes" of the Church, it is a question of the essence of Christ's Church. Is this actual community, that is, the Catholic Church, really the Church of Christ? This question addresses itself to every Christian community.[9] The argument proposed by the First Vatican Council is concerned directly with the image of the Church, with the lineaments of her face as they manifest themselves to the observer, even the unbelieving observer, without making any appeal to the historical foundation of the Church by Christ with the "notes" or dimensions willed by him.

In the enumeration which it makes, the Council, without pretending to be exhaustive, proposes five of these observable traits (and not four, as in the case of the "notes") which belong to the phenomenon of the Church, that is, her *marvelous* expansion, her *eminent* holiness, her *inexhaustible* fruitfulness, her *catholic* unity, her *invincible* stability. The five adjectives which accompany the nouns insist on the uncommon character of these manifestations. The Church appears in the world as a phenomenon which is unusual, exceptional, astonishing.

It is clear from the history of the text that these traits are to be considered, not each in isolation, but as a whole and qualitatively. As in the case of Christ it is a matter of a *multiform* convergence. It would therefore be foreign to the mind of the Council to think that any one of these characteristics, taken by itself, is enough to constitute the sign of the Church. It is all of them, taken together, which make of the Church a sign which is immense and luminous, an analogue of the sign of Christ.

One can group the characteristics enumerated by the Council

---

9. Some writers, like Hans Küng, prefer to the term *notes,* the term *dimensions*: "Where are the dimensions of the Church founded by Christ realized?" Cf. H. Küng, *L'Église* (2 vols., Paris, 1967), vol. 2: 381: English translations, *The Church* (New York, 1968; London, 1969).

and give them a logical arrangement in different ways according to the point of view one adopts. If we are envisaging the forces of destruction which menace human society, we can say that the Church, thanks to the principle of unity and cohesion which she has received from Christ, that is, the Spirit, triumphs over internal division (unity), and over external division, the effect of human particularity (catholic unity), and that she triumphs over the limits of time and history (invincible stability) and over the limits set by natural wear and tear and age and death (holiness and fruitfulness). Again, we can say that the sign of the Church, like the sign of Christ, touches man in his entirety, in his *spatial condition* (expansion, catholicity), in his *temporal* condition (stability, permanence) and in his *humanity* itself (unity, holiness, martyrdom).

The text gives an indication also of the value which the Council recognizes in the sign of the Church. On the ontological plane, she is a "great and perpetual motive of credibility." She is a *great* motive of credibility since in reality it is a question of a multiplicity of particular and converging signs, as in the sign of Christ. Because of this complexity and convergence, her motive force is of great weight, that is to say, it is singularly effective in convincing and persuading men of good will. She is a *perpetual*, that is to say permanent, motive of credibility, in that she is spread out before the eyes of all generations. The Church, continues the text, constitutes "an undeniable witness" to her divine mission. The argument is undeniable, in the sense that the sign in itself possesses a real and objective consistency, which makes it as *valid* for non-believers as for believers, as is said in the following sentence, which serves as a conclusion to the Council's exposition: "So she herself, like a standard set up among the nations (Is 11:12), draws to her those who have not yet believed, and in her own children increases their assurance that the faith they profess rests on a solid foundation."

On the subjective plane now, therefore, that is to say, on the plane of man confronted by the sign of the Church, the text states that this sign *strengthens* the faith of those who believe and *draws* those who do not yet believe. Faith today, then, rests not only on the signs of antiquity, which accompanied historical revelation in Christ, but also on the sign which is always actual and present, the sign of the Church. For those who are outside the Church, this sign acts as an *appeal*, an *invitation*, not as a compulsion or constraint. The appeal is more or less persuasive, more or less effective, according to the variable brilliance of the sign in the course of the centuries and according to one's experience of the Church.

As in the case of historical revelation in Jesus Christ, more-over, this exterior appeal is matched by the inner call of grace, which is given so that the exterior appeal of the sign of the Church may bear fruit. "To this witness," says the Council, "is added the effective help of grace from above. For the Lord of love stirs the hearts and guides the path of those who err, so that they may come to the knowledge of the truth (1 Tim 2:4), and he strengthens with his grace those who have been called out of darkness into his marvelous light (1 P 2:9), so that they may persevere in this light, this Lord who never leaves us except when we leave him." That is, grace *supports* from within the action of the exterior sign. Grace *strengthens* the faith of those who believe; grace *stirs* and *helps* those who are far from faith or on the way which leads to it. Like the signs of historical revelation in the time of Christ, the sign of the Church acts in a climate of grace.

The First Vatican Council's formulation does not pretend to be definitive, or above reproach; it does not claim to preclude any subsequent attempt at a formulation which will be fuller and more precise. In this connection, it may be asked if the Council's formulation as it stands shows sufficient awareness of the actual complexity of the sign of the Church. The sign of the Church is in fact more ambiguous than the sign of Christ. The unity of the Church is real, but it is a wounded unity, needing to be healed, a unity needing to be protected and always needing to be made more complete; her stability is al-ways under threat; her catholicity is subject to perpetual ten-sions; her holiness rises against a background of sin. The First

Vatican Council's formulation has doubtless to be understood in the sociological context of the nineteenth century, when the Church was conceived as a perfect, autonomous, transcendent society, which escaped the vicissitudes to which human societies are a prey. One thing is certain: it hardly allows us to suspect that what we are concerned with is a tissue of *paradoxes* (unity —universality, permanence—temporality, holiness—sin) which make of the Church a riddle to which we must find the key. The Church of the First Vatican Council seems an abstract Church, an ideal Church with absolute attributes, rather than a community of believers on a journey, fragile and prone to sin. The qualifying adjectives added to the traits of the Church (marvelous, eminent, unbreakable, inexhaustible) are of an intensive rather than a paradoxical order. Hence this formulation by the First Vatican Council lends itself with difficulty to apologetic use, especially in the context of the twentieth century.

Let us call to mind how the Second Vatican Council, sensitive to this difference in context, has modified perspectives and formulation while preserving the doctrine.

To make the sign of the Church more luminous, more brilliant, such it would seem was the motive which led John XXIII to undertake the work of the Second Vatican Council: "We shall present the Church in all her splendor, *sine macula et sine ruga,* and say to all those who are separated from us, 'Look, brothers, it is the Church of Christ.' "[10] In the thought of John XXIII, the Church, purified, renewed, become young again, is to constitute a sign capable of manifesting the authenticity of her origin and her mission, and of inviting those who do not belong to her to find in her the place of salvation.

John XXIII, however, when he evoked the sign of the Church, did so with great discretion, stressing, in what goes to make up the sign, unity and charity. "It will be," he said, in the encyclical *Ad Petri cathedram,* "... a marvelous spectacle of truth, unity and charity, the sight of which, we are sure, will be for those who are separated from this apostolic see, a gentle invitation

---

10. *Documentation catholique,* t. 56 (6 Sept. 1959), col. 1099.

to look for again, and to find, this unity for which Jesus Christ prayed so earnestly to his Father." [11] John XXIII did not speak of compelling proof but of persuasive sign. [12]

We have seen that the Second Vatican Council often referred to the text of the First, but without ever citing it in full. It is noticeable too that, in most of the passages in question, the sign of the Church is brought back in practice to the sign of unity in charity. The Church is the sign of the coming of salvation among men in the measure in which she reflects in our world the unity of love in the life of the Trinity. We have seen also that the Second Vatican Council, by a process of personalization which extends to the whole economy of revelation and its transmission, speaks of witness, personal and common, whereas the First Vatican Council speaks of the marvelous *attributes* of the Church. It is through people themselves, through their lives of holiness, through Christian communities, through their life of unity and charity, through the whole People of God, through its life in accord with the gospel, that men will understand that the Church is the home of salvation.

2. *Contemporary points of resistance to the Sign of the Church*

There is no doubt that the value of the sign of the Church has been stressed by the last two Councils, different though their perspectives and formulations were, more abstract in the case of the First Vatican Council, personalist and more discerning in the case of the Second.

Yet in proposing this sign to the men of our time, we ex-

---

11. "Id profecto mirabile praebebit veritatis, unitatis caritatisque spectaculum; spectaculum dicimus, quod ii etiam cernentes, qui ab Apostolica hac Sede sejuncti sunt, suave, ut confidimus, invitamentum accipient ad illam unitatem quaerendam assequendamque, quam Jesus Christus a coelesti Patre flagrantibus rogavit precibus" (AAS 59 [1959]: 511).

12. H. Holstein, "L'Église, signe parmi les Nations," *Études,* October 1962, p. 47.

perience, we must all confess, a certain embarrassment. For as
a result of publicity, which makes of the smallest local event
a world-wide event, we are more aware of the weaknesses of
ecclesiastics and ecclesiastical institutions. We know, from
the periodicals and newspapers, from radio and television, the
complaints which are daily made against the Church. We are
also more sensitive than we were to errors which are simply
historical.

The charge made by Mr. Charles Davis, in the book in which
he recounts the genesis of his own inner struggle,[13] is directed
precisely against a Church which has, in his eyes, ceased to be
a sign and become a counter-sign. Mr. Davis's argument amounts
to this. To say that the Church is a motive of credibility is to
say that one finds in her the life of faith, hope and charity
which distinguishes the Church of Christ. "But," he says, "I do
not perceive within the Roman Catholic Church signs enough
to support her claim to be, as the Church of Christ, the visible
incarnation of faith, hope and charity. In fact there is solid evidence to the contrary."[14] Mr. Davis considers that the Church,
as a social structure, is the enemy of the Christian *faith*, since
she has become a zone of lies, lacking any respect for the truth,
that she has become an obstacle to Christian *love*, since she
oppresses and destroys persons, and that she shatters *hope* to the
point of compromising her mission.[15] If the Church is thus
lacking in faith, hope and charity, this fact is to be attributed,
in Mr. Davis's [16] judgment, to her anachronistic hierarchical structure, and to the attitude which it inspires: extreme and oppres-
sive authoritarianism among clerics; among the faithful in
general, immaturity, frustration, agony and fear.

These accusations are made, not only by those who have left
the Church, like Mr. Davis, but also by Catholics themselves,
by bishops, theologians and lay people.

---

13. Charles Davis, *A Question of Conscience* (London, 1967).
14. *Ibid.*, p. 118.
15. *Ibid.*, pp. 64-117.
16. Apropos of Charles Davis's book, see Gregory Baum, *The Credibility
of the Church Today, a Reply to Charles Davis* (New York, 1968).

In the Council itself the liaison between the Church and the powers of money and exploitation was denounced in open forum, as was the position of a Church who is herself a financial power. The Church was accused of being confined, at least in the great nations of the west, to some millions of those who are both rich and white, of being present only in certain social classes, which have a tendency to consider her as their own property. For a century the Church has been blind to the poverty and distress of the working class: she has not denounced the injustice of which it was the victim, and she has lived on the offerings of those who ground it down. The Church has not chosen the royal road of the cross.[17]

Many theologians and lay people reproach the Church with her slowness in discerning the signs of the times, and adapting herself to historical conditions; with her constant diplomatic delay in the face of necessary decisions or calls for intervention; with her resentment against the social universe within which she has—at least in the last century—gone through her evolutions; with her lack of understanding and even harshness with regard to those who carry on research in her service; with her centralizing spirit and her encroaching legalism; with her bureaucracy, which so easily becomes greedy for honor and power, and sometimes too intent on providing careers for its members; with her tendency to dominate and her preoccupation with prestige; with her lack of collective humility; with her desire to level and make uniform in order the better to dominate; with her clinging to Latin and western ways and thought-forms; with the scandal given by the widespread defection of religious and priests.[18]

---

17. There is a great deal of episcopal testimony to this in: P. Gauthier, *Consolez mon peuple* (Paris, 1965), and *Jésus, l'Église et les pauvres* (Paris, 1962). See also the inquiry conducted by the review, *Esprit*, October 1967.

18. A list of these grievances can be found collected by H. Küng, *The Church;* K. Rahner, *Est-il possible aujourd'hui de croire?* (Paris, 1966), pp. 42-45; English translation, *Faith Today* (London, 1967); Italian translation, *La Chiesa nella situazione d'oggi* (Brescia, 1969); J. B. Metz, "Théologie politique et liberté critico-sociale," *Concilium*,

Criticism is particularly severe upon the attitudes of church-men. There is the lack of sincerity, the refusal to admit that the Church, in the course of the centuries, has not always been in command of the situation, and that she has indeed been mistaken, has not understood, has sinned and needs to be converted and reformed. There is the official practice of lying, coolly accepted for the "good" of the institution, which is conceived as an absolute, an end in itself. There is authoritarianism, which will admit of no truth but that which corresponds to the official opinion, the opposite opinion being immediately censured, forbidden, stifled: this is the transformation of authority by means of domination, after the manner of civil and political authority. There is the lack of any real sympathy for people, their problems and their sufferings, and of any real understanding of them.[19] The Church, observes Mr. Morris West, is more like a "corporation" than a family.[20]

Those who base their arguments on history recall the persecutions of the Jews and the crusades, the processes of the Inquisition and the burning of witches, the wars of religion and the night of St. Bartholomew, the evasions of the Church when confronted by the questions of war and slavery and poverty and the rest. It is enough to read Barth and Bonhoeffer, Péguy, and

n. 36 (1968): 9-25 trans., English edition; R. Laurentin, *Enjeu du deuxième synode et contestation dans l'Église* (Paris, 1969), pp. 83-90; J. Bonnefoy, *Inconfortable Église du XXe siècle* (Paris, 1969); H. De Lubac, *L'Église dans la crise actuelle* (Paris, 1969); Y. Congar, *Au milieu des orages* (Paris, 1969); J. Daniélou, *La foi de toujours et l'homme d'aujourd'hui* (Paris, 1969); trans., *Faith Eternal and the Man of Today* (New York, 1970); L. Bouyer, *La décomposition du catholicisme* (Paris, 1968); trans., *The Decomposition of Catholicism* (New York, no date); H. U. von Balthasar, *Cordula ou l'épreuve décisive* (Paris, 1968); P. Eyt, "L'élément politique dans les structures sociales," NRT 92 (1970): 3-25.

19. See on this subject: John L. McKenzie, *Authority in the Church* (London-Dublin-Melbourne, 1966); *Ibid., Myths and Realities* (London, 1963), pp. 3-34; H. Küng, *Truthfulness, The Future of the Church* (New York, 1968).
20. Morris L. West, "Causes for Anxiety in the Church," *Concilium*, n. 51 (1970): 15-16.

Bernanos, Kierkegaard and Dostoievsky, to be aware of the end-less list of charges against empty traditions—a fixed and authori-tarian dogmatism, bereft of any historical sense or biblical in-spiration, and a morality cut off from life and steeped in casuis-try; against opportunism, intolerance, formalism, legalism and the sleek officiousness of ecclesiastical dignitaries of all degrees; against the lack of a creative spirit and initiatives held up.[21]

These complaints, besides the fact that they represent only one aspect of ecclesial reality, and that a very limited one, do not take sufficient account of the Church's concrete situation. They err often through idealism. Let us acknowledge, never-theless, that they are in part well-founded. And it would be too simple a solution to conclude that their authors are all rebels, schismatics and imps of Satan, just as it would be too simple to suppose that all reactionaries are tyrants, torturers and agents of the Inquisition. We must not allow ourselves to be abused by language. We need to be attentive, I think, not so much to the way the criticisms are expressed or even to the criticisms themselves, but rather to the spirit which inspires them.

Let us begin by recognizing that the Church today is subject to extreme and painful tensions. Certain of these tensions, how-ever, are not peculiar to the Church: they belong to the whole of human society and civilization, which is in a state of muta-tion. There is for instance a dispute going on in which the blame is laid upon the *structures* of society and the tradition

---

21. To make the inventory of criticism directed against the Church still more complete, mention may be made of grievances raised by other religions. At this level the most severe criticism comes from *Hinduism*, which holds against the Church her dogmatism, which it finds intolerant. The idea of an authority whose function is to guard the truth of faith is unacceptable to Hinduism, and it rejects the idea of a unique revelation or of a religion which declares itself to be the religion *par excellence*. And finally Hinduism reproaches the Church with not having kept her promises, since Christ has come, but the world is no better. *Buddhism*, for its part, is not opposed to the idea of the Church, or to the idea of authority, but rather to the absolute and external character of the message of salvation; for it sees religion as above all a personal and interior experience.

which society transmits. Is it surprising, then, that by a sort of mimeticism this dispute has repercussions within the Church and even against the Church? Though she is a divine mystery the Church is also, in her human aspect, an institution, a tradition, and consequently vulnerable and open to attack.[22]

Within the Church herself, moreover, the equilibrium which has been regained between the Church as a hierarchy and the Church as the People of God, has had, as its immediate consequence, an awareness on the part of the laity of the responsible share which is theirs in the life and action of the Church. This redressment of the balance could hardly take place without evoking inevitable manifestations of the liberty which has been regained, manifestations which involve sometimes extreme language and aggressive attitudes and actions.[23]

Some of the criticisms levelled against the Church are made by serious, competent and responsible men, anxious for just reforms and necessary adaptations. I am thinking of men like Fr. Congar, Fr. Rahner, Fr. Chenu, Fr. de Lubac, Fr. Schillebeeckx. In them, criticism is a sign of interest and anxiety to serve. It springs from an awareness that the Church is constantly in need of reform, an awareness too that new forms of life and thought cannot arise without the appearance of divergences: these divergences, as long as they damage neither the unity of faith nor the communion of charity, are signs of vitality. The Second Vatican Council was the first to put into practice salutary and constructive self-criticism of this sort.

But then, equally, one is sometimes forced reluctantly to recognize that there is, in certain criticism directed at the Church, the manifestation of an attitude habitually bitter, vindictive, surly, even spiteful, which has decided in advance to spare nothing, but to make a universal havoc and reduce to dust everything past and present in the Church, an attitude which systematically throws into the background all that there

22. H. De Lubac, "L'Église dans la crise actuelle," *NRT* 91 (1969): 582; Y. Congar, *Au milieu des orages* (Paris, 1969), p. 65.
23. R. Laurentin, *Enjeu du deuxième synode et contestation dans l'Église* (Paris, 1969), pp. 180-182.

is of authentic renewal and true charity, all that is an expression of renewed youth, especially among the Christian communities of the east and of Africa and the "occupied" countries, where the faith is taken seriously. Reading certain articles and books, one cannot get rid of this impression of a settled determination to destroy, which crops up on every page, of an attitude like that of a beast in search of prey. Sometimes those who are called "conservatives" would gladly welcome new forms of Christian living if they had not been deterred by so much speech and action designed to kill.

Lastly there is another genus of criticism which proceeds from a sort of love-hate, or from affectionate aggressiveness. I have in mind the criticism which though extreme in tone and maladroit in expression is rooted in a deep love of the Church. The attitude which inspires it corresponds to that of prophecy. In the criticism of many Catholics, especially the young, there is, at bottom, a denunciation of all that deviates, in the Church of today, from the message and spirit of the gospel, all that is a distortion or falsification of this message and spirit, all that will not fit in with it, a denunciation of the Church's compromise with the powers of this world, and of the contradiction between her Mystery as the Body of Christ and the spectacle she offers to men. There is here a desire to return to the freshness and purity of the Church's source.[24]

If many of our contemporaries are unhappy, harsh or even violent before what they see as disfigurements in the Church, it is from a desire and need of the Church, but of a frank, authentic Church, a living and receptive Church, renewed according to the spirit of the gospel, a Church who is the servant of mankind; in short they desire and need a Church who is really a Witness to the charity of Christ. With many, if the Church is under attack, it is because they recognize in her a value essential to our faith in Christ, a necessary sign in the world of the salvation brought by Christ. In opposition of this

---

24. M. D. Chenu, "Un Peuple prophétique," *Esprit*, 35 (1967), 608; R. Laurentin, *Enjeu du deuxième synode et contestation dans l'Église*, p. 85.

"prophetic" sort, there is, certainly, a possibility of illusion. There is a danger of falling into the kind of triumphalism which consists in doing away with, "on principle," whatever the conservatives persist in upholding; there is a threat too of a fundamental nonconformity which could lead to conflict and rupture rather than unity. These dangers are real, but they should not prevent us from recognizing the signs of health and renewal and creativeness which lie behind many disputes whose virulence may be astonishing.[25]

This said, and whatever may be the spirit which inspires many of the complaints against the Church, one thing remains: it is becoming more and more difficult, not to say impossible, to present the Church to our contemporaries as a *visible sign* that salvation has come into the world. In doing so, we feel we are falling into the triumphalism so often denounced by the fathers of the Council. In the face of Protestant theologians who insist on a theology of the Church firmly planted on Calvary before the cross, and on a Church which is a community of sinners, ceaselessly needing to ask forgiveness and to purify itself, we hesitate to speak of the Church as a sign lifted up before the nations. At all events, we have not the

---

25. One can distinguish, today, in the context of actual debate, *five* types of Christian. There is (1) *the conservative,* whose motto is "the same today as yesterday." He is the man who ignores the Council and finds himself today in anguish and unable to cope. He is under the impression that everything is going to ruin in the Church. There is (2) *the reformer,* who sets out to follow a regular procedure, respecting the law. The creators of the Council fall into this category. There is (3) *the marginal Christian,* who abandons the institutional Church, since it seems to him an outmoded super-structure. There is (4) *the disputant* (the *contestataire*), who wants a radical change in structures while remaining inside the Church. He makes his protests in words and by means of active demonstrations. There is (5) *the underground Christian,* who rejects the institution but does not dare to confront it directly. He wants to stay inside the Church. Secretly and under cover he takes initiatives which are necessary in his eyes to prepare for the Church of tomorrow. The three types of critic distinguished in the text more or less correspond to (2), (3) and (4) as described here. Cf. R. Laurentin, *Enjeu du deuxième et contestation dans l'Église,* pp. 79-82.

assurance of Cardinal Dechamps at the time of the First
Vatican Council, who saw in the Church a sign which was efficacious and easy to recognize.

Among some Catholics there exists even a sort of practical
scepticism with regard to the sign of the Church. Far from
seeing in it a support for their faith, they denounce in it what
constitutes an obstacle. "The Second Vatican Council," remarks
G. Mollard, "after expressing itself magnificently in words, has
been unable to translate these into strong action. It would need
strong action for the evangelical renewal desired by the fathers
to become evident to everyone. That the pope has given away
one of his tiaras, that bishops are wearing more modest rings,
these do not constitute strong action, but are gestures without
any great significance, since they do not involve their authors.
It is precisely because the Council has not been able to express
itself in action which all can see, that today, as before, the
Church is not recognized as the sign of Christ and his gospel.
For the unbelieving and the indifferent, she remains an obstacle
to faith rather than an invitation.... For many Christians the
situation can be defined today as before the Council: faithfulness to Christ in the Church, in spite of the Church." [26] In
February 1967, at a theological meeting held in Rome to prepare for the synod of September, Mgr. Blomjous mentioned
"the crisis of credibility" which is shaking the post-conciliar
Church and creating a malaise in her. "Many think," he said,
"that the Church does not keep her promises, because the
hopes raised by the Council and the principles of reform which
it enunciated are still unrealized.[27]

Observing that this state of mind is wide-spread enough
among Catholics today, Fr. Malevez remarks: "As often as
one has to praise the zealous hope of seeing the Church refuse
to compromise herself with the sources of secular power, and

---

26. G. Mollard, "Après le Concile," _Esprit_, October 1967, p. 359.
The same writer adds, "Charles Davis's crisis of conscience is that of many
Christians, even if it be not absolutely for them a question of leaving
the Church." (_Ibid._, p. 359).

27. _Esprit, October,_ 1967, p. 359.

conform herself instead to the purity of her Master, one has
to dread seeing Christians deliberately shut their eyes to the
spiritually authentic characteristics which she has never ceased
to show. For—let us not forget it—it is in her that the majority
of men find and must find a valid motive for following Christ:
since a number of them are incapable of tracing her origin
back directly to the sign which is the Jesus of history . . . it
is to be presumed that it is in the lives of their fellow-Christians
and in the Church as a whole as she exists before their eyes
that they should recognize the foundation of their faith. If, by
the opinions you hold, you do away with the spiritual value
of the Church, in her members and in her essential organs,
you will, by the same token, cut from under the feet of most
men the most accessible ground of belief." [28] Then he adds, "Far
from conceding the validity of throwing up our commission
in this way, we should say rather that the sign of the Church
which is always present, is still waiting for theologians who
will demonstrate its full force." [29] Fr. Karl Rahner, for his part,
deprecates the fact that the sign of the Church is not sufficiently
studied in theology, especially in fundamental theology. And,
he points out, "the experience of the action of the Holy Spirit
in the concrete life of the Church is also, let us remember, an
historical experience, and can be reflected upon. And if in traditional fundamental theology this experience has in practice
played no part at all (in spite of the efforts of Cardinal Dechamps and the teaching of the First Vatican Council), it is
becoming in the 'new' fundamental theology a theme which is
central and given preference." [30]

---

28. L. Malevez, "Jésus de l'histoire, fondement de la foi," NRT 89
(1967), 786-787.

29. Ibid., p. 787.

30. Karl Rahner, Est-il possible aujourd'hui de croire? (Paris, 1966),
p. 207. This new fundamental theology which Fr. Rahner talks about
covers both more and less than fundamental theology. It covers more,
since it studies not only the fact but the content of revelation, that is,
the different Christian mysteries; it covers less, since it makes a choice
among the problems of classic fundamental theology. Its criterion is
this: it studies the mysteries and motives of credibility which have an

Do not the difficulties which we experience with regard to the sign of the Church arise, in great part, from the fact that, as Malevez points out, theology has not yet succeeded in proposing a valid way to treat it? Up to now, indeed, fundamental theology has applied, without differentiation, to all the signs of revelation, the schema—*ne varietur*—of the physical miracle. In this way we have lost sight of the specificness and dynamism of each of the signs, and to that extent impoverished the scope of supernatural semiology. One thing is certain: a history of the argument from the sign of the Church and its use during the hundred years which separate the First from the Second Vatican Council reveals that there does not yet exist any satisfactory monograph on the subject. It is essentially a matter for research.[31]

3. *Towards a way of approach*

The first problem is that of finding a way of approach which is valid in itself, and valid in the eyes of contemporary man, a way of approach which is in accordance with his mentality.

At the outset, let us remember that since what is intended is *theological* research into the sign of the Church, this sign must be envisaged in its totality, that is both on the ontological plane (the reality of the sign) and on the subjective plane (the human subject confronted by the sign). Equally, I think, we need, after the example of the Second Vatican Council, to envisage the sign from a point of view which is at once dogmatic and apologetic.

The *dogmatic* way of looking at things asks, in the light of revelation and faith, the secret of this radiance which shines in the face of the Church: it is in the Spirit of Christ, the source and principle of the Church's union, cohesion and expansion.

---

existential repercussion in the lives of men *today*. To tell the truth, it is more a fundamental dogmatics, of a synthetic and existential sort.

---

31. M. Grand'maison, *L'Église par elle-même motif de crédibilité* (Rome, 1961), pp. 7-9.

The *apologetic* way of looking sets out from the Church as an observable Phenomenon, complex and paradoxical, encompassing space and time. It gathers together the data provided by this Phenomenon and asks, in a methodical and critical theological discursus, which must be valid even in the eyes of the unbeliever, what are the facts which can make of the Church a sign which is really consistent in its ontological reality and really capable of fulfilling its function intentionally. The apologetic way of looking then studies the dialectic of the sign's discernment, at the spontaneous level and at the reflective level. Lastly it asks under what conditions the sign can be discerned by those who do not believe: what the necessary intellectual and moral dispositions are on the part of the subject confronted by the sign, and what experience of the Church he needs, and what dispositions are required also on the part of those who pose the sign, that is, Catholics themselves, for it to constitute a really effective and compelling appeal.

In the study of the *Church as a Phenomenon* which follows, two approaches are avoided, which seem to me for different reasons inadequate, the *comparative* approach (at least as a direct approach) and the *transcendent* approach.

The comparative approach consists in comparing the Church with other religious communities (the Christian communities separated from the Church, or the other great religions of salvation, Buddhism, Hinduism and Islam) and declaring that the Church manifests in relation to these an unequalled superiority, especially at the level of unity, universality, permanence and holiness. This obviously presupposes that one recognizes, outside the Catholic Church, elements of salvation and "Church," but that the Church represents an excellence, a fullness of sanctification which does not seem to be realized to the same degree in the other communities of salvation. This approach seems to me complicated, not very satisfactory, and open to very serious risks. In particular, it is difficult for it to escape the accusation of being ignorant, inexact, prejudiced and even unjust, since the man who practices it is always tempted to minimize the importance of the facts he comes up against in order to make Catholic superiority more striking. I do not deny that this approach has elements of value, but I think it has, above all, a *confirmatory* value. And if we have not succeeded in showing the objective and internal consistency of the sign, it is in vain that we shall have recourse to the comparative method in order to refloat the ship which is already lost.

Equally, the *transcendent* approach is avoided, at least in the way formulated by the First Vatican Council, which sees in the Church a phenomenon whose transcendence is analogous in the moral order to the transcendence of physical miracle, and attests directly the divine origin of the Church and her mission. To describe to our contemporaries the *marvelous* expansion, the *eminent* sanctity, the *inexhaustible* fruitfulness, the *catholic* unity and the *invincible* stability of the Church is to provoke for no good reason an uncontrollable allergy. It would be impossible not to raise the phantom of a triumphalist Church.

The approach suggested, then, is by way of *internal intelligibility*, of a *search for meaning*. This method sets out not from the Church's absolute and glorious attributes, but from the *paradoxes* and *tensions* which constitute her concrete reality. It seeks to understand these paradoxes and tensions, in themselves and in their mutual relationships, and in relation also to the explanation which the Church offers of herself. The consistency between this explanation and the facts observed (nature and dimension) leads us to think that the Church's testimony is true. She is really, in our world, the sign of salvation in Jesus Christ. The intelligibility of the *Phenomenon* is in the *Mystery attested*. The miraculous attributes of the Church are not the point of departure; the Church's transcendence appears rather as a conclusion to the analysis of her tensions, as the key of intelligibility, necessary in order to understand the Phenomenon in her totality and complexity.

4. *The Church as a mystery of faith*

A theological reflection on the sign of the Church must

unite, as was suggested, in one complementary vision, the dog-matic and apologetic aspects of the sign. Let us look first at the Church as a mystery of faith.

As well as, and much more than, being a society defined by juridical connections, the Church is a mystery of *communion,* the word meaning here all that belongs to the union of per-sons, in the Trinity as in the Church. *Communion* designates the mystery of our relationship with God, with the divine Persons, with Christ, with the Spirit, and with the other members of the Body of Christ.[32]

Of all the themes to which the Second Vatican Council ad-dressed itself, that which renews most deeply our vision of the Church is precisely this theme of the Church as a mystery of communion. It orients and inspires the whole of the constitution *Lumen gentium;* it might even be said that it throws on every point of ecclesiology a totally new light. The ecclesiology of communion, especially alive and fruitful in the Churches of the east, has been, in the west, not disowned or ignored, but for a long time left in the shade, in favor of an ecclesiology of in-stitution, hierarchy and authority. What the Second Vatican Council has done in restressing the ecclesiology of communion is simply to recover an essential element of the Christian heri-tage.[33]

By an ecclesiology of *communion* is meant an ecclesiology which envisages the Church as an organic and living whole, constituted by all those internal and spiritual bonds (the gifts of the Spirit, the theological virtues) and all those external and visible bonds (profession of faith, sacraments, ministry) which unite in the Spirit those who believe, and by which all the faithful scattered throughout the world form the *Ecclesia,* the assembly. This ecclesiology brings itself to bear on all the essential elements of the Church, but each of these is considered

---

32. J. Hamer, *L'Église est une communion* (Paris, 1962), p. 178: trans., *The Church is a Communion* (New York, 1965).

33. R. Latourelle, *Théologie, science du salut* (Bruges and Paris, 1968), p. 259; trans., *Theology, Science of Salvation* (Alba House, New York, 1969), pp. 259-260.

as it encourages, helps, accomplishes or perfects the communion which is the Church.[34]

Through the possession of all these means in common, the faithful form the ecclesial communion, which thus has a double aspect, an aspect of mystery and a social and institutional aspect. But the social and institutional character of the Church exists in order to serve the reality of the mystery. In the ecclesial communion, the social structure discloses the internal life from which it proceeds and to which it is ordained. From the indissoluble union of these two elements arises the communion of the faithful as a unique organism.[35]

This mystery of communion has its exemplar and source in the Trinity; for the Church is at once the work of the Trinity (it is the unity of the Trinity which encompasses and embraces mankind in the Church) and a sharing in the communion of the Trinity. God, that is, wished through grace to introduce us into the mystery of love which is the communion of the Trinity. The decree on ecumenism says of this mystery of the Church that its "supreme model and principle is the unity of the one God in the Trinity of persons, Father, Son and Holy Spirit" (UR 2). God desired that men, who are divided and scattered, children of wrath and sin, should be brought together again and united in the Spirit of love after the example of the divine persons. Through the Church, he wished to make of all mankind one family, one People of God, one Body of Christ, one Temple of the Holy Spirit (Eph 4:1-6), and he willed that the principle of union, cohesion and expansion in this People should be the very love with which the Father loves the Son and the Son the Father. The Church is a mystery of communion in the Spirit.

Without Christ and his Spirit, men are divided and set against one another. It is as the fruit of the life and death of Christ, immolated to "gather together in one the children of God that were scattered abroad" (Jn 11:52), that mankind passes from a state of division and hatred into the unity of charity. In this

---

34. G. Thils, *L'Église et les Églises* (Louvain, 1966), p. 30.

35. A. Antón, "Unità e diversità nella Chiesa secondo il Vaticano II," *La Civiltà Cattolica*, 4 October 1969; pp. 25-26.

unity, Christ is our only Mediator. By being lifted up on the wood of the cross, he has deserved to "draw all men to himself" (Jn 12:32). He is the only way, the only shepherd, the only door to the fold. He gives all men the power, through baptism into his death and resurrection, and through faith in the gospel, to become children of the Father and to approach the Father in the one Spirit, so that they can say "*Abba*, Father," in the Spirit of the Son (Gal 4:6), and love other men as Christ and the Father love them.

The Church, then, is a mystery of *communion*. She is "the people made one by the unity of the Father and the Son and the Holy Spirit" (LG 4). In this mystery of communion, the bond which unites Christians to one another and to God is a bond of love and a personal bond, the *Spirit* of God (UR 2). What God purposes in his Church is to make us share in Christ's sonship, to *in-spire* his Spirit into our hearts, so that all men, children of God and brothers among themselves, may constitute one People of God, one Body of Christ. In her life on earth the Church must witness to the one triune God, so as to be "the visible sacrament of this saving unity" (LG 9), that is, both "the sign and means of inner union with God and of the unity of all mankind" (LG 1).

If the source of the Church's communion is the Holy Spirit, who is the Spirit of God before being the Spirit of the Church, one can understand how, given life and unity and strength by this Spirit, sustained and directed by him, the Church can face time and space and human egotism. "You shall receive power when the Holy Spirit has come upon you, and you shall be my witnesses in Jerusalem, and in all Judea and in Samaria and to the uttermost part of the earth" (Acts 1:8). "I am with you always, even to the end of the world" (Mt 28:20). "Make disciples of all nations" (Mt 28:19). It is because the principle of the Church's communion is the very Spirit of God, that she can, in so far as she opens herself to his action, be a reflection in our world of the Trinity's life of union in love, and a sign of the salvation brought by Christ. Without this divine principle, which never ceases to give and renew her life, the Church, like earthly societies, would be in jeopardy and indeed die.

5. *Paradoxes and tensions in the Church*

After considering the Church from the point of view of faith, let us see now how the presence of the *Church as a Phenomenon* in the world can awaken us to the presence of the *Mystery* which she constitutes. In what sense can the Church be a sign for contemporary man, leading him to think that she is the place of salvation?

First of all it needs to be said that the sign does not arise from her being a wisely ordered and wisely administered hier-archical society, a sort of sociological ideal, a society, that is, whose structure would be superior to that of contemporary hu-man societies. It is not the human aspect of the Church which makes her a sign. The sign begins to appear when one notices that the Church, while possessing characteristics common to all structured and organized societies, is distinguished from other societies by certain astonishing peculiarities which originate in *paradox*.[36]

Thus we can distinguish in the Church at least three major paradoxes: the paradox of *unity*, the paradox of *permanence* and the paradox of *holiness*. These paradoxes are not simple, as we shall see. Each, in fact, is constituted by an *ensemble* of *tensions*, of which certain are powerful enough to shatter any society which had to submit to them and at the same time face the test of duration. This general effect of *paradox* and *tension* makes of the Church an enigmatic sign, to which it is necessary to find the cipher or key.

Through the simultaneous existence in her of traits apparent-ly incompatible—in the eyes of human experience and human history—and yet traits which are harmonized in herself, the Church suggests something of the great paradoxes of Christ's

---

36. H. Holstein, "L'Église, signe parmi les nations," *Études,* October 1962, pp. 48-49.

presence in the world: simplicity and authority, humility and the unheard of claim of him who declared himself the Son of man, the Son of the Father, the Savior of mankind, the eschatological Judge, without sin, and yet having more than anyone else a sense of sin, and of its universality. The Church, like Christ, is a *riddle* to be *solved*.

The study of paradoxes and tensions in the Church is not an abstract undertaking. It is in history, and by the methods of history, that theology must grasp all that goes to make up each one of these paradoxes. On the basis of the data thus gathered together, theological reflection can then be built, and can discover, beyond and behind the *Church as a Phenomenon*, the mysterious *action of the Spirit*.

CHAPTER V

The Paradox and Tensions of Unity

The first of the great paradoxes of the Church is that of unity. From a superficial point of view the unity of the Church can be reduced to a unity of baptism, creed and authority. In reality this unity masks multiple and prodigious tensions. There have been periods in the Church when theology emphasized Catholic unity, but without any great ability to perceive all its complexity. Our own time is more sensitive to the *diversity* and *complexity* which go to make it up. That Catholic unity should subsist in spite of all these tensions excites astonishment and creates questioning. In the light of phenomenology and history, the unity of the Church is distinguished in the following ways.

1. *A complex and demanding unity*

Every society is characterized by, at the very least, some unity, that is, the unity which results from the common pursuit of the same end, the same ideal. But one notices that the more demanding and complex the ideal pursued is, the more difficult it is for it to gain acceptance by the many, and to survive the test of time without losing something of its purity. History proves that if an ideal is high it tends to become lower, and to become simplified in order to accommodate itself to the greatest number. If it tries to remain too pure, it reaches only individuals, or else it dissolves into sects of the lowest kind and ends by disappear-

ing altogether. Now it is one of the first facts observable in
the Church that her unity is not just any sort of unity, a superficial unity, but a unity of a *complex* sort. That is, the Catholic
faith is not simply a vague religious attitude, sentimental and
making little demand on those who hold it, nor is it simply the
adherence to a certain number of exterior observances, but a
faith in mysteries which turn human reason upside down: the
Unity of God in the Trinity of persons, God incarnate, man's
divinization by God's communication of himself to his creature,
salvation through the cross, the resurrection of the body, the
sacramental eating of Christ's body and blood and so on.
The Christian message is a scandal to the Jews, and, to the
Greeks, foolishness.

The complexity of Christianity lies also in the *balance of
opposites* which it accomplishes, especially in the philosophical
options which it takes up: the way, for instance, it holds in
equilibrium, in its conception of man, incarnate spirit and
spiritualized body, person and community. In the spiritual life
there is an equilibrium between love of God and love of one's
neighbor, between personal prayer and liturgical prayer, between
action and contemplation, between marriage and virginity. In
the idea of salvation there is respect for the person, who is
neither absorbed, dissolved into the Absolute, nor separated
from God, but called to a communion with the divine persons.

This complex unity is also a *demanding* unity, which asks
man to submit to Christ not only his exterior actions, but his
most secret thoughts and deepest desires. It lies in the exigence
of a choice which can go as far as martyrdom. The choice of
martyrdom is in fact at the horizon of every Christian life. "If,"
says *Lumen gentium,* "this privilege falls to the lot of few, all,
nevertheless, must be ready to confess Christ before men, and
to follow him in the way of the cross, through the persecutions
which will never be lacking to the Church" (LG 42).

Now in spite of the complexity and demanding nature of
her unity, and in spite of its demand that she should preserve
her original message unchanged (a demand which is often a

cause of complaint against the Church, when she is accused of intransigent dogmatism), the Church has, in the course of the centuries, received and incorporated into herself multitudes of human beings. This belonging to the Church, which is generally accompanied by a deep integration of personality, gives rise among her members, however unknown or isolated in time and space they may be, to a "communion." According to the testimony of the faithful themselves, the source and principle of this cohesion and communion in the Church is the union of all her members to and in Christ and his Spirit.

This is the first of the elements which go to make up the paradox of the Church's unity: the unity of faith in the same gospel in spite of the complexity of its message and the demands it makes.

2. *Faithfulness to the message and constant adaptation to time*

In what the message of faith consists was definitively established by the evidence of the apostles, the witnesses of Christ's inner mystery. And yet, under pain of becoming a word without resonance, this message has to remain always as alive as on the day of its proclamation. The man of the twentieth century must feel as vividly that it is addressed to him as did the Jew or Greek or Roman of the first. For the aim of the gospel is to initiate a dialogue which will end only with the end of time. The word which was spoken in a particular *milieu*, at a precise moment of time, must meet the men of every time, in their own historical setting, each time unique, and provide the answer to their questions and their anxieties, in order to lead them to God. The Church must be attentive both to the word of God and to the voice of time.

It follows then that there will be an inevitable tension between the *present* and the *past*. On the one hand, the Church must not be attached to the letter of the past, to the point of falling into a sort of primitivism or romanticism about her historical origins. On the other hand, she must not, under the pre-

text of fulfilling the aspirations of the contemporary world, sacrifice the substance of Christ's message, after the manner of Bultmann or the liberal Protestantism of the last century.

The Church is constantly exposed to this double danger:
of neglecting necessary adaptation in the name of fidelity to the
deposit of faith, or of compromising over the message itself,
with the excuse of a perpetual need to revise it. The Church
can be the victim of stagnation, or inability to move, or she can
be the victim of fashionable ways of talking or the transient
thought-forms of a particular period. But it has to be confessed
that she has often in the past transferred to the realm of dis-
ciplinary and practical problems the demand of revelation that
it must remain unchanged, and so failed to meet urgent needs
for adaptation. One thing is certain: there is an inevitable
tension between what is given, and possessed in peace, and the
adaptation which is still obscure and confused, hovering on the
threshold of the present or imminent future. The Church is
condemned to live in a state of *precariousness*. For a Church living in hope is a Church ceaselessly finding the future in the
present, discovering today the fidelity of tomorrow.

Fidelity and adaptation: the Church responds to this double
prerequisite in her double concept of tradition and development.[1]

In fact, the Church does, in her preaching, manifest the
desire to lose nothing of the message she has received, not to
alter it, or introduce into it anything new, but to keep it intact,
to defend it and to propose it according to its real meaning.
And on the other hand she does recognize the obligation to
understand the gospel afresh, so that she can draw from it
new answers to new questions. She has to preach the same
gospel as the good news for *today*. She should, says *Ecclesiam
suam*, "try to express the Christian message in terms of the
philosophical concepts, the language and culture, the customs
and thought-forms of man as he actually lives and moves and

---

1. Constitution *Dei verbum*, II.

has his being on earth today." [2] *Gaudium et spes* recognizes that the Church is passing through a new era, and that it is her duty, at every moment, "to scrutinize the signs of the time and interpret them in the light of the gospel," so that she can answer the questions of each generation (GS 4). She has to interpret the *same* gospel of Jesus Christ as attested by the apostles, from the point of view of a new cultural context and new questions. These new problems stimulate the People of God to discover how God's word impinges on each epoch and what demands it makes.

This work of actualizing in new contexts the unique and unchangeable word of Christ is part of a tradition which goes back to the origins of the Church and has never been interrupted. The actual text of the parables, for instance, in our gospels, is already a re-reading and realization of the Lord's words in the slightly different context of the early Church. The Council of Trent, with its eighteen years of preparation, sought solutions to new problems. The Second Vatican Council, on a multitude of points, confronted the gospel with questions that earlier ages could scarcely ask, since they arise against a different background.

If this actualization is the work of the magisterium, it is still more the work of the preacher and the theologian. Theology represents the Church's constant effort to live in contact with the world and with the problems, the doubts and the projects of the world. It is through theology that the encounter between the faith and the contemporary world takes place. And it is to theology also that there belongs the task of showing that the Church has not, in this work of actualizing the message of Christ, betrayed it, but has, as she claims, been unfailingly faithful to it.

---

2. "Nonne Concilium ipsum, ex eo quod sibi proposuit, pastorali munere, illuc contendit jure meritoque, ut christianus nuntius in cogitationes influat, in verba, in cognitiones, in mores, in sensa hominum, qui in terrarum orbe hodie vivunt et animis aestuant?" (Paul VI, *Ecclesiam suam,* AAS 56, [1964]: 640-641).

That the Church should be faithful to the past without being a slave to it, that she should manifest equally and tenaciously
the will to preserve her fidelity to the unique message of Christ
and the will *to actualize it in new contexts* in order to answer
the questions of each new time, this is not one of the least
paradoxical aspects of the unity of the Church. To realize the
seriousness of this tension, it is enough to consider the difficulties
of many Protestant communions: some grimly attached to the
letter of the gospel but without any real creativeness (Protestant
communities of the fundamentalist type), others, on the contrary, too much preoccupied with contemporary man and his
philosophy, and prepared to sacrifice to it the essentials of the
Christian faith.

3.   Unity of faith and theological pluralism

The problem of actualizing the word in new contexts is
closely bound up with that of interpreting the faith and with the
plurality of ways in which our understanding of it may be expressed.

Theological pluralism [3] is a matter of fact. It means the
formulation of one and the same faith, one and the same mystery,

---

3. On theological pluralism and the problems it presents the following
are useful: G. Philips, "A propos du pluralisme en théologie," *Ephemerides
theologicae lovanienses,* 46 (1970): 149-169; K. Rahner, "Theological
pluralism and the Church's unity of faith," *Concilium,* n. 46 (1969): 93-
112; *Ibid., Magistero e Teologia* (Brescia, 1967); M. Flick, "Pluralismo
teologico e unità della fede," *La Civiltà Cattolica,* n. 1 (1970), pp.
323-333; Z. Alszeghy and M. Flick, *Lo sviluppo del dogma cattolico*
(Brescia, 1967); J.-P. Jossua, "Immutabilité, progrès ou structurations
multiples des doctrines chrétiennes," *Revue des Sciences philosophiques
et théologiques,* 52 (1968): 173-200; *Ibid.,* "Règle de foi et orthodoxie,"
Concilium, n. 51 (1970): 57-66 trans., English edition; M. De Certeau,
"Y a-t-il un langage de l'unite?" *Concilium,* n. 51 (1970): 77-89; trans.
English edition; E. Schillebeeckx, *Révélation et théologie* (Brussels and
Paris, 1965), passim: trans., *Revelation and Theology,* 2 vols. (New York,
1967 and 1968); G. J. Pinto De Oliveira, "Église, orthodoxie et societé
pluraliste," *Concilium,* n. 51 (1970): 91-100, trans., English edition.

in different intellectual registers, whose diversity is the result of differing *milieux*, historical, philosophic and cultural. This diversity introduces into the language of faith necessary and fruitful differences, which nourish, enlarge and renew its universe of discourse. Pluralism, nevertheless, carries risks, especially that of a tension between unity of faith and theological pluralism. Just how far is it possible, in pronouncements of faith, to allow a diversity of expression which will leave intact the unchanging unity of divine revelation?

Often, in talking about theological pluralism, people oppose it to the monolithic structure of neo-scholastic thought. In point of fact, pluralism has always existed. What, for example, is probabilism, in moral theology, if not a form of pluralism? Much more, there is already in scripture, if not pluralism, at least a plurality and complementarity of perspective in presenting the same mystery. There is, that is, a synoptic approach, a Johannine approach and a Pauline approach to the mystery of Christ. In the synoptic tradition, Christ's revealing work is connected with the titles of Messiah, Teacher, Preacher. The epistle to the Hebrews compares the economies of the two covenants and celebrates the pre-eminence of Christ's revelation. St. John sees in Christ the perfect Witness to the Father. If, indeed, one can talk about a theology of Mark, or Matthew, of Luke or John, it is precisely because of this plurality of perspectives, categories and vocabulary which exists already in scripture.

When, with the patristic era, we have the beginnings, no longer of revelation, but of theological reflection, pluralism is even more in evidence. In the scholastic period schools are formed, proliferate and even oppose one another: Thomists, Scotists, Suarezians. Systematizations appear with noticeably different orientations. The faith is one, but what a difference there is in the theologies of Justin, Cyprian, Origen, Augustine, Thomas and Duns Scotus.

Theological pluralism is due to many different factors. First of all, *different mentalities and different cultural milieux* engender different sorts of sensibility. The east developed an ecclesiology of communion, while the west elaborated an ecclesiology of institution.

Secondly, differences are produced by the choice of *different basic philosophies*—Platonism, Aristotelianism, personalism. Patristic theology of the Trinity, for instance, or of divine exemplarism, creation, moral perfection, the vision of God, is unintelligible without a knowledge of Platonic and neoplatonic concepts and modes of thought. Modern thought, marked as it is by personalism and dialogic relationship, has influenced the theology of the Trinitarian life, of the Incarnation, of grace, of sin, of faith. An evolutionary vision of the world obliges us to re-think the theology of creation, original sin, redemption.

Thirdly, *different intuitions and initial preoccupations* result in different systematizations, Dominican, Jesuit, Carmelite, Franciscan and Benedictine, for instance.

Fourthly, sometimes it is an affair simply of a *difference in emphasis,* either in treating a particular question or in the whole of a systematization. The same *datum* of faith turns, as it were, on a different pivot. In Trinitarian theology, for instance, the eastern Church sets out from the Trinity of persons in order to arrive at the unity of nature, emphasizing the divine processions and being consequently more dynamic. The western Church stresses the Unity of nature and goes on afterwards to the plurality of persons, so that the axis of the whole is in the divine relations and the conception more static. St. Augustine, in applying the anthropological analogy to the Trinity, developed both the psychological schema of spiritual dynamism (thought and love), and the personalist schema of mutual gift. Later, the personalist schema was given preference by Richard of St. Victor and the medieval Franciscan tradition, while St. Anselm gave preference to the psychological model. St. Thomas took his point of departure in the psychological, but in order to make a synthesis of the two. The re-stressing of the psychological schema in the theology of the schools is generally attributed to Duns Scotus. The swing of the pendulum has brought us back in contemporary theology to the personalist.

Lastly, a *perspective* freely adopted can inspire the whole of a systematization, the theocentric systematization of St. Thomas, for instance, the Christocentric systematization of kerygmatic theology, or the anthropological systematization suggested by Fr. Rahner. Each system represents an effort to interpret and express the same *datum* of revelation. None is reducible to another, except on the plane of the mystery all seek to understand, or on the plane of the Church who recognizes all as valid. Each can be made more perfect, and each is susceptible of progress.

Since dogmatic expressions are the result of theological reflection, it is legitimate to speak not only of theological pluralism but also of a pluralism—or better of the possible plurality— of dogmatic expression. Dogma is the authentic ecclesial expression of a revealed truth; dogmatic definition is the attestation of a saving reality, but in terms which are connected with a particular cultural, sociological and historical context. We need, then, to distinguish, in a dogmatic formula, between what is, in the proper sense, attested, and its expression in human terms, which are bound up with a particular period and a particular mentality, a fact which would justify subsequent formulations which were more complete, more sensitive to fine shades of meaning and more in correspondence with the reality of the mystery. Theology today is, more and more, discovering the part played by the problem of language in the declarations of the magisterium.

Dogmatic formulas, moreover, being often directed against a specific error, are susceptible of a stress proper to the situation in which they were made, which has to be understood; it can happen that they emphasize one way of looking at a thing to the detriment of another, and leave without explicit expression important aspects of revealed truth. The Council of Trent, for instance, on the subject of justification, does not even mention adoptive sonship; apropos of the Mass it stresses exclusively its sacrificial character and preserves complete silence on its aspect as a commemorative meal; in speaking of the priesthood it mentions the power to celebrate the Eucharist and absolve sins, but does not mention preaching or spreading the good news of the gospel. These omissions and restrictions are explained when we remember that the Council wished simply to exclude Protestant errors, without any claim to be giving a complete and exhaustive exposition of doctrine.[4]

There is a place, then, in the Church for new, more perfect formulations, and even for a certain reinterpretation of dogma, in, for instance, purifying later formulations of imperfections which have been able to attach themselves to formulations in the past, or in a rectification of perspectives such as that which the Second Vatican Council was able to make in the way it presented the Church, revelation and faith. More than that, if one admits the co-existence of parallel theologies, equally legitimate, there is a place, it would seem, for parallel dogmatic formulations, on condition, obviously, that they do not conflict, or contradict the *meaning* of previous dogmatic formulations.[5]

If theological pluralism has always existed in the Church, it assumes today dimensions which make of it a phenomenon at once traditional and without precedent. In the past, among the scholastics and neo-scholastics, the pluralism of schools and systems was expressed in a language which, if not in every case identical, was at least near enough to be understood. The philosophical horizon and the choices on which a system could be based were easy to recognize. The orthodox and heterodox

---

4. G. Philips, "A propos du pluralisme en théologie," *Ephemerides theologicae lovanienses*, 46 (1970): 158.

5. How are parallel theological or dogmatic formulations to be judged and how is it to be verified that they do not contradict previous formulations? This verification belongs, it would seem, to a *total hermeneutics*, that is, to a hermeneutics which would take account of (a) words and their meaning in the present day context; (b) the relationship of the formulation in question to the continuity of faith in the Church; (c) the analogy of faith; (d) the analogy of the documents of the magisterium; (e) the *praxis* to which the formulation in question leads. The magisterium itself, in order to express itself and make itself understood in a pluralist context, would need to produce a hermeneutics of its own, dealing with the terms it uses, explaining them and justifying them, just as a civil legislator takes into account in formulating the law, the different ways in which language is used at the time.

could meet and contradict one another, and at the same time identify one another and identify the sources of their disagreement. It is not like that today.

Pluralism today arises from the mass of material accumulated by every discipline and from the diversity of the methods employed. Philosophy has become pluralist, and the sciences have emancipated themselves from philosophy. The result is that theologies are ranged not face to face, but side by side, disparate, without a common horizon of thought. We find ourselves in the presence of theologies which call themselves *Christian*, which propose themselves as a reflection on the same creed, but which constitute a different universe. We are confronted by wandering galaxies. How, for instance, are we to assess and situate in relation to Catholic theology, the theology of Barth or Bultmann? There is an analogous diversity among Catholic theologians themselves. Consider the discussions on the Eucharist, on Christology, on original sin, on eschatology, on the resurrection. Philosophic worlds and universes of discourse are so different that we no longer understand one another. And, moreover, the development and exigencies of hermeneutics makes us more aware of the differences in horizon, culture, history and mentality which separate us from the texts of the past. There follows the phenomenon of a *re-reading* of scripture, of the Fathers, of the documents of the magisterium, but according to modes of thought and expression which become more and more different.

Theological pluralism is inevitable. It is even an advantage, and the Second Vatican Council recognized both its legitimacy and its fruitfulness.[6] It is, nonetheless, undeniable that it pro-

---

6. The decree on ecumenism declares: "What has been said above about a legitimate diversity in matters of worship and discipline should be applied also to the theological formulation of doctrine. In point of fact, in the effort to understand revealed truth in depth, the methods and means of knowing and expressing divine things have been different in East and West. It is hardly surprising then that certain aspects of a revealed mystery have sometimes been better understood and better expressed by one or the other, so that these different theological formulations must often be considered as complementary rather than opposed" (UR 17). *Gaudium et spes* says: "the deposit of faith or revealed truth is one

vokes a continual tension, which can reach a critical point, between a legitimate diversity and the unity necessary to safeguard the faith. That is, if it is true that theology more and more keeps its distance in relation to the official formulations of the magisterium, how are we to be sure that all still profess the same faith and acknowledge the same mystery revealed in Jesus Christ? In a pluralism which takes many forms and is directed to many ends, there is a risk of progressively eliminating the content of faith and preserving nothing but its intention. Unity, softened by the recognition of so much diversity, can arrive at the point where it dissolves in it. How are we to believe in the one God revealed in Jesus Christ, if the witnesses who attest him no longer have anything in common among themselves, and if the term "Christian" covers meanings which are strange to one another—if, for example, it is affirmed that the Son did not exist before the Incarnation, that there is no question of two natures in Jesus Christ, and that his resurrection happened only in the consciousness of his disciples?

There is no doubt at all that pluralism sometimes creates extreme tensions. And one may legitimately ask oneself how a society submitted for centuries to tensions such as these, can subsist, without either becoming dislocated or disappearing. We are in the presence of a riddle.

4. *Wounded unity and ecumenical desire*

That the inner tensions to which unity is submitted can arrive at a critical point and damage the equilibrium of the Church is not simply an hypothesis, but an historical fact.

Wounded unity

The Church's unity was maintained for a thousand years; and then it suffered two especially serious historical ruptures, the

---

thing, the way in which these truths are expressed is another, provided their sense and meaning is safeguarded" (GS 62). See also LG 23, UR 4, AG 22.

schism with the East in 1054, and Luther's Protestant Reformation in the sixteenth century. The responsibility for both these ruptures is a shared one, and the decree on ecumenism openly recognizes it: "Communities of a considerable size were separated from full communion in the Catholic Church not without the fault of those on both sides" (UR 3).

In the schism with the East various factors played a part and resulted in oppositions which became more and more impossible to overcome.[7] There were factors of *ecclesiastical politics* (the growing opposition between Constantinople and Rome, and the taking of Constantinople by the crusaders with their itch to Latinize in all spheres), *religious and cultural factors* (a difference of language and mentality, resulting for both East and West in intellectual isolation, and a diversity of rite which implied for the East a diversity in the whole style of Christian life), and *theological factors* (the development of a more rational and discursive theology in the West in contrast to a more contemplative theology in the East, a thirst to define and dogmatize in the West in contrast to a greater reserve and flexibility in the East, and the theological tendency in the West to centralize and make uniform, in contrast to the theological pluralism of the East). Attempts to restore unity had only an ephemeral success. The Council of Lyons, in 1274, under Gregory X, led to a reunion of the two Churches, but from 1282 onwards there was a new break. The Council of Florence, in the fifteenth century, under Eugene IV, reached an agreement proclaimed on 6 July 1439, but the hierarchy of the East rejected the Council and its decrees with violence. The schism has lasted ever since, consummated by the isolation imposed by Turkish domination, which has continued to keep bitterness alive.

In the same way, the Catholic Church and the Reformed Church share responsibility for the break in the sixteenth cen-

---

7. On the Eastern Schism see especially: Y. Congar, *Neuf cents après. Notes sur le schisme oriental* (Chevetogne, 1954), trans., *After Nine Hundred Years* (New York, 1959); H. Küng, *L'Église*, 2: 392-394; English translations, *The Church* (New York, 1968, London, 1969).

tury, as witness Pope Adrian VI's letter to Chieregati, the nuncio
sent in 1522 to the Diet of Nuremburg, where the German
princes assembled to decide on a common attitude to Luther
and the nascent Reform. "You must say," said Adrian, "that we
freely acknowledge that God has permitted this persecution
because of men's sins, and especially those of priests and prelates . . . we know that even in the Holy See itself, and for a
number of years, many abominations have been committed:
abuse of holy things and transgression of the commandments in
such a way that everything has turned to scandal. All of us,
prelates and churchmen of all degrees have turned aside from
the way of justice." [8]

The break with Protestantism coincided in fact with the
decline of the papacy and the moral depravity of the Renaissance popes, with the decadence of the Church in general
(wealth in the hands of the prince-bishops and monasteries, an
impoverished and uneducated clergy, popular superstition, sti-
fling legalism, a religion of observances and exterior practices),
and with the decadence of theology (the quarrels of the schools
over peripheral subjects and their neglect of the main questions—
such as justification, the word and the sacraments, the law and
the gospel and so on). The Church decayed. The Christian
communions of Africa and Asia were no longer in communion
with the Church of Rome: the Church had become European,
and even so much reduced; for the Russians were now part of
the Eastern Church, while the Balkans and part of Spain were
under the Mohammedan yoke. This shrinking of the Church only
made her resent the more the losses she suffered in the sixteenth
century at the hands of the Reformation, with the defection of
the Danish, Norwegian, Swedish, English and Scottish Churches,
and of large parts of Germany, Switzerland and Hungary. A
Reformation was indeed urgently required.

This explains why Luther's appeal, with its desire to return
to the true spirit of the gospel, found so large an audience and

---

8. Text cited by R. Schutz, *Dynamique du provisoire* (Taizé, 1965),
pp. 119-120; English translation, *The Power of the Provisional* (London,
1969).

met with such success. Luther touched the Christian conscience at a sensitive point, where it was aspiring after a truer worship, a more interior devotion, in a less ostentatious, less legalistic Church. Christians who took their faith seriously had a nostaglia for a Church deeply renewed.

The unfortunate thing about the Protestant Reformation was that it went beyond its intentions. It was oriented more and more towards a radically different conception of the Church. Little by little, its reformation extended to the domain of doctrine, the sacraments and the ministry. *Political* motives, moreover, played still more part in this reform than theological or ecclesiastical motives. Certain it is that Luther, in his appeal, in 1520 to the German nobility, repudiated the distinction between spiritual power and secular power, refused to allow the pope's power to convene councils, rejected the Mass and the sacraments, except for baptism and the Supper of the Lord, and denied the right of either pope or bishop to impose a point of doctrine on the faith of Christians. In 1522 religious vows and the priestly obligation to celibacy disappeared, and also the practice of saying Mass in private.[9]

Luther wished to reform the Church, but he broke her unity and opened the way to more and more division, and to doctrinal variations without end. In practice Protestant communities fragmented. In the World Council of Churches, which does not include all, there are more than two hundred and twenty-five separate communions. Though they all believe that Christ's Church is *one* and seek sincerely for unity, they are at variance on a multitude of points.[10]

In the current of thought, therefore, which led to the Protestant Reformation, one can recognize a real desire for a more personal contact with Christ and the gospel, a deeper religious life and a more biblical dogmatics. But the Reformation went too far in building up a theology based on faith alone and scripture alone, and in undermining the authority of the magisterium.

---

9. R. Post, "L'Église a la veille de la Réforme," *Concilium*, n. 27 (1967): 53-64; trans., English edition.

10. H. Küng, *L'Église*, 2: 383; English translations, *The Church*.

The Catholic Church, for her own part, took some time to gather together her spiritual energies for putting into operation the necessary reforms. It was only with Paul III (1534-1539) that the first indications of a renewal appeared, with the creation, in 1538, of a commission of cardinals charged with working out projects for reform. Finally, in 1546, the Council of Trent opened. The authenticity of this reform must be judged by its fruits, and these are to be found not only in the texts elaborated by the Council, but also and above all in the actual reform of men and institutions which is the real test of any reform. The restoration of the Catholic Church began in the era of the Council itself, with the nomination, by Paul IV, of cardinals who supported reform, among whom were the future Pius V, a canonized pope, and Charles Borromeo, equally canonized. Then came the reform of the Roman curia, the battle against simony, the reform of the monasteries, the reform of the old orders (the Camaldolese, the Franciscans, the Capuchins), the foundation of new communities (the Theatins with St. Gaetan, the Barnabites with St. Anthony-Mary Zaccaria, the Somasques with St. Jerome Aemilius, the Jesuits with St. Ignatius of Loyola, the Oratorians with St. Philip Neri, the Eudists and the Sulpicians, the Catholic reform in Germany (with St. Peter Canisius), the mystical movement (with St. Teresa of Avila and St. John of the Cross), the missionary movement in India and Japan (with St. Francis Xavier) and in Africa and North and South America, the organization of seminaries for priestly formation, the foundation or reform of the Catholic universities of Salamanca, Rome (the Angelicum, 1577; the Anselmianum, 1687; the Gregorian, 1585; the Propaganda, 1622), Innsbruck and Louvain and so on.[11]

Unity to be restored and ecumenical desire

Though the Church has preserved her unity (of faith, of worship and of government) and has been reformed, it does

---

11. L. Christiani, *L'Église à l'époque du Concile de Trente,* in Fliche and Martin, *Histoire de l'Église,* n. 17 (Paris, 1948); L. Willaert, *La Restauration catholique, Ibid.,* n. 18 (Paris, 1960).

not follow that she has not been wounded by these great historical divisions. If the storm has not overthrown her it has weakened
and impoverished her: she is like a tree from which the wind
has torn off several major branches, and she has sometimes lost
her balance, her sense of proportion. And the separated communities, for their part, are not dead branches: they continue
to live by the Spirit of Christ and his gospel. Often indeed
they have placed more value than we have done on the spiritual
treasures which they have conserved, among Protestants the
sense of scripture as the word of God, the sense of the transcendence of God and the gratuity of grace, and among the Eastern
Churches the sense of mystery and the meaning of liturgical
prayer. The history of the Church can show us that in fact
the separated communities have deeply influenced the life and
development of the Catholic Church, in theology, in spirituality,
in liturgy, and in art.

The first reaction of the Church, after the great historical
breaks, was to withdraw and take up a defensive attitude in
order to protect her threatened unity. Then misconceptions, prolonged lack of understanding and doctrinal divergences, with
the emotional charges which accompanied them, hardened the
attitudes taken up and created between the Church and the
separated communities a scandalous division. And yet the Church
has never resigned herself to these divisions. Throughout the
centuries, the popes (especially Innocent III, Eugene IV, Julius
III, Gregory X, Gregory XIII, Gregory XV and Urban VIII)
have made many attempts at *rapprochement*. But it is, above all,
since the nineteenth century that this ecumenical effort has
become particularly intense and sustained.

Among the gestures which the Catholic Church has made
towards the Eastern Churches we should note particularly the
letter *In suprema Petri Apostoli Sede,* of Pius IX (1848), the
encyclical, *Praeclara gratulationis,* of Leo XIII (1894), and the
creation by the same pope of a commission *Ad reconciliationem
Dissidentium cum Ecclesia fovendam* (19 March 1895), the
creation by Benedict XV of the Congregation for the Eastern
Church (1 May 1917) and of the Institute for oriental studies

(15 October 1917). In our own time, on December 7th 1965, Paul VI lifted the excommunication exchanged for nine centuries between the pope and the patriarch of Constantinople.

On the Protestant side the problem of unity did not present itself acutely until the beginning of the nineteenth century, with the first attempts at missionary evangelization. It was in fact when Protestants set out to preach the gospel in missionary countries that they grasped the seriousness of the scandal brought about by the multiplicity of existent Christian confessions and their deep doctrinal differences. At the conference held at Edinburgh in 1910 it was discovered how much harm divergencies of faith can do to the missionary apostolate. In China, for example, more than sixty confessions calling themselves Christian were working side by side. It was the same in India and in Japan. In the face of this scandal, the Protestant Churches understood the urgency of mending their broken unity.

The history of the ecumenical movement is therefore the history of the overtures towards one another and groping attempts at *rapprochement,* made by the separated Christian communities. An important stage was reached with the forming of the Ecumenical Council of Churches at Amsterdam in 1948. This Council, the World Council of Churches, held important meetings at Evanston in 1954, at New Delhi in 1961 and at Upsala in 1968. Although the Council is not a Church, it opens up wide vistas upon the possibility of a gathering together of all Christian communities in the one Church of Christ. Today, the ecumenical movement among our separated brethren exhibits two distinct tendencies, towards establishing closer and closer links between different communities on the level of dialogue and collaboration, and towards defining the essential elements of that unity which Christ desired for his Church.[12]

On the Catholic side interest in the problem of unity is the result of several factors.

The first attempts at a *rapprochement* between Catholics

---

12. G. Thils, *Histoire doctrinale du mouvement oecuménique* (Louvain, 1962).

and Protestants date from the days immediately following the French Revolution, when French Catholics emigrated to England, that is, towards the end of the eighteenth century. In the nineteenth century, the landmarks are the Oxford Movement, with Newman and Pusey, and Leo XIII's letter *Ad Anglos,* 14 April 1895, to encourage the pioneers of unity in England. The movement had begun. It gained strength in the twentieth century, with the prayer for unity suggested by Paul Wattson, an Episcopalian, who soon became a Catholic. In 1909, Pius X gave his blessing to the celebration of the octave for unity. A year later the conference at Edinburgh took place, bringing to birth the Protestant ecumenical movement.[13]

From then onwards, ecumenism developed with the help of the problem posed by evangelization in territories where Catholics and Protestants worked side by side. It was encouraged by the Malines Conversations between the Church of England and the Church of Rome (1921-1926), by the influence of charismatic individuals, like Cardinal Mercier, the Abbé Couturier, Dom Beauduin, Cardinal Bea and John XXIII, and by the research of theologians like Fr. Congar, who reconsidered the schism with the East and the Protestant rupture in the light of history and faith.[14]

The foundation of a Secretariat for Unity, in 1960, and the Second Vatican Council's decree on ecumenism showed, on the Church's part, a firm and sincere desire for dialogue and fellow-

---

13. G. Boyer and D. Bellucci, *Unità cristiana e movimento ecumenico* (Rome, 1963).

14. Y. Congar, *Chrétiens désunis* (Paris, 1937); *Ibid., Neuf cents après. Notes sur le schisme oriental*, trans., *After Nine Hundred Years*. In the history of the ecumenical movement, an encyclical like *Mortalium animos* (6 January, 1928), seems to mark in its severe tone a regression. Pius XI is concerned to utter a warning against a pan-Christianity which would be accomplished at the price of doctrinal concessions unacceptable to the Church. Certain Catholics, on the grounds that all religions were equally valuable, were in favor of a communion including every dissident opinion, at the price of serious doctrinal concessions. The pan-Christians wanted by means of doctrinal compromise to set up a sort of confederation of all religions. The encyclical is a vigorous rejection of this excess. To be understood it needs to be seen in the context of the time.

ship with the separated Churches. Pope Paul's friendly gestures
towards the Patriarch Athenagoras and Archbishop Ramsey gave
concrete expression to the attitude expressed in the texts. In the
decree on ecumenism, the Catholic Church publicly acknowledged her share in the responsibility for the great historical
divisions; she recognized the salvation and abundant life to be
found in the different communities; she avoided the wounding
terms schismatic and heretic; she spoke of ecclesial communities
or Churches; she declared, with more attention to fine shades
of meaning, that the one Church of Christ *subsists in* (rather
than *is*) the Catholic Church; and she asked of all the faithful
a change of heart and the witness of a life of holiness, since
the mystery of unity is a mystery of love and supplication.

The Church, then, is conscious of her unity and her identity.
But she is conscious also that this unity has been wounded,
in part through her own fault, and that division is a scandal.
There is, therefore, no question here of a triumphant or final
unity, but rather of a unity which is internal and real, and
which yet works and prays not only to incorporate into itself
new members but also to rediscover those who have left it.
It is a unity that is broken and to be restored, a unity still to
be made perfect. If the Church did not show this ecumenical
dynamism, her unity would be lacking in an awareness of the
seriousness of the divisions which have actually come about, and
also in an awareness of the prayer of Christ: "That they all
may be one" (Jn 17:21). Such an absence of ecumenical desire
would be the condemnation of the Church. And that the Church
is conscious of her wounds and at the same time anxious to recover the fullness of her ancient unity is an indication of a
salutary tension in her. Division has impoverished the Church.
Reconciliation would enrich her, and give her a new vitality.

5. *Unity and catholicity*

The history of the divisions and doctrinal variations of the
Protestant communions—a history which often coincides with the
history of the regions or nations where they have developed,

shows how difficult it is for the Church to be really universal, ecumenical, catholic, without sacrificing something of her internal unity, especially her doctrinal unity.

Unity and catholicity seem to contradict each other. Unity, in effect, implies the elimination of elements of differentiation. Unity, especially a unity which wants to be enduring and consistent—such as the unity of the Jewish people on whom God imposed the rejection of all that was foreign, easily becomes authoritarian, intransigent, centralizing in tendency, and sacrifices legitimate elements of diversity; or else, in order to protect itself, it becomes transformed into a closed sect. While unity easily sacrifices universality and diversity to ensure internal cohesion, catholicity on the contrary, which implies receptiveness and communion, readily allows divergences, sacrificing if need be internal unity, especially doctrinal unity. Catholicity is prepared to simplify, to adapt, provided that there is some common denominator, even of an inferior sort, which can form a rallying point for the greatest number.

The paradox is that the Church seeks both *unity* and *catholicity*. Not only is she called together, assembled (internal unity), but—as witness the history of the missions—she calls together and assembles all men on earth. Catholic unity tries to triumph over the divisions of the spirit and of the flesh. It transcends the biological community, with all the powerful bonds which unite the family; it transcends the nation, the political and cultural community, and strives to create the community of the children of God, in Christ and through Christ (AG 12). It seeks to construct, over and above earthly geography, another geography, which, in embracing the whole earth, unites all men, without distinction of language, color, race or institution.[15] It builds up the Body of Christ, in which there is "no longer Jew or Greek, bond or free," but the children of the Father, "made to drink of one Spirit" (1 Cor 12:13). The Church is built, not in contradistinction to men, but in a union of love with all men.

---

15. C. Dumont, "Unité et diversité des signes de la Révélation," NRT 80 (1958): 148.

What it is important to notice in this universality is not so much the phenomenon itself (the space taken up or the number of members) but its quality. We are concerned with a universality in the unity of faith, sacraments, ministry and authority, with an expansion which is accompanied by a transformation at depth of the mind and heart, as the result of a free choice, and which is brought about not by force of arms but by the attraction exerted by love: the love of God in Jesus Christ.

6.   *The Church universal and the local Churches*

The tensions between unity and catholicity are many and take many forms, even within the Church. As long as they do not touch the unity of faith, sacraments, ministry and charity, there is no division; unity remains intact. More than that, tensions such as these are fruitful and a source of progress; for they make it possible to envisage new perspectives. The history of the Church reveals inner tensions of this type and at different levels.

There is, first of all, the tension among *local Churches*. The New Testament already illustrates in the Church a coexistence of unity in plurality. There were *local Churches* with their individual structures, relatively autonomous: the Church of Jerusalem, the Church of Corinth, the Church of Antioch and so on; there were *regional* Churches—of Asia, Palestine and Greece. Some Churches, moreover, had their own gospels, Mark for the Romans, Matthew for the Jewish converts, Luke for the Greeks, John for Asia Minor. There was also a diversity of language, customs and mentality. Unity is not uniformity. There is even tension to be found between Jerusalem and the diaspora, between Jewish converts and Gentile converts. But in spite of this regionalism, the Churches preserved among them a communion of faith and sacraments, a communion of bishops (by means of synods and councils) and a fellowship of love. There were local Churches but there was a communion of Churches.

A similar tension appears in the course of the centuries between local Churches and the *universal* Church, created by the communion of all the Churches. These two lines of force, as it were, have been sometimes in a state of *rapprochement* or synthesis, but sometimes in opposition or even conflict. To the extent to which the Church, as a society, is organized and structured, with a central administration and all the organs which belong to it, a canon law and canon lawyers, there is a tendency to think of the local Churches as branches of the one great universal Church, this being composed of all the faithful throughout the world united under the authority of the pope. The West has given preference in the Church to the aspect of unity and universality which is guaranteed by institutional and juridical unity, but without always paying enough attention to the variety and diversity of local Churches. In the East, on the other hand, the fundamental unity is the local Church, where the essence of the Church is fully realized, an assembly brought into being and bound together by the word, the Eucharist and the Holy Spirit, and also by the bishop, who is at the basis of this unity. Collegiality lies in the dialogue of the local Churches, who realize diversely, but totally, in each place, the fullness of the Church: this is the foundation of unity. Over this συνεργια presides the successor of Peter.

Tension is inevitable between an ecclesiology of the universal Church and an ecclesiology of the local Churches. The Second Vatican Council took as its point of departure, in *Lumen gentium,* the universal Church as the communion of all the faithful with the pope and the body of bishops.

There is no doubt that an ecclesiology of the universal Church encourages unity. Last century for instance, the idea of unity as bound up with the primacy prevailed, while the notion of collegiality took second place. This sort of unity has its dangers. There is the danger, for example, of falling, in order to secure the triumph of unity and primacy, into an exaggerated centralization, of abolishing regional differences and turning unity into uniformity. These is a danger also of making the pope the only bishop, of attributing to him in practice the prerogatives of the whole Church, and reducing the regional bishops to the status of functionaries. There is the danger of turning the local Churches into administrative branches of a sort of religious "confederation" called "the Church universal." There is the danger of legislating without taking account of mentalities, of local customs and local problems. A unity which succumbed to these dangers would constitute a *counter-sign;* for it would abolish the plurality which constitutes the Church, and constitutes mankind.

An ecclesiology which takes its point of departure in the local Church sees in it the universal Church *in act,* the privileged place of the life of the Church; for it is in the local Church, the living cell of the universal Church, that the faithful are united to receive the bread of the word and the Bread of the Eucharist. The Eucharist, above all, which is the sacrament of communion with God and communion with men, and the act in which each assembly enters into communion with the universal Church, takes place in the local Church. The local Church is not the whole Church, but it is completely the Church; for all the elements of the Church are realized in each local or regional Church. The universal Church is created by the communion of all the local Churches, in one and the same Lord, one and the same gospel, one and the same authority.[16]

An ecclesiology centered in the local Church also has its dangers, which, equally, are facts of history: the dangers of a Church enclosed within her own national frontiers, excessively attached to her own prerogatives, bound up with, that is to say, compromised in, the politics of the country, arrogant and intractable in her dealings with the successor of Peter. In short there are all the dangers of particularism, of a ghetto Church. An extreme inflation of the local Church is a menace to catholicity. Such, to speak only of the past, was the case of the Gallican Church.

So the maintenance of unity in diversity is a source of

---

16. *Lumen gentium* says apropos of local Churches, "It is in them and through them that the one unique Catholic Church exists" (LG 23).

tension between the universal Church and the local Churches, between the primacy óf the pope and the collegiality of the bishops. It is true that the Church is endowed with all the organs capable of ensuring both unity and diversity. The function of the primacy, for instance, is to maintain unity, while collegiality guarantees universality in the plurality of local Churches, and safeguards unity through the communion of the bishops with one another and with the pope. Primacy and collegiality are designed to support and complete each other, and represent two real dimensions in the Church, horizontal and vertical. By a horizontal dimension each local Church is connected with the others, while by a vertical dimension she is united to the vicar of Christ, the center and summit of the universal communion. A monarchical principle and a collegial principal are combined, then, in a paradoxical unity.

A certain dialectical tension between unity and diversity, nevertheless, inevitably remains, and it is impossible wholly to absorb it. An exaggerated concern for unity leads to a belief in autocracy, and to a process of levelling down; an excess of diversity leads to the disintegration of unity and to anarchy. What we need is unity without uniformity, plurality without division. The swing of the pendulum between base and summit, between center and circumference, between the universal Church and the local Churches, between primacy and collegiality, belongs to the very reality of a Church which is at once transcendent and immanent in the world.[17]

In this respect, no other society is comparable to the Church.

---

17. See especially: A. Antón, "Unità e diversità nella Chiesa secondo il Vaticano II," *La Civiltà Cattolica*, 4 October, 1969, pp. 23-35; *Ibid.*, *Primado y Colegialidad* (BAC, Madrid, 1970); *Ibid.*, "Episcopato e primato garantiscono la diversità e l'unità nella Chiesa," *La Civiltà Cattolica*, 18 October, 1969, pp. 110-124; Y. Congar, "De la communion des Églises a une ecclésiologie de l'Église universelle," in: Y. Congar and B.-D. Dupuy, ed., *L'Episcopat et l'Église universelle* (Paris, 1962), pp. 227-260; G. Thils, *Unité catholique ou centralisation à outrance?* (Louvain, 1969); G. Baum, *The Credibility of the Church Today* (New York, 1968), pp. 129-141; B. P. Prusak, *Canonical Concept of the particular Church before and after Vatican II* (Rome, 1967).

The most far-seeing prescriptions of canon law would never
succeed in preventing the inevitable controversies and conflicts.
The paradox is rather that, in the midst of such tensions and
so many of them, the Church survives.

7. Internal unity and missionary unity

Unity belongs to the Church as Christ's gift to his Bride.
But this unity demands to be stretched to the dimensions of
the whole earth, and to include the whole of time. The unity
of the Church is a *dynamic* unity, like the work of redemption
itself (LG 13). The missionary unity of the Church is not simply
proselytism, the result of the devotion of a certain number
of her members to increasing the Church numerically, but a
demand of nature. The Church would not be herself, that is,
"the universal instrument of salvation," "the universal sacrament
of salvation" (LG 9, 13, 48; AG 1), if she were to limit herself
to a continent or a nation. She would not reveal her true nature
in a way that could be seen.

The missionary activity of the Church prolongs in time
the movement of Trinitarian love begun by the mission of the
Son and the Spirit; it reveals, visibly, the saving love of God
which appeared in the Savior Christ. If the Church were not
one, she would not be the new People of God Christ came
to gather together; and on the other hand, if she were not
missionary, she would not be the sacrament of salvation for all
men.

The history of the missions shows that missionary activity
is, *in fact*, one of the dominant characteristics of the Church,
although in this history we can distinguish times of weakness
and times of strength.

The first century, with the extraordinary *élan* provided by
the apostles, and particularly by St. Paul, was both the springtime of the Church and the springtime of missions. The third
century (and the beginning of the fourth) marks the evangelization of Africa. From the seventh century onwards there is a

slowing down, owing to the barrier of Islam, and owing also to ignorance as far as the New World was concerned.

In the thirteenth century the missionary movement gathered force again, with the Franciscan penetration of China. At the end of the sixteenth century, with the great voyages of discovery and the reform of Trent, there was an outburst of missionary activity: missions were established in India, in China, in Japan, in the Philippines and in America. During most of the seventeenth century this initiative was maintained, but weakened towards the end. The eighteenth century is a blank time, owing to the persecutions, and to the suppression of the Society of Jesus. But in the nineteenth century, missionary activity soared again in an extraordinary way, with the foundation of more than twenty missionary congregations. In the twentieth century the movement continued, but there has been for some years now a tendency to withdraw, owing to the self-determination of the nations of the Third World, the crisis in vocations and also, it has to be said, the rather unenlightened attitude of certain theologians, who under the pretext of stressing the value of universal salvific grace have come to put in parentheses the will of Christ and the very nature of the Church as the "universal sacrament of salvation."

8. Unity pursued and always in flight

The history of salvation is the history of a unity to be realized. Through Christ this history entered its final and eschatological stage; for Christ decisively made his own, mankind and the whole of creation. Through the Incarnation, the cross and the resurrection, unity was definitively obtained. And yet, in ourselves, this unity remains incomplete, for our tending towards the integration of our whole being in the grace and love of God is never over. In the world also unity remains incomplete; for the world is still disordered by sin, and always menaced by division. The unity of the Church herself is always to be recovered because always threatened, from within by the scandalous behavior of Catholics, from without by persecution in a thousand forms.

The task of bringing men together in the unity of charity seems always to be defeated. The Church's efforts give the impression of issuing in failure, persecution, absurdity. The action of Christians seems to shatter itself against the fact of death; it never succeeds in imposing itself permanently on a situation. The Church cannot operate in expectation of a once for all victory. The task which has been entrusted to her, of bringing men together in unity, will never be accomplished, however long this world lasts. Her unity is always lacking; it is a *needy* unity.

It is also a *tireless* unity. Indeed that is one of the most widely acknowledged characteristics of Catholic unity: the Church is never exhausted, never despairs, never gives in to scepticism, in spite of having perpetually to begin again, because of war, open or concealed persecution, the desertion or sloth of men. The Church never resigns. She takes up her position midway between Utopia and despair. She pursues unremittingly her work of unification and salvation. She aims at summing up all the peoples of the earth, and she takes up her task afresh in each new century.

Consider, from this point of view, the patient work of evangelizing the Hindu world, the world of Islam, the world of atheism. Catholic unity is the more difficult to achieve in that Christianity is never unincarnated. The first Catholics were Jews; then there were the Greeks; then the Romans; then national Churches. The Church strives to incorporate into unity every human diversity. A hundred times it would have been reasonable to despair and give up. Think of her efforts to implant the faith in China, only to see herself turned out as soon as she had done so. Denied, repulsed, rejected, scoffed at, deported, the Church begins again, to devote herself with patient stupidity to building up, by the same means of love, the Body of Christ. There is something deeply moving in this attitude which never succumbs to despair, and which refuses at the same time the optimism of expecting a final triumph in this world.

9. *Conclusion*

This complex and demanding unity, founded on freedom
and love; this unity which is at once faithfulness to Christ's
message and constant actualization in new contexts, in order
to remain in touch with the world and its needs; this unity
of creed in a plurality of perspectives, formulations and systematizations; this unity wounded but repentant, reformed and
seeking to re-establish communion with the separated Churches;
this unity in catholicity, in spite of every particularity; this
unity of the Church universal in the diversity of local Churches;
this unity which is at once an inner unity and a missionary unity;
this precarious unity always threatened but never discouraged,
which has pursued its end for two thousand years: all this constitutes a *paradox*, an *enigma* offered to the eyes of the man
of good will, to help him to recognize the Mystery which is
hidden beneath the Phenomenon. All these tensions, that is, belong to the Phenomenon of the Church: all are observable and
submitted to the gaze of witnesses and the judgment of historians.
A single one of them would suffice to break the Church. And
yet, she remains. It was said of Christ, "Who is this man?" It
might be said of the Church, "What is this?"

CHAPTER VI

The Paradox and Tensions of Temporality

The First Vatican Council suggested this second great paradox of the Church when it mentioned, among the astonishing characteristics which made of the Church a sign, her invincible stability (*stabilitas invicta*). The expression means two different things. It means, first of all, that the Church has stood the test of time and that she continues to subsist: this is properly speaking the *permanence* of the Church. It means also that the Church has survived without losing her internal unity. Not only does she subsist, but she is also resistant to the corrosive and disintegrating forces which would otherwise have been able to damage or dissolve her internal unity. She *endures* in *unity* in spite of her *temporality*.

This permanence in a state of unity is an important aspect of the total paradox of the Church. It means that though the Church travels through history, she preserves her internal cohesion, especially doctrinally, in spite of oppositions from within (conscious and unconscious errors, individual and collective passions), and oppositions from without (persecution and the many forms of imperialism). While societies and religions in general change with time, either disintegrate and die or else succumb to a hospitable but levelling syncretism, the Church conserves her complex yet demanding unity.

In trying to assess this paradox of permanence in the midst of temporality, I have renounced, as in the case of unity, the comparative approach. This approach, which consists in com-

paring the twenty centuries of the Church's life with the duration
of the other great religions of salvation (Hinduism and Buddhism
in particular), indeed works out to the Church's advantage, but
is of little significance, since what is important is not so much
the duration, but the character of the duration; it is the complexity and seriousness of the problems faced in its course, and
especially the substantial matter of the Church's involvement
in the history of mankind. So again the approach preferred is
by way of internal intelligibility, the study of the paradox in
itself, with all the tensions which go to make it up, in order
to seek afterwards an adequate explanation of the phenomenon
observed.

The Church cannot escape from history. Although she is
distinct from the world, she cannot isolate herself from it by
taking up the attitude of a meta-historical observer. Being-in-
the-world belongs to the essence of the Church; for the salvation
brought by Christ is for the world and offered to the world.
It is precisely this world in perpetual growth and in search of
its own identity that the Church has a mission to lead to God;
it is precisely these men in their historical setting and at each
moment of historical duration that she has to understand and
save. How is she to save them without talking to them in order
to know them? And how is she to talk to them, unless she meets
them in their own *milieu,* in the institutions within which
they are in the course of evolving, in the temporal and historical
structures of their time?

The Church proceeds from a divine, gratuitous initiative, irreducible to the laws of this world. What is specific in her is the
supernatural salvation which she offers to the world in Jesus
Christ. But on the other hand, the world and its history are
the ground in which she takes root; they are the loaf which she
has to leaven. Sent into the world in order to save it, she has
to insert herself into the world, but this insertion is not without risks.

In her encounter with time and history, the Church is constantly threatened by two dangers: one may well ask oneself
which is the worse, too deep an insertion into the world or a lack

of insertion. On the one hand, the Church is obliged to enter the life of mankind. She has to meet men at the level of their own problems, to understand them in the setting in which they live and work, in the structures which unite them to one another—social, political, juridical, economic. But if this entering into men's lives is a source of strength to the Church, it is also a source of danger. For the more the Church enters into the history of a period, the more she adopts its rhythm, its structures, its modes of thought and action, the more she risks losing her own identity and sinking into the phenomena of the age. On the other hand, if, in order to avoid the risks of temporality and be faithful to her spiritual mission of sanctification and salvation, the Church isolates herself from the world, and lives in a ghetto, she risks not being able to understand those to whom she speaks; she risks talking to them in a language they cannot interpret, and so losing them. History is a witness that this double danger has always been before the Church, the danger of being absorbed by temporality and guided by it, and the danger of being cut off from the world and at last reduced to silence.[1] In antiquity and in the medieval period the Church nearly perished by entering too deeply into the juridical and political structures of the time. In recent centuries she has almost died of isolation. The surprising, the paradoxical thing is that she has always, as if by grace, survived. Let us look, not at all, but at some of the moments in the Church's history when the tension between an excess of insertion and an absence of insertion into the world has reached a critical point.

1. *The threat of Judaism*

The first danger which the Church had to face in her mission of becoming universal, came from the very nation where she had taken root. The Church was in fact born in the midst of Judaism, in the middle of a People which regarded itself as

---

1. In the course of the centuries this menace to the Church of either too great an insertion in the social structures of the world or a lack of insertion has taken different names. So one may talk of a Church

the chosen race, a People whose long religious history turned on strongly established institutions. The Law, circumcision, the Temple, Jerusalem, these were unassailable elements of Jewish religion; for they expressed concretely the very election of Israel.

The Law or *Tôrah* was the name for the whole mass of rules and regulations which governed the relationships of the Jews with God and with one another. But the word designates more particularly the Pentateuch, which includes God's instructions to his people on the conduct of its moral, social and religious life (the decalogue, the code of the covenant, Deuteronomy, the law of holiness and the priestly code). The Law, and especially the decalogue, was the charter of the covenant, election in its concrete form. It made of Israel the holy people of a holy God, set apart, to live in communion with God, to adopt the style of life required by this communion and to collaborate in God's design for salvation. The Law, inseparable from the covenant, inseparable from election itself, had for the Jews the importance Christ has for Christians. It was holy, an object of veneration, so much so that Jewish speculation ended by identifying the Law with the divine Wisdom. *Circumcision,* especially after the exile, was the distinctive mark that a man belonged to the Jewish community and to Yahweh. It became absolutely obligatory, not only for Jews, but also for proselytes (Acts 15:5ff; 16, 3; Gal 2:3). At the time of the New Testament the obligation to be circumcised was more important even than that of keeping the Sabbath (Jn 7:22-23). Finally, the Temple was the religious center of Israel, and if Jerusalem was a holy city, it was because it possessed the Temple. Just as the great feasts of Jewish worship recalled the events of the Exodus, and the ark of the covenant recalled the alliance between God and his People, so the Temple was the sign of

---

which is socially compromised, or, on the other hand, of a Church afraid to become involved, of a liberal Church, or of an intransigent, integrist Church, closed to all dialogue, and so on. The terminology varies, but the problem remains the same.

the presence of Yahweh, and the memorial of his choice.[2]

Now what had been up to this time the salvation of Israel was in danger of becoming, for nascent Christianity, a mortal embrace. For strict Judaism, defacing little by little the original meaning of the covenant, had come to separate the Law from its author, Yahweh, the only author of salvation, and to make of it an absolute, to think that observing its precepts, especially that of circumcision, was a means of coercing God, in the spirit of *do ut des*. In the same way, strict Judaism had come to see in Jerusalem and its Temple the unique *locus* of the divine presence. Such an attachment was in danger of imprisoning the early Church within the boundaries of a single nation, of allowing it, certainly, to be a religious revolution, but one that was a phenomenon in the history of Judaism, and bound up with the Jewish nation. In order to free herself from the Synagogue and from Judaism, and become herself, that is a universal religion, the early Church had to undertake a long and painful process of *disentanglement*. She almost became the victim of her necessary insertion into Judaism, which had prepared the way for her and given her birth.[3] In this process of disentanglement it is convenient to distinguish four stages.

1. The first factor in this liberation was the existence of the Hellenists, that is, the Jews of the diaspora. While the ordinary run of Judaizers or rigorists retained of Jesus' message only that "salvation is from the Jews" (Jn 4:22) and sought to impose

---

2. R. De Vaux, *Les Institutions de l'Ancien Testament* (vol. I, Paris, 1957), pp. 79-82, 221-250; (vol. II, Paris, 1960), pp. 166-173; trans., *Ancient Israel: Its Life and Institutions* (New York, 1961), and *Ancient Israel* (London, 1965); J. Bonsirven, *Le judaïsme palestinien au temps de Jésus-Christ* (Paris, 1950), pp. 77-92; E. Hamel, *Les dix Paroles* (Bruges and Paris, 1969); J. Jeremias, *Jerusalem zur Zeit Jesu* (Gottingen, 1962); trans., *Jerusalem in the Time of Jesus* (London, 1969).

3. J. Daniélou and I. H. Marrou, *Nouvelle histoire de l'Église*, vol. I, *Des origines à Saint Grégoire le Grand* (Paris, 1968), pp. 59-69; trans., *The First Six Hundred Years* (London, 1964).

on non-Jewish converts the same obligations incurred by Jews of the Synagogue, the group of Hellenizers, living in a Greek *milieu,* exhibited a more open frame of mind. It was these Hellenizers of the diaspora who helped the Church to disentangle herself from a narrow and rigorist exclusivism. The seven deacons (Acts 6) were all Hellenists—Nicholas was even a Greek convert from Antioch (6:5). These deacons constituted one of the most dynamic elements in the early Church, and helped to accelerate the process by which it opened out into the non-Jewish world. We can see this from the influence exerted by Stephen and Philip. *Stephen* is the incarnation of the new spirit, oriented towards gaining the world for Christ, and ready for the necessary breaks. It was for this reason that he encountered the opposition and hatred of the Sanhedrin: "This man never ceases to speak words against this holy place and the law" (6:13). Persecution scattered the Hellenists throughout Judea and Samaria, while the apostles remained in Jerusalem (8:1). *Philip,* the Hellenist deacon, preached the good news to the Samaritans (8:5), and then at Caesarea (8:40). The gospel had already crossed the frontiers of Palestine.[4]

2. It was then that the second event important for the future of Christianity took place: the episode of the conversion of the centurion Cornelius (10). In the actual account of this incident two distinct centers of interest can be discerned. The first has to do with the problem of the relationships between Jews and non-Jews. Could a Jew sit down at table with a pagan? It was to this question that Peter referred first, on entering Cornelius's house: "You yourselves know how unlawful it is for a Jew to associate with or to visit anyone of another nation" (10:28). But the vision of Joppa had made Peter understand that he must go beyond the precepts of legal purification and clean and unclean food. He knew that he could sit down at the centurion's

---

4. M. Simon, *Les premiers chrétiens* (Paris, 1967); *Ibid., St. Stephen and the Hellenists in the Primitive Church* (London, 1958); *Ibid., Les sectes juives au temps de Jésus* (Paris, 1960); trans., *Jewish Sects at the Time of Jesus* (New York, 1967).

table (10:28). It was precisely at this point that Peter attracted criticism from certain Christians in Jerusalem: "Why did you go into the house of uncircumcised men and eat with them?" (11:1-3). Peter explained and justified his conduct, referring to the vision of the sheet (10:11-16).

The second center of interest concerns the *baptism* of the centurion and the admission of Gentiles into the Church. Peter, seeing that God had renewed for the Gentiles the miracle of Pentecost, decided to baptize Cornelius and his household: "Can anyone forbid water for baptizing these people, who have received the Holy Spirit just as we have done?" (10:47). At Jerusalem, Peter used the same argument: "If then God gave the same gift to them as he gave to us when we believed in the Lord Jesus Christ, who was I that I should withstand God?" (11:17). God himself had abrogated all difference between Jews and Gentiles, in giving his Spirit to all alike. Christ is "the Savior of all" (10:36). "Whoever believes in him receives forgiveness of sins through his name (10:43), whether he is Jew or Gentile. This is already the doctrine which Peter is to make prevail at the Council of Jerusalem (15:9-11). The precedent of the centurion of Caesarea was definitive for Peter, and would give weight to the decision which was to ratify conclusively, at the Council of Jerusalem, Paul's activity in admitting Gentiles to the Church.[5]

3. The foundation of the community of Antioch, the first Christian center after Jerusalem, marked the third stage in the disentanglement of the Church from Judaism. The foundation of the Church at Antioch dates back to the years 36–37, that is to the time of Stephen: "Those who were scattered because of the persecution that arose over Stephen travelled as far as Phoenicia and Cyprus and Antioch speaking the word to none except Jews. But there were some of them, men of Cyprus and Cyrene, who on coming to Antioch spoke to the Greeks also, preaching the Lord Jesus. And the hand of the Lord was with them and a great number that believed turned to the Lord"

---

5. J. Dupont, *Étude sur les Actes des Apôtres* (Paris, 1967), pp. 75-81; 409-412.

(11:19-21). In this community at Antioch Jewish and non-Jewish Christians lived side by side, and in time, it seems, came to eat at the same table (Gal 2:11-14).[6] This posed in a new form the problem of a choice between Jewish particularism and Christian universalism. In 42, in the face of this development in the community, the apostles sent Barnabas there, and he, a Greek by birth, reported the success of this expansion of the Church, seeing in it the work of God (Acts 11:23). Antioch, the capital of Syria, the third city of the Empire, after Rome and Alexandria, was to become the center from which Christianity would set out for the Greek and oriental world.

4. Lastly, Paul, the Apostle of the Gentiles, was the instrument through whom the Church finally freed herself from the slavery of Judaistic observances (the Law, circumcision, legal purification). A Jew and a Pharisee, but born in a Greek *milieu*, Paul defined and formulated the way in which the Christian conscience moved at depth (15:1-35). When he provoked the Council of Jerusalem in 49, he placed the Church face to face with the question of the relationship between Judaism and Christianity. What Peter had consented to for the centurion Cornelius, what the community of Antioch had increasingly introduced into the practice of its life had to be made the very principle of Christian expansion. Let Jews, when they became Christians, keep their legal observances (circumcision in particular)—agreed. But let no one impose on pagan converts the Jewish stage of salvation, which Christ had completed and gone beyond. The decree of Jerusalem comprised two parts. The first part freed pagan converts from the obligation to circumcision. The second allowed only four prohibitions: Christians were to abstain from food sacrificed to idols, from blood, from the flesh of strangled animals and from fornication.[7] Paul had

---

6. This was certainly so in 51, but it seems that the habit of eating together had been introduced into the community some years before. This at least is what the text of Galatians implies.

7. It is generally thought that the Decree of Jerusalem was drafted after the Council of Jerusalem. Its formulation betrays a slight concession

disengaged the Church from her Jewish background and effected the universal sowing of the seed of the word.

In the eyes of rigorist and intransigent Judaism this disentangling of the Church from the Law and from Jewish institutions was equivalent to the annihilation of the true Israel, the chosen race, and made Christ appear as the destroyer of the nation. Hence the opposition of this party among the Jews to Christ and to Christians.

The majority of the Jews did in fact refuse to acknowledge Christ and the gospel. They did not recognize the Messiah. They refused the new covenant in his blood. They would not acknowledge the new temple of his body. They would not acknowledge the fulfillment of the Law in the gift of the Spirit. They remained obstinately attached to race and blood. They would not abandon the perspective of a national community in order to enter upon that of the choice of a universal community, as wide in its dimensions as mankind.

The Epistle to the Romans tried the Law. Salvation was, henceforth, for every man, Jew or Gentile, bound up only with faith in Jesus Christ. Christ now took the place of the Law (Rm 10:1-13). It was not belonging to a particular race, not the observance of the Law, not circumcision, which determined whether a man belonged to God's People, but *faith* in Jesus Christ. Israel's vocation was revealed in Jesus Christ, the unconditional grace given to the whole of mankind, including Israel. The design of God was the salvation of all men, Jews and non-Jews alike.[8]

So the early Church overcame a double danger: the defection

---

on the part of James and the moderate elements to the more rigid Judaizers.

---

8. It is equally necessary to stress the influence of the Gospel of St. John (at the end of the first century), revealed in its transcendence of the frontiers of Judaism, its universal conception of faith and salvation and its recourse to the category of the Logos, which is nearer to the Greek mentality in its Stoic and Platonist forms and in Philo, although radically different in its identification of the Logos with the divine Person of the incarnate Son.

of Jewish Christians, who, under pressure from Jewish nationalism, were in danger of returning to Judaism, and the suppression
of non-Jewish Christians, who were in danger of abandoning
their new faith rather than remaining confined within the framework of ancient Judaism. If the early Church had listened to
the Judaizers, she would have remained a miserable Jewish sect
and become a historical curiosity like the Essenes. In freeing
herself from the Synagogue and rigorist Judaism, the Church
surmounted her first great danger.

2. The weight of the Roman Empire

After escaping the danger of becoming too deeply involved
in her original *milieu,* Judaism, the Church had to face persecution, both from fanatical Jews within her own confines, and,
above all, from the paganism of the Empire. For nearly three
centuries she lived under the threat of persecution, in an atmosphere of irony, or of suspicion and hatred, with periods of actual
harassment alleviated by periods of comparative calm. This
constant threat of persecution explains the voluntary semi-
effacement of the Church from the official life of the time. Public
opinion and the law obliged her to live at the margin of society.
But if Christianity could not be openly proclaimed in public life,
it was nonetheless very active. The Church's life was a concentrated life. She gained individuals one by one. She penetrated society at every level. She infused new blood into it.
She transformed its soul. The day would come when the Empire
would acknowledge itself Christian.

Officially this change in the situation coincided with the
Edict of Milan, in 313, which, in proclaiming for all the liberty
to practice the religion of their choice, Christianity or paganism,
put an end to the persecutions and officially recognized the
Church. The obstacles which had up to this time been placed
in the way of evangelization were removed. Free from now
onwards to do so, the Church inserted herself into the history of
the Empire. She grew with it, accepted its protection and gave
it her support. She shared the universal belief in the permanence

of Roman civilization and the Roman Empire, and her insertion into it was so nearly complete that its fall only just failed to involve her in a common ruin. The Church of the Empire of Constantine was in danger on a double front, political and cultural.

The political danger

On his conversion Constantine gave the Church religious liberty. But in practice he took up a position which favored Christianity. He even sought through his legislation to direct pagans to the new religion. He forbade, for example, the practices of divination and magic; he had the temple of Aphrodite destroyed because of the sacred prostitution that was carried on there. In general, however, he showed himself tolerant as far as pagans were concerned, preserving his friendship with them and even confiding to them important duties. It was with Constantine's sons, especially Constance, and later Theodosius, that the attitude towards paganism was to harden and turn into persecution.

Constantine's attitude was, nevertheless, not without ambiguity. Though converted, he retained his Roman notion of authority. Now according to Roman mentality the emperor is the supreme pontiff, having the right to intervene in all religious questions, especially in the nomination of the flamens, and even in private worship. No doubt in becoming a Christian Constantine had left a considerable part of this mentality behind, but he nevertheless continued to regard himself as Head of the Church, the representative of Christ, the equal of the apostles. He encouraged the faith, he encouraged Christian morality and Christian worship. Through his liberality and his fiscal exemptions he helped the Church to rise from the ruins where persecution had left her. Christian churches multiplied, some of them on a grandiose scale. He gave his support to the bishops. Little by little, he became recognized as the propagator of Christianity. But at the same time, he made use of the Church for imperial ends. Constantine supported the Church, since he saw in her the only force capable of giving the decadent Empire a new vitality and saving it. It was for this reason that he associated the Church intimately in his remodelling of the State. The highest offices of the State, the consulate and the prefecture, were filled by Christians. The imperial palace was a palace where bishops and priests were numerous, and often charged with civil functions, to the benefit of the unity of Church and State. Gradually an imperial régime was elaborated which in its union of Church and State anticipated the Holy Roman Empire of the Middle Ages. With Constantine, and later with Theodosius, the Church passed from the position of a persecuted religion to the position of a state Church. Protected and overwhelmed with favors, she practically included the Emperor in her hierarchy among the superiors designed by God. The Emperor, on his side, naturally regarded himself as the Leader of the Christian People, a new Moses, a new David. Above him there was no authority but God. The Church became, as it were, liable for the State, and cooperated in the defense of the Empire—a compromising situation. There was an obvious danger of the Church's being contaminated by the State. In accepting and associating herself with the centralizing and totalitarian politics of the Empire, the Church was laid open to the danger arising when a State, even a Christian state, becomes the paramount consideration. She risked being the first victim of imperial protection: in golden chains perhaps but in chains nevertheless.

In fact, Constantine, full of deference to the bishops, intervened constantly in the affairs of the Church. He summoned the Council of Nicea, for instance, assumed the chairmanship of it, had the agenda submitted to him, guided the discussions, imposed the credo, forcing the bishops to sign it, and taking up a threatening attitude towards recalcitrants, and gave orders to the bishops to ensure that the decisions of the Council were carried out.

The Church, for her part, adopted, in her own ecclesiastical structure, the structures of civil society: provinces, metropolitan sees, dioceses, prefectures, the centralized type of administration in use in the Empire. It followed that the seat of civil power and the seat of ecclesiastical power were intimately related and enjoyed equal prestige. So, when the seat of imperial power was moved from Rome to Constantinople, the see of Constantinople would come to rival the pontifical see of Rome. This connection between the seat of ecclesiastical power and the seat of civil power would, in the end, lead to the schism with the East. It has to be added that Christianity, having become all-powerful through the favor of Constantine and his successors, would in her own turn become intolerant and a source of persecution, hunting out pagans and making schism and heresy crimes punishable by the State. Scarcely freed from oppression, the Church was submitted to a still more grueling test, that of protection by the State, and she in turn became an oppressor.[9]

The cultural danger

In the cultural sphere, the Church's insertion into the Greek world led to a crisis of a different sort, but a no less serious one. For a century the Church was divided by Arianism.

When Christianity, expressed in Semitic categories, encountered the centers of Greek culture, especially Alexandria, the Church was obliged to express her faith in terms which the Greek world understood and could assimilate. The mystery of the Trinity, in particular, was a source of difficulty. How was she to stress the Trinity of persons without sacrificing either the Unity of God or the equality of the persons? And how was she to express the mystery discursively, according to the terminology of the time, without making it a slave to the meaning

---

9. On the political danger to the Church under Constantine see: J.-R. Palanque, G. Bardy, P. De Labriolle, *De la paix constantinienne à la mort de Théodose*, in: A. Fliche and V. Martin, *Histoire de l'Église* (vol. III, Paris, 1947); G. Barbero, *Il pensiero politico cristiano dai Vangeli a Pelagio* (Torino, 1962); M. H. Shepherd, "Before and after Constantine," in: *The Impact of the Church upon its Culture* (Chicago, 1968), pp. 17-38; J. Daniélou and I. H. Marrou, *Nouvelle Histoire de l'Église* (vol. I, Paris, 1968), pp. 263-372; trans., *The First Six Hundred Years* (London, 1964); J. Gaudemet, *L'Église dans l'Empire romain* (Paris, 1958).

7

which this terminology conveyed? As, for instance, the doctrine of God the Word, the Logos, is central to Johannine theology, the neo-platonic and stoic Logos was called in to express the relationship between the Logos and the Father. But the transfer was not without danger. The generation of the Logos was in fact explained by making a distinction between the Logos ἐνδιαΘετος, the primary state of the Logos, immanent in God as a sort of divine attribute, depersonalized, and the Logos προφοριχός distinct from the Father as a person, having a mediatory function in creation and revelation, but inferior to the Father. At the end of this process of thought one arrives at the heresy of Arianism.

Arius, in fact, wanted to safeguard, in the inner life of the Trinity, the privileges of the Father: one, eternal, alone in being without birth or origin, incommunicable; for if he communicated himself he would be subject to division and change. It followed that anyone beside the Father was a creature, including Christ. Jesus Christ, the Son, was not God as the Father was, that is he was not eternal or uncreated like the Father, since it was from the Father that he received being and life. He was not God in essence, but a perfect divine creature, an exception. But if Christ is not God, there is no longer Incarnation or redemption; and the whole of Christianity falls to pieces.

Constantine intervened because he saw in Arianism a danger to the unity of the Empire. For a united Empire there must be a united Church. He therefore summoned the Council of Nicea in 325. The Council, following Athanasius, declared that Christ was true God and true man; that he was the Son of God, consubstantial with the Father: ὁμοούσιος. After Nicea, far from quieting down, the conflict rebounded in reaction to the term *homoousios,* and the crisis lasted until the end of the fourth century. It ended, as far as the Church was concerned, under Pope Damasus, in 377, and, as far as the State was concerned, under the Emperor Theodosius in 380-81.

Nicea, and later the First Council of Constantinople, represent the confrontation of Christianity, born on Jewish soil, with the Greek cultural *milieu,* and the effort of the Church and her theologians to give a new and precise semantic content to words materially identical with those in use, but now charged with a different meaning. The theology of the first few centuries was a long and patient work of purifying and achieving focus, in order to express according to Hellenic categories the fundamental mysteries of Christianity: the Trinity and the Incarnation. In this work, the contribution of Athanasius, Hilary of Poitiers, Ambrose and the Cappadocian Fathers was decisive.[10]

3. *The enslavement of the Church by feudalism*

Identified with the Empire, the Church seemed destined to perish with it. But with a mysterious start, at the very moment when the Empire was foundering, she undertook the evangelization of the conquerors and the task of opening the way of salvation to new peoples. In less than three centuries, with men like St. Remigius of Rheims, St. Avitus, and Pope Gregory the Great (in the sixth century), the Church won those who were called the Barbarians. In this connection, the baptism of Clovis, like that of Cornelius earlier, has the value of a symbol: the Church, in the West, disentangled herself from the Empire at the moment of its destruction. She entered anew into the life of nations, but not without running another danger, perhaps the most serious in her history.

The Church had led the Barbarians to the gospel of Christ. As a result monasteries and local churches and sanctuaries bene-

---

10. On the cultural danger see: J. Daniélou, *Message évangelique et culture hellénistique aux IIᵉ et IIIᵉ siècles* (Tournai, 1961); trans., in: *History of Early Christian Doctrine before the Council of Nicaea* (London, 1964); G. Prestige, *God in Patristic Thought* (London, 1936); M. Spanneut, *Le stöicisme des Pères de l'Église* (Paris, 1957); G. Aeby, *Les missions divines de Saint Justin à Origène* (Fribourg, 1958); B. Lonergan, *De Deo uno et trino,* pars analytica (Rome, 1961), pp. 15-113; A. Orbe, *Hacia la Primera Teología de la procession del Verbo* (2 vols., Rome, 1958); I. Ortiz De Urbina, *Nicée et Constantinople* (Paris, 1963).

fited from the liberality of the great. Kings shared their authority with prelates, who became temporal princes. So much wealth and honor, far from being a source of strength to the Church became a supreme danger. After enriching the Church, feudalism would seek to absorb and enslave her. In this respect the policy of Otto I, in the tenth century, was typical and had a determining force.

King of Germany and soon Emperor (in 962), Otto I intended to be so *in fact*, and not simply in name. Profiting from the vacancy of four ducal sees, he immediately entrusted them to members of his own family. Then, in order to weaken the authority of the secular princes, he decided to associate the Church intimately with the politics of the Empire. He granted to bishops, abbots and other dignitaries the rights and privileges of temporal princes. Thanks to this policy, the new counts and marquises were free as far as the secular princes were concerned, while their celibacy (at least according to law) ensured that the king would have their benefices at his disposal when they died. Since the ecclesiastical princes were indebted to the king for their benefices and their lands, he could exact from them all the services he desired. As a result of the dignity of temporal princes which he had conferred on them, moreover, the king exercised a growing authority over the nomination of bishops, and abbots, whom he chose according to his interests from among his most faithful friends and his own chaplains and ordinaries.

There followed for the Church an inversion of her situation which was absolutely abnormal. It was the king who chose the candidates for ecclesiastical dignities, the canonical election having no more than a confirmatory value. The bishops were first and foremost princes and vassals of the king, and priests afterwards: they were subject to the State, administrators of vast landed property and free in practice of any connection with Rome. More than that, for a century (from 962 onwards), the kings of Germany arrogated to themselves the right to nominate the sovereign pontiffs. The Church became an annex of the State. The pope was an imperial chaplain and the bishops were ordinaries of the court. The upper reaches of the hierarchy were open only to sons of the ruling families. The Church was caught up in the feudal system.

This enslaving of the Church by feudalism extended to all levels of the clergy and put the Church in a position of dependence on the holders of temporal power which has never since been equalled.

The Germanic nobility and the Germanic squires, who were primarily warriors and land-holders, had no *penchant* for towns, and there was therefore an exodus of the urban population to the country. Now according to Roman law, the owner of the soil is the owner also of all that is to be found on it, and consequently of the churches on it. So the feudal landlord, lord also of the buildings and benefices attached to his land, acquired the habit of choosing himself the priests for his "own church." Up to this time priests had depended on the bishop; from now onwards they were to receive both office and living from the squires and lords temporal: it was *lay investiture*.

Such a system, it goes without saying, was disastrous. Chosen by the whim of their patrons rather than by vocation, priests were bewilderingly ignorant, scarcely knowing how to read or write, vaguely acquainted with the essentials of sacramental rites. And since the living was more important than the office, the office itself became an object of financial speculation. The sacraments were bought and sold, as ecclesiastical dignities were. Simony was accompanied by other immorality: married priests and priests with concubines were an every day affair and no longer even created scandal.

Save in exceptional cases, the higher ranks of the clergy were recruited from the nobility, and, as in the lower ranks, office and benefice coincided. The bishop received from the king or prince the *honor episcopatus,* which included both the office and ecclesiastical jurisdiction. Afterwards, he had himself consecrated. Abbeys and bishoprics, being regarded as the personal property of the king or of the princes, were bought and sold, exchanged, offered as a dowry or a present like any other temporal possession. Those in the ascendant, in order to keep the wealth of the Church within their own hands and extend their influence over people in general, bestowed on their younger sons, even at a tender age, bishoprics and monasteries richly provided with livings. Unworthy and incapable bishops were the plague of the Church of the time.

The Church of feudalism, before the reform of the eleventh and twelfth centuries, glided towards the abyss. Having lost the power to choose her own ministers and hierarchy, from the pope to the ordinary priest, she was no longer in control of her destiny. The fact that the living had become more important than the office gave rise to simony and other immorality. The bishops, who were feudal overlords rather than bishops, had no pastoral considerations of any sort, and left their people to rot in ignorance. The use of the sacraments scarcely existed. Devotions, processions and pilgrimages were disproportionately inflated and took the place of dogma. The time was ripe for heresy and schism. In fact, in the eleventh century, the Albigensian heresy appeared, accompanied by a swarm of sects and superstitions of all kinds. It was in the eleventh century also that the great schism took place, which separated the two worlds to which the Roman Empire had given birth: the West, and the Byzantine and Slavonic East. Never perhaps had the situation of the Church seemed so desperate. Her insertion into the social and political structures of the time had become absorption by these structures, the loss of her freedom and the decay of her spiritual dynamism.[11]

4.   The greatness and ambiguity of medieval Christendom

The situation was desperate. And yet, the Church recovered and lived. The new life began at the tenth century Benedictine

11. On this period see: F. Kempf, in: *Handbuch der Kirchengeschichte*, Vol. III 1, pp. 219-461; G. Dawson, *The Making of Europe* (London, 19-32); *Ibid., Religion and the Rise of Western Culture* (Garden City, Doubleday, 1958); E. Amann and A. Dumas, *L'Église au pouvoir des laïcs*, in Fliche and Martin, *Histoire de l'Église* (vol. VII, Paris, 1943); M. D. Knowles, and D. Obolensky, *The Middle Ages* (London, 1969).

Abbey of Cluny, and thanks to Cluny's abbots, several of whom were indeed saints, it spread gradually throughout the monasteries of France, Italy, Spain, England and Portugal. Monks would go to Cluny to be initiated into and formed in the monastic life, or else monks from Cluny would be asked to stay in the monasteries of other regions to reform them. Founded in 910, Cluny counted in 1100 more than ten thousand monks dispersed in fourteen hundred and fifty monastic houses, having swarmed throughout the whole of the West. Though it did not attack directly the problem of lay investiture, Cluny's influence was nonetheless decisive; for it infused into the Church a spirit of prayer, of discipline and of holiness, which prepared Christians as a whole to desire reform.

Little by little the reform radiated and spread throughout Christendom, sustained and propagated by saints like St. Romuald, the founder of the Camaldolese, St. John Guilbert, founder of the abbey of Vallombrosa, St. Peter Damien, one of the most vigorous reformers of the time, and, in the following century, St. Bernard, the amazing abbot of Clairvaux. It was supported by synods like those of Augsburg (952), Poitiers (1000), Limoges (1031), Pavia (1022) and Bourges (1031), which fought against simony and Nicolaitism, and above all by popes like Leo IX, Gregory VII and Urban II.

Without any shadow of doubt, the chief artisan of reform was Gregory VII. Small in stature, but with a gigantic personality, an iron strength and an incandescent zeal, Gregory VII understood at once that in order to save the Church, and give her back her holiness, it was necessary to make her *free*. He understood, moreover, that only the pope, at this moment of history, could undertake such a task.

His programme of reform was clear-cut: to fight simony, Nicolaitism, and above all lay investiture. To the mind of Gregory, all the faithful—kings, emperors, princes, bishops, clerics and the ordinary laity, were subject to the pope, who had universal authority and responsibility. Already, by the decree *De electione pontificia*, in 1059, Nicholas II had withdrawn papal elections from lay influence and imperial interference.

Gregory VII, in his synods (1075-1078), forbade kings, princes or any other laymen whatsoever, to confer on any man the least ecclesiastical dignity. A fearful conflict ensued, lasting fifty years. In the end, by the Concordat of Worms, on September 23rd, 1122, the Church's right was recognized. The freedom of canonical elections was guaranteed, from that of the pope downwards, and the Church's usurped possessions were restored.

Otto I, in order to escape from the power of the secular princes, had made of bishops and abbots temporal princes completely bound to his own person. At the same stroke, the temporal power of the emperor placed the Church in tutelage and curbed her spiritual dynamism. With the Concordat of Worms, the situation was reversed.

Free from now on as far as the temporal princes were concerned, the authority of the pope grew from day to day. The Church tended to be organized as a strongly centralized monarchy, with her curia and her nuncios. The pope, at the head of Christendom, and invested with imperial splendor, took sovereign decisions in matters of faith and discipline. He exacted canonical obedience from all the bishops. He could judge the emperor, depose him, excommunicate him, and dispense his subjects from all bonds of loyalty. Not only was the pope a temporal sovereign of the papal state, but also the suzerain of several states. The first Crusade was a holy war created and directed by him. It made of him the first man of his time, the Head of Christendom, and assembled about his person the whole of the West. The element of cohesion in the unity of the Christian West was no longer the emperor but the pope, as Head of the Church.

So, for nearly three centuries, that is from 1050 to 1350, the Church seemed to have succeeded in constructing on earth, as it were, a divine domicile: Christendom. She was surrounded by an unheard of prestige. Cathedrals were built; men set off for the conquest of the Holy Sepulchre, or to fight Islam; they threw themselves into discovering the world. The pressure of monastic orders has something almost stupefying about it: Cistercians, Premonstratentians, military and hospital orders, Franciscans and Dominicans. In 1316 the Franciscans numbered fourteen hundred houses and more than thirty thousand religious. The Dominicans, in 1303, had six hundred houses and ten thousand religious. It was the period when Aristotelianism gradually penetrated the whole of culture and fertilized the sacred sciences; it was the period of the great theological syntheses of St. Bonaventure and St. Thomas Aquinas, the period of Dante and of Roger Bacon.

In this Christendom the pope was the supreme arbiter. "The papacy," writes M. Jean Guitton, "educated all consciences, controlled all powers and taught all teachers, even the profane. There was no more a place where the unbeliever could lodge himself in this system than there had been a place for the Christian in the pagan system. The heretic was treated as a traitor. Peoples were mobilized in the interests of the faith. Catholicism now entered into the very viscera of western history." [12] After being dominated by the State, the Church herself became dominating.

If, in effect, in this Christendom, the two powers (temporal and spiritual) were distinguished, the same grounds and the same finality were assigned to both, that is the guiding of the People of God towards supernatural salvation, in conformity with the institutions and rules of the Christian faith. Everything in a word came back to the supremacy of the Church, since the ordering of all things to their supernatural end affected not only the individual but society also, and regulated public life and its structures. The whole world, including the cultural and scientific world, was monopolized and, as it were, confiscated by the Church and her vision of life, which is that of scripture. [13]

The medieval inheritance lay heavy upon the Church. It plunged her into a state of profound ambiguity. Since activities

---

12. J. Guitton, *L'Église et l'Évangile* (Paris, 1959), pp. 381-382; trans., *The Church and the Gospel* (London, 1961).

13. Y. Congar, "Église et monde dans la perspective de Vatican II," in: *L'Église dans le monde de ce temps* (coll. "Unam sanctam," n. 65, 3 vols., Paris, 1967), vol. 3: 15-18.

which are purely human and profane were developing under her aegis, she found herself liable for all that was done in her name. The mistake made by Galileo's judges would have been simply an episode in the history of science, if his judges had not believed themselves to be speaking in the name of the faith. It has taken centuries for the Church to dispel the ambiguities created by such a situation, in the spheres of war, of science, of politics, of philosophy and theology. The crusades, the Inquisition, Copernicus, Galileo, Descartes, Pascal, Leibniz, all these are so many facts and names which express this ambiguous situation, a situation sometimes painful and even tragic.[14]

5. *The modern nations and neo-Caesarism*

In the relationship between Church and State, a variety of situations is possible. The State may oppose the Church for ideological or political reasons (as in the period of persecutions up to the fourth century); or State and Church may live side by side, in peaceful neutrality, each operating on its own account in its own domain (which is more or less the situation in the free West today); or Church and State may be associated. This association may in turn have very different *balances of power*. The Church may enjoy the protection of the State, but this protection may be such as more or less to paralyze her freedom (as in the Constantinian Church); or the State may set out to dominate the Church and in the end enslave it (as feudal society did); or the Church through her spiritual power over individuals may finish up by dominating the State and herself become a sort of super-state (like medieval Christendom). In practice, the swing of the pendulum, from Constantine to the French Revolution, has been in favor of the State.

From the fourteenth century onwards, the power of the State, partly eclipsed by the universal and dominating power of the

---

14. On medieval Christendom, see: L. Génicot, *Les lignes de faîte du Moyen Âge* (Louvain and Tournai, 1962); trans., *The Contours of the Middle Ages* (London, 1967); M. D. Knowles and D. Obolensky, *The Middle Ages*; Daniel-Rops, *L'Église de la Cathédrale* (Paris, 1952).

medieval papacy, regained at a national level an autonomy, and then an authority, which rapidly became absolute, and then aggressive and hostile.

In every domain the *élan* of the Church gave way. The crusade was a thing of the past. The enthusiasm of the cathedral builders flagged. Theology simply repeated itself and lost its creativeness. The taste for luxury was like a gangrene among the clergy and even among the religious orders. And, above all, the unity of Christendom began to break up. The ambitious image of a society intellectually and religiously united, using Latin as the common language of its liturgy and its schools, was rapidly waning. Paris was no longer the only great university center. Oxford, Prague, Salamanca and Coimbra were in full flower and becoming her rivals. Intellectual life had ceased to be a clerical monopoly. National languages were competing with Latin and becoming more and more the medium of instruction as well as the medium of literary art.

And this linguistic revolution was only the sign of a still more profound revolution, that of *nationalism*. The pope's right to control the nations of the West was being contested by young states which claimed for themselves the civilizing mission assumed up to now by the Church, and refused to hold at her hands their temporal power.

The principle which gave birth to the modern nation state had, to tell the truth, been at work for a long time. Indeed the School of Bologna, from the eleventh century onwards, spread the cult of the emperor Justinian's *Corpus juris civilis*. In this code the sovereign's authority is recognized as absolute: his will is law. The legal scholars of the Middle Ages transposed this doctrine into their theses, and propagated an ideal of government which gradually gained ground among the princes of the time. The Middle Ages, thanks to the buttress of the papacy, resisted their tentative efforts, but the principles of neo-caesarism ended by very nearly imposing themselves. Already at the beginning of the fourteenth century with Philip the Fair, whose ministers were professors of Roman law, medieval Christendom was shattered. Temporal power had gained its autonomy.

Philip the Fair was the first of the sovereigns of the modern European nations: France, Germany, Spain, Portugal, England, Austria and the rest.

In the face of these pretensions, the papacy reacted to the opposite extreme. Those who defended the power of the state provoked those who defended the pontifical power, who went as far as sustaining that all things temporal as well as spiritual, are ruled by the Church. This stiffening in the attitude of the Church gave birth to a painful conflict between royalty and papacy, particularly in France. Philip the Fair, like his jurists, was convinced that the temporal government of the kingdom belonged to him alone, and that in this domain he had no superior but God. Thus the principle of a separation of powers was enunciated, the domain of the State separate from the domain of the Church. The attack on Boniface VIII at Anagni showed that the medieval order, founded on the supremacy of the Church as the arbiter of power as well as of conscience, was giving way. Another conception of the world was in process of gestation. The era of nationalism had openly come, and the Church was obliged to take account of it. With the Reformation, moreover, royal absolutism doubled; for it implied confessional absolutism, according to the principle: *cujus regio, ejus et religio.*

Since the nations of the west had reached self-consciousness, and detached their identity from the medieval dream of Christendom, it was henceforth within the framework of nationalism that the Church was obliged to pursue her task and insert her life. This was a new sort of insertion, which carried with it new dangers, from within as well as from without.

In mission countries, nationalism had sometimes disastrous results. The Church took the risk of associating herself with the daring enterprises of the great discoverers who set out under the patronage of the western states: Spain, Portugal and France. Immediately the missions found themselves bound up with royal administration—so much so, that the bearers of the word of Christ too often appeared to the natives of the country as agents of white penetration, delegated to establish outposts of the conquering and colonizing State. Since it was marked by this ambiguity, missionary activity often met with resistance, and even hostility, especially in China and Japan—an attitude which was the more justified in that the European states, in spite of the efforts of the Congregation for the Propagation of the Faith, never ceased to interfere in missionary undertakings in order to use them for their own ends.

At home, the Church was involved in the life of the *nation.* And the progress of absolutism posed her with grave problems. In the Spain of The Most Catholic King, as in the France of The Most Christian King, the weight of neo-caesarism made itself increasingly felt. Nothing is more typical in this respect than the position of the French Church before the Revolution. The clergy, with the nobility and the third estate, constituted one of the three orders of the realm. The higher ranks of the clergy were composed almost entirely of noblemen: of a hundred and thirty bishops only one was a commoner. A commemorative medal struck by the clerical assembly, in 1655, showed the royal sceptre and the episcopal cross intertwined and surrounded by the legend *una salus ambobus*: "only one salvation for both." In fact, at the heart of the centralizing, authoritarian regime of the King, who was God's representative, the Church was part of the machinery of state. After the Concordat of 1516, bishops were nominated by the King, and provided by him with benefices and titles; they were peers of the realm and royal counsellors.[15] Once again, after entering into the life of the State (this time pluralized) the Church was domesticated by it. In practice this putting of the clergy into tutelage separated them from Rome. The swing of the pendulum was in favor of the State.

6. *The Renaissance, humanism and cultural insertion*

Much more than a simple return to the study of classical art and letters, the Renaissance denotes a revolution which affected western society at every level, social, moral, aesthetic and philo-

15. P. Blet, *Le Clergé de France et la monarchie* (2 vols., Rome 1959), vol. 2: 431.

sophical. It characterizes a whole epoch (from the fourteenth to the sixteenth century) and is defined by a new spirit, in opposition to the spirit and society of the Middle Ages. The Renaissance is not yet a total emancipation of man as far as God and Christianity are concerned, but rather a passionate affirmation of man and of his value as man. At the historical level it tends to explain events by concrete and immediate circumstances rather than by carrying them back to the first Cause.

The literary and cultural element in this revolution is *humanism*. Humanism proposed to form man (the grammarian, the orator, the poet, the pedagogue, the philosopher) by means of classical, that is to say Latin and Greek literature. The humanist was distinguished by, as it were, a cult of letters, by the love of wisdom, by confidence in man, by the desire to unite culture and piety. He did not reject original sin or grace, but he stressed all that is good and beautiful in man. He had a cult of form, and he expressed it through the imitation of antiquity.

Before becoming European phenomena, the Renaissance and humanism were Italian phenomena, with their principal centers first in Florence, and then in Rome, Naples, Pavia, Ferrara and Venice. And it should be added that if the influence of humanism has been so considerable in Italy, it is due to the fact that papal Rome, under Nicholas V, Sixtus IV, Innocent VIII, Alexander VI and Leo X, welcomed, encouraged and propagated the new spirit.

One can discern in the history of humanism two distinct phases: a first phase, which extends from the fourteenth century and on through the first half of the fifteenth with Petrarch as its point of departure, and a second phase, which extends from the second half of the fifteenth century and on up to Erasmus. European humanism, in France, Germany, England and Spain, belongs to this second phase.

Taken as a whole, the humanist movement was not a pagan movement, and it cannot be held directly responsible for the immorality of the Renaissance, which existed long before humanism and flourished in circles where humanist culture was a stranger. It must nevertheless be recognized that in allowing the Christian ideal and the pagan ideal to co-exist in them, the humanists took up a position of permanent ambiguity. In fact, in the course of time, the cult of man which they preached was to end by taking the place of the gospel, and setting up man as a rival to God.

The Church, especially in the upper reaches of her hierarchy, accepted the new world. In this, the pontificate of Nicholas V was decisive. Nicholas had lived in Florence in the midst of the *élite* of the movement from a literary and generally artistic point of view, and, once pope, he dreamt of making Rome the intellectual and artistic capital. He summoned artists from the whole of Italy, from France, Spain and Germany; he surrounded himself with humanists and intellectuals in general; and he took in hand the setting up of the Vatican Library, and the reconstruction of St. Peter's, the Vatican and Rome itself in unparalleled splendor.

In itself it was right of the Church to associate herself thus with the cultural movement of her time, and to keep in touch with its *élite*. Unfortunately she did not know how to resist the disintegrating elements which the new culture carried within it. With the art of antiquity and the cult of antiquity, she absorbed the spirit of antiquity, and allowed herself to be caught up in a style of life whose dominant values were those of money and luxury, pleasure and pride. In time, moreover, side by side with that of believing and Christian *literati*, who saw in their culture a means of enlarging their faith, there developed a pagan humanism, which daily encroached more and more on the life of the Church.

The disastrous results of this change in mentality were exhibited in the popes themselves. For fifty years, under Sixtus IV, Innocent VIII and Alexander VI, the papal court set the example in outrage, as far as lust and provocative display were concerned. In this respect, the pontificate of Alexander VI, a Borgia (1492-1503), was indubitably the most deplorable of all the pontificates of history. The Church sank to the lowest depths of immorality and crime. It was the period when poisons and daggers acted with remarkable efficiency, and when Savonarola, in Florence, demanded reform, and announced God's judgments upon an adulterous Church.

While Alexander VI succumbed to the luxurious paganism of the Renaissance, Julius II yielded to the temptations of temporal power—the temptation of politics. His ambition was to make the pope sole master in Italy, and Rome the center of an artistic, intellectual and spiritual unity. But this *"casqué"* and military pope let venality and corruption thrive in his own *entourage*, and delayed the hour of reform.

Finally, Leo X succumbed to the temptations of art. A Medici, whose mind had been formed in Florence, in an atmosphere of brilliant worldliness and intellectual refinement, he brought to Rome all the pride of the Medicis. The greatest Maecenas of his time, he surrounded himself with artists, and made Rome the capital of the world of beauty, the point where all creative energy converged. Three names enshrine this unparalleled apogee: Leonardo da Vinci, Michelangelo, Raphael. But no more than Alexander VI or Julius II did Leo X know how to read the signs of the times, and realize the urgency of reform. Instead of the sacred tiara, the Church wore another, the three-fold crown of science, poetry and the visual arts.

During all this time the protracted complaint, which for two centuries had risen from the depths of the Christian conscience, remained without response. Pilgrims who passed through the eternal city returned to their countries sickened by the venality and cupidity, the luxuriousness and debauch of churchmen, and even of the popes themselves. The scandal of papal Rome deeply discredited the whole Church.

There is no doubt that it is possible, at least in theory, to distinguish between an ecclesiastical function and the man who exercises it. But neither Savonarola nor Luther did so. The Church and churchmen were confounded in the same universal reprobation. The scandal of Rome spread in the Church, bringing back all the evils of the tenth and eleventh centuries: among the people ignorance and superstition, and the primacy of devotions over devotion, in the higher ranks of the clergy the accumulation of benefices, Nicolaitism and nepotism, simony, pastoral absenteeism, ostentatious luxury and pride, and in the lower ranks, ignorance and decadence. There were nevertheless, sound values which resisted these influences: integrity of faith in the popes, and above all the presence of sanctity, in St. Catherine of Genoa, St. Antony, St. Francis of Paola, St. Lawrence Giustiniani, and St. Catherine of Bologna.

Notwithstanding, the Church was in urgent need of reform, on the institutional plane and on the plane of discipline and morality. Tentative efforts were made before the Council of Trent: some not always orthodox or balanced (like those of John Wiclif and John Huss), others ineffectual and short-lived (like those under Pius II, Paul II, Sixtus IV, Innocent VIII, Alexander VI and Julius II). Only certain basic elements in the Church, particularly the religious orders (Benedictines, Dominicans, Augustinians, Carmelites and Minims), went on to accomplish a redress which was a prelude to the Council of Trent and constituted a force in reserve for the future. The real reformation, with all the dimensions demanded by the situation, was put off. Elaborate projects remained a dead letter, because the curia (the popes, the cardinals, the bishops), did not—with an efficacious desire—want reform, *inner* reform. They knew their duty, but they did not do it. Reformation would come, but it would come late, when the initiative was no longer in the hands of the Church, and it would end in the drama of Luther and the loss of half of Europe. The Church had inserted herself into Renaissance culture and the Renaissance way of life, but she had done so to the point of being stuck fast in it, in an odor of putrefaction.[16]

---

16. R. Aubenas and R. Ricard, *L'Église et la Renaissance*, in: Fliche and Martin, *Histoire de l'Église* (vol. XV, Paris, 1951); L. Pastor, *Histoire des Papes* (vols. I-III, Paris, 1901-1903); trans., *A History of the Popes from the Close of the Middle Ages* (London, 1952); K. Burdach, *Riforma, Rinascimento, Umanesimo* (Florence, 1935); Daniel-Rops, *L'Église de la Renaissance et de la Réforme* (Paris, 1955); L. J. Rogier, R. Aubert, M. D. Knowles, *Nouvelle histoire de l'Église*, vol. III, *Réforme et Contre-Réforme* (Paris, 1968).

7. *The nineteenth century and lack of insertion*

After a period of excessive insertion in the culture and political life of the European nations, the Church, in the nineteenth and early twentieth centuries, was in a new, more subtle danger, that of absence. For a century and a half she was indeed like a stranger in the world, and consequently slow in understanding it. As far as modern philosophy and science were concerned, she developed a curious and painful inferiority complex.

The society to which the French Revolution gave birth went through rapid transformations. Work was no longer confined to the soil, but took place in workshops, factories and mines. Capitalism developed at the same time as industrial life, since it was indispensable to it. Side by side with the bourgeoisie a new social class appeared, the proletariat, the anonymous mass of workers, at the service of employers and machines, a class living under oppression, awaiting the hour of revenge. The word "liberal" was on everyone's lips, but it was a word loaded with equivocation. The Church was faced with a form of civilization which disconcerted her, and then alarmed her. She shrank from new ideas; then she condemned them. She accepted the support of the bourgeoisie, which represented the new form of power, and at the same time she lost the working class. The pontificates of Gregory XVI and Pius IX well illustrate the widening gap between the Church and the world.

With a speculative rather than a political cast of mind, Gregory XVI was, both by temperament and by formation, suspicious of novelties. His secretary, Lambruschini, stiffened this attitude, and involved the pope in a policy of hostility towards the modern world. Gregory was persuaded that any concession to the spirit of the age would put in peril the very foundations of the Church. This can be seen well enough in the affair, or rather the drama, of Lamennais. Lamennais considered that if the Church were to be really free and assume her real mission, she must be separated from the State, and from politics, and free herself from the powers of high finance represented by the bourgeoisie. These ideas were prophetic, but at the time ill-understood. In particular, the radical separation of Church and State, of politics and religion, seemed a heresy, in that it seemed opposed to the whole tradition of the Church. Gregory XVI's two encyclicals, *Mirari vos* (1832) and *Singulari nos* (1834), condemned the ideas of Lamennais and of the newspaper *L'Avenir*, and gave Gregory the reputation of being an anti-liberal pope.

To tell the truth, in the colossal confusion of ideas and terminology, it was not easy to separate wheat from tares. By *liberalism*, Gregory XVI understood any opinion which declared itself in favor of absolute liberty from authority: in theology (the setting up of reason in opposition to dogma), in politics (the separation of Church and State), or in the sphere of the press and free associations (with no distinction between believers and unbelievers). No doubt it was useful to recall to men's minds that there are limits to the liberty of the believer, constituted that is, by his submission of himself to the gospel, to dogma and to the legitimate authority of the Church and the pope. Unfortunately Gregory XVI's encyclicals did not distinguish between legitimate aspects of this authority and aspects which are injurious to freedom. Hence the pope appeared to be the enemy of modern society, the champion of a dead past, opposed to any sort of novelty. Gregory, moreover, passed over in silence the question of economic liberalism, the most urgent of all, and so gave the impression that he was deaf to the cries of the working class in its slavery to capitalism.

In this context, his successor, Pius IX, rapidly created the impression of being a liberal pope. Indeed, at the beginning of his pontificate, Pius IX intended to show that the Church favored progress, and that, without sacrificing any of her dogma, she was open to the aspirations of her time. The new pope seemed determined to throw the Church into the current of history.

It was, however, a *détente* of brief duration; for soon the situation between the papacy and the new movements grew more rigid, perhaps because the Church, conservative by tradition, felt incapable of co-operating with men who wished to transform the world in the name of the principles of 1789, perhaps because the revolution itself, in its three-fold manifestation as liberal, national and social, went too far, and made an issue of interests which the Church regarded as sacred. In fact, there is no doubt that both these reasons represent real aspects of the problem.

One thing is certain: after his forced exile of seventeen months in Gaeta, Pius IX returned to Rome considerably disillusioned. Rather in spite of himself, owing to the hostility he had encountered, his pontificate took a different turn. His interest and his efforts henceforth were directed to problems of doctrine, organization and internal discipline. He worked with enthusiasm at centralizing the Church. The curia became the center of Catholicism. Through the Roman congregations, through nuncios who intervened more and more in the life of local Churches, through the nomination of bishops completely devoted to the Holy See, through the imposition of the Roman rite on the entire world, and finally through the foundation of *La Civiltà Cattolica* and *L'Osservatore Romano*, Pius IX, in practice, identified himself with the Church, and imposed everywhere, in the concrete, a papal absolutism. In order to resist the tendency of modern states to exclude the Church from public life, he pursued a policy of concordats (with France, Spain, Austria and Russia), a policy already practiced by Gregory XVI, but fleetingly and without success.

In the *doctrinal* sphere, the pope was convinced that the despoilers of the papal states and the defenders of liberty who wanted to remove religion from public life were all heirs of the philosophical schools of the eighteenth century. The protagonists of the rights of man arrived in the end at denying the rights of God. The principles of liberty led to an overthrow of everything: they were therefore to be condemned. It is in this context of confused ideas that Pius IX's interventions have to be understood. What attitude should be taken with regard to the world the Revolution had brought into being? How was the regimen of modern liberties—political liberty, liberty of conscience, the freedom of the press, freedom of worship—to be judged? Should these liberties be approved, tolerated or resisted? The confusion was all the greater in that the principles of liberty had been elaborated outside and in opposition to Christian tradition. From the moment "Catholic liberalism" appeared, questions of this sort kept Catholics, liberal and *intégriste,* in a state of permanent conflict, which gave the pope deep pain. Pius IX considered that he had to speak.

He did so by means of the encyclical *Quanta cura* (1864) and the *Syllabus* (1864), a table of eighty propositions pinning down and condemning all the errors of the time. The encyclical condemned the principle of the lay State which governed without taking religion into account, the principle of liberty of conscience and freedom of worship, the principle of the sovereignty of the people considered as a supreme law. It proclaimed, moreover, the absolute independence of the Church in respect to the civil power, and her right to form consciences, especially those of the young. Finally it asserted papal authority to the full, even in spheres which did not directly impinge on dogmas of faith or morals. The *Syllabus,* for its part, condemned rationalism, pantheism, indifferentism, gallicanism, statism, socialism, communism and, in particular, liberalism, which thus found itself without hope of appeal.

Among the Church's enemies, Pius IX's intervention provoked a veritable outcry, among liberal Catholics a deep deception. In reality the pope did not wish to reject the whole of modern civilization and progress, but to anathematize "liberty," "progress" and "the modern world" as unbelievers conceived them, that is as ammunition against religion. He intended to condemn excesses and deviations. And in point of fact, beneath the words "revolution," "republic," "modern world," "liberty," there lay at the time a rejection of any submission to an authority superior to the individual conscience. Many Catholics, nevertheless, would wish that the pope had equally recognized what is valid in our age.

To do Pius IX justice, it should be remembered that the nineteenth century was the time when the wave of rationalism, after being more or less contained for two centuries, broke on Europe. In the eighteenth century, the French *philosophes* and encyclopedists, the English and French deists, and the German promoters of the *Aufklärung* were already agreed in setting up man against God. The revolutionaries were disciples of the eighteenth century *philosophes*, and inspired by their principles. Indeed throughout the nineteenth century irreligion increased in depth and extent. It became sectarian and aggressive, determined to eliminate not only Christ and the Church, but God himself. It was this vast offensive against God that the Church had to confront. Let it suffice, in order to evoke the period and the atmosphere, to recall a few names.

There was the criticism directed against the Christian faith by men such as Reimarus, Strauss, Renan, Kähler, and Wrede, who were precursors of historical criticism after the manner of Bultmann. There was the evolutionism and transformism of Darwin, first applied in the realm of the sciences and then generalized and applied to man, institutions, morality and religion, to become at the end of the process a refusal to accept any revelation except that of permanent consciousness of man's progress. There was rationalism, or the religion of science, encouraged by the enormous progress in technology. While twentieth century science works at its own level and has no philosophical ambitions, nineteenth century science was philosophic in inspiration and, like the philosophy which inspired it, anti-Christian. In short, the humanism of the nineteenth century was an atheist humanism. The Christian conception of man was resented as a yoke imposed on him, and so, in order to enter into possession of itself, humanism tended to eliminate God and substitute for him man and humanity in general. This attitude, which had evolved as a result of ideas which appear first at the Renaissance, was developed in the eighteenth century and formulated in the nineteenth, in the philosophy and writings generally of Hegel (1770-1831), Feuerbach (1804-1872), Marx (1818-1883), Comte (1798-1857), Taine (1828-1893) and Littré (1801-1880).

In the face of this rising tide of rationalism, the Church had at her disposal only an apologetics more remarkable for goodwill than soundness. Polemical and poorly equipped at a scientific level, it threw itself into what seemed most urgent: it stopped

up the breaches, and resisted assailants as best it could. It would
have needed a vigorous exegesis, philosophy and theology to
have answered the historical and philosophical criticism of the
time. And Catholic science in the nineteenth century was weak
and in decline; it was out of date, and incapable of making a
synthesis of the old and new. Against the theses proposed by
rationalism the Church could only enter a plea of *non-recevoir,*
and call in question the motives at work. In the countries of
the third world the civilizing powers abandoned the elementary
schools to the Church, but the class which would come ultimately to power was to receive its higher education in the great
European universities, Oxford, Cambridge, Paris and Louvain.

In the lay ideas of the nineteenth century—liberty, equality,
democracy, the separation of politics and religion, historical and
literary criticism—there were, without any shadow of doubt,
along with doubtful ingredients, valuable elements which the
Church could have assimilated. But in the face of attacks,
she refused them all *en bloc.* For nearly a century she heaped
up anathemas. She clung to the possession of a few Italian
principalities, and confounded in the same reprobation those
who were defending right principles and those who were attacking her dogmas. Pius IX, in particular, was unable to adapt himself to the evolution which was in process of radically transforming society. Obsessed by the liberal and national revolution
he was blind to the social revolution. It was only towards the
end of the century that Catholic social doctrine was at last set
in motion, under Leo XIII.[17]

One can, to be sure, find explanations for the Church's attitude. But the fact remains: the Church of the nineteenth
century, confronted by a world in the making, withdrew. More
and more she became isolated. After being involved too deeply
in the social, political and cultural structures of the past, she
now ran the risk of not being involved enough, of no longer

17. If it is true that the nineteenth century Church as a whole took
time to turn her attention to social justice, it has to be remembered that
local initiatives had already been taken by certain bishops. In 1848,
for example, Ketteler in Germany wrote a pastoral letter on social justice.

making herself understood by the world she was to lead to the gospel, and of breaking off all dialogue with it. Her life was concentrated within itself, and on itself, but she became more and more *absent* from the world, more and more isolated, and consequently without any real impact on the world. Lack of insertion is, for the Church, no less serious a risk than excessive insertion.[18]

On the other hand, it has to be recognized that this withdrawal of the Church within herself had aspects not wholly negative. In recollection, in gradually and painfully detaching herself from her temporal ambitions, she was purified, and rediscovered her own identity as a spiritual presence in the world. In solitude, the way for renewal was prepared, a renewal which was to be manifest in the twentieth century in the outburst of religious and missionary life. Certain gestures made at long intervals (ecumenical gestures for instance, and gestures towards a *rapprochement* with the working class) allowed it to be understood that the Church's isolation was accompanied by reflection, and that these presaged a change of attitude.

8.   *The twentieth century: in search of new forms of presence and engagement*

After a long period of protest against the modern world, and then of isolation, the twentieth century Church has, since the last war and especially since the Second Vatican Council, undergone a veritable *metanoia* in her attitude towards the world. It is a conversion with many manifestations. Instead of being suspicious, the Church has become accessible and welcoming: we have only to think of the gestures of John XXIII and Paul

---

18. On the nineteenth century Church see: R. Aubert, *Le pontificat de Pie IX*, in: A. Fliche and E. Jarry, *Histoire de l'Église* (vol. XXI, Paris, 1952); E. Hocedez, *Histoire de la théologie au XIXe siècle* (3 vols., Brussels and Paris, 1949-1952), vol. I: 13-21; G. De Lagarde, *La naissance de l'esprit laïque* (5 vols., Louvain and Paris, 1956²-1963); H. De Lubac, *Le drame de l'humanisme athée* (Paris, 1949); trans., *The Drama of Atheist Humanism* (New York).

VI (to the United Nations). She has changed from a policy of prestige to a policy of discretion, even of self-forgetfulness. Before, she claimed to give without receiving, to know all there was to know, without having anything to learn from the world. Today, she acknowledges that she receives a great deal from the world, and learns considerably from it. She recognizes the world as a free partner in an open dialogue. She recognizes other cultures, other mentalities, and has confidence in them. Dialogue with present day philosophy, long interrupted, has been resumed. The Church engages in dialogue also with the separated Christian communities, with the great world religions, and even with modern atheistic humanism. With communist régimes she looks for forms of cooperation or at least of mutual understanding.

This conversion is the result of grasping more completely the mystery of the Church. In seeking to define more precisely her own nature, the Church has been led at the same time to define more precisely her relationship to the world, since she is, by vocation, "sent" to the world.

Medieval Christendom conceived the relationship of Church and State in terms of *power*, the power of the priesthood culminating in the pope, and the power of the State in the king or emperor. In this perspective, the temporal was subordinated to the spiritual, as the body to the soul—a subordination which usually turned into domination. In *Gaudium et spes*, the Second Vatican Council rejected this conception. We are, henceforth, concerned with the relationship between the faith professed by the Church and the history of mankind. The Church does not seek to dominate men's earthly activity, but to relate the world and its history to eschatological salvation. And eschatology is not, in relation to history, dominant, but unitive; for it simply expresses the *total* and *ultimate* meaning of human history and the human vocation.

Hence the Church and the world are no longer to be conceived as two powers side by side, or one above the other, but rather as concentric circles united by the Word, who is both the Creating Word and the Revealing Word. The first circle includes the whole of mankind and its history, and the

whole of creation, while the second includes all those who have
accepted the gospel and constitute the Body of Christ. The world
is mankind waiting and implicitly asking for the gospel; for
the Church is that reality which reveals to the world the final
meaning of its activity and its history. The world is not something concurrent with the Church, but the *milieu* where the
presence of Christ and his Spirit is in hidden labor to bring
the Church to birth. The Christian faith does not enter into
competition with social, political, cultural or economic realities;
for its function is not to dominate, but to animate and give
ultimate meaning to everything. That is why the Church no
longer seeks to exercise a power over the State; [19] she no longer
even asks to be officially recognized by it. Her action in the
world is real, but in accordance with her true mission of sanctification. She acts in society, not in dominating it, but by means
of *being present* and *giving life*. What is active in the world is
the whole People of God, mixed up with other human beings
(like the leaven in the loaf), giving to all the activities and
aspirations of mankind (power, knowledge, the relation of men
to things, and to one another and so on) a *meaning*, which is
that of the gospel, and leading a life which is in accordance
with the gospel, that is to say, exercising that silent but efficacious
sort of action which we call *witness*.[20]

It goes without saying that the Church does not the less for
that cease to pursue in the world her work of evangelization proper, inviting men to become members of the People of God, members of the Body of Christ. By that means, the world becomes the
Church. But what is new in the twentieth century Church is
the very conception (at the level of reflective consciousness) of
the Church and society, and consequently the revision of their

---

19. The decree *Ad Gentes* observes: "the Church has no desire to
meddle in any way in the government of the earthly city. She claims
no other right than that of being at men's service ... through her charity
and faithful service" (AG 12).

20. Y. Congar, "Le rôle de l'Église dans le monde de ce temps," in:
Vatican II, L'Église dans le monde de ce temps (coll. "Unam sanctam,"
n. 65, 3 vols., Paris, 1967), vol. 2: 305-327.

mutual relationship; it is the broadening of the notion of the temporal, which no longer simply signifies temporal power in relation to the spiritual power of the Church, but all that man, linked with the cosmos, does and undertakes in order to realize a more human world and to realize himself; what is new, in short, is the estimation in which human and earthly realities in themselves are held. Since the Second Vatican Council gave explicit expression and formulation to this new consciousness, in *Gaudium et spes,* let us look at the essentials of the positions it takes up.

1. The Church recognizes the *autonomy* of the world and its values (GS 36). She describes the world as it is, and accepts it as it is. At the time of medieval Christendom the world scarcely existed, so completely did it espouse the Church's point of view. Today, the world enjoys a full autonomy. It follows its own progress and creates its own structures. The Church remains distinct from the world, since she has her mission, her means, in God's initiative of grace, culminating in the sending of the Word and the Spirit. But she recognizes in the world its own value and respects it.

2. The Church and the world are, after all, engaged in the same task, that is, in developing man and making him a success. The Church and the world are working on a common matter, man, and both seek his perfection, though by different means. And the same God who is man's creator is also the God who reveals himself to man and saves him. It is because human history and revelation both seek man's perfection that the Church offers herself to the world to serve it. In the Middle Ages the Church claimed to *govern* the world. Today she wants to serve it, to be in *diaconia,* in service to mankind, just as she is the *servant* of the Word (DV 10).

3. The Church wishes to serve the world not only in offering it the gospel, which would change its condition into that of the People of God, but also in so far as it is the world. What is

meant here is that service which the Church offers to the world to help it attain its own object, not, to be sure, in all domains, but where the truth about man is concerned. *Gaudium et spes* (41, 42, 43) gives precise details of the sort of service that the Church can in this way offer to the world. To every man she discloses the ultimate meaning of his vocation as a human being: "The Church, who has received the mission of making manifest the mystery of God . . . reveals to man at the same time the meaning of his own existence, that is, the essential truth about himself" (GS 41). She reveals to man the dignity and freedom of the human person. In relation to society, she contributes to strengthening the bonds of unity and communion among men; for the Spirit by whom she is led is a Spirit of unity, cohesion, and charity (GS 42). Finally, the Church, in her members, co-operates in the activities of other men, even at the level of their secular work, and has respect for the laws proper to each different discipline (GS 43).

4. Aware as she is of the help which she brings to the world, the Church recognizes also the help which she receives (GS 44). Never before has the Church made such a declaration. She receives from the world the richness and diversity of its cultures, and these offer her a language in which she can present the gospel to the men of each different time and each different *milieu*. The Church, moreover, realizes that the progress of mankind on a cultural, economic, social and political plane, and in the sphere of family life, contributes to the unity and progress of the ecclesial community. Even persecution and opposition from the world help the Church to purify and renew herself.[21]

5. To the account of the help which the Church receives from the world must be added *signs of the times*. In the very fact of its existence, the world, with its values, is charged with intelligiblity. The events and phenomena which go to make up

---

21. Y. Congar, "Le rôle de l'Église dans le monde de ce temps," in: *Vatican II, L'Église dans le monde de ce temps*, vol. 2: 305-327.

the course of human history and scan the progress of mankind constitute an implicit language, which the Church can and must read. The rise of the working class, for instance, the emancipation of colonized peoples, the forming of an international conscience, all these express deep human aspirations. When they are under- stood in the light of the gospel they have the value of *signs*.[22] "Moved by faith . . . the people of God tries to discern among the events, demands and desires of our time . . . which of them are authentic signs of God's presence or purpose" (GS 11). These are, as it were, so many *appeals* addressed to the gospel, to the Church, and to theology, so many stimulants to their action. They are "openings" for the gospel, points at which the world, being there more "penetrable," more easily allows Christianity to enter. To read the signs of the time is to perceive the relationship beween the values of the world and the message of salvation. The world's questions, Fr. Congar observes, "are so many knocks on the cover of the gospel to make it open at the relevant page, so many piercings of the side of the Church so that the saving water and blood may flow out through her." [23] The Church needs, therefore, by a sort of prophetic intuition, to become aware of the event which is a sign and of what it means. And this awareness is possible only if the Church, as once the prophet was, is intensely present in the world, so that she can discover in the world's activities the signs of the progress of the kingdom of God. The discerning of signs presupposes that the Church is concretely involved, that she is in "com- munion with the problems and hopes and tragedies of the world." [24] The Church should go out to meet the men of her time, to find and disclose the grace of salvation at work in the tissue of their history.

---

22. M.-D. Chenu, "Les signes des temps," NRT 87 (1965): 29-39; *Ibid.*, "Les signes des temps," in: K. Rahner, and collaborators, *Gaudium et Spes. L'Église dans le monde de ce temps* (Paris, Mame, 1967), pp. 97-116; G. Langevin, "Intelligence de la foi et lecture des signes du temps," in: *La foi et le temps* (Bruges and Paris, 1969), pp. 11-30.
23. Y. Congar, "L'Église et le monde," *Esprit*, 33 (1965): 346.
24. M.-D. Chenu, "Un Peuple prophétique," *Esprit*, 35 (1967): 605.

So, more conscious of her true nature and of the nature of her relationship to the world, the twentieth century Church is in search of new forms of presence and engagement.[25] This is a difficult matter; for the world in whose life she is to engage is itself searching, searching for a language, for new social and political structures, new terms of reference, a new image of the cosmos. It is in the life of this world where the only defining element is the undefined, the unforeseeable, that the Church has to engage. The Church, moreover, lives in a cultural context, a civic, political, scientific, economic and artistic context, which is no longer the work of Christians alone. Christians live in a state of diaspora in a secularized world. The life of faith is, in consequence, no longer an affair of inheritance or background, but an affair of personal decision, of unceasing victory over odds. In this new world, the Church must be a Church with living members, operative and responsible, carrying within themselves the gospel and the spirit of the gospel, in the midst of their social, professional and family life. This sort of action belongs to the influence which is called witness, and which is exercised in animating a *milieu*, by infusing meaning into it, by living within and radiating life. And this action has to penetrate and give life to all *milieux*, at every level of society. In this respect enormous progress remains to be made. For example, the Church is still very little involved in the international world, in the working-class world, in the university world, in the world of international politics (the world of the United Nations) or in the world of international economics (the world of the Common Market).

Besides this kind of influence, the Church can, as a visible, historical, social reality, affect the way the secular world develops and thus co-operate with it for the good of mankind. There is here a new field of action for the Church. It is, indeed, impossible for her to remain indifferent to the world's discussions, on peace, for instance, or on over-population, or on help for

---

25. The word engagement is more appropriate here than insertion, since we are concerned with a new relationship to the world based on a deeper understanding of the mystery of the Church.

undeveloped countries. The answers to problems of this sort cannot be derived directly from revelation: the solutions proposed by the Church, however much inspired they may be by the spirit of the gospel, are chosen from an analysis of the actual situation of the Church and the secular world today. It is a matter of suggesting, in collaboration with the secular world, certain orientations or certain limits of a practical order, which might help the progress of the world to take a course which would constitute progress towards salvation. This advisory *rôle* which the Church can take up in relation to the secular world, is a service to the world as such, and at the same time is part of the prophetic function of the Church.[26] These new forms of presence and engagement in the secular world carry with them, it hardly needs to be said, dangers which can already be discerned.

1. The chief danger is that of reducing Christianity to a form of *humanism* (anthropologism, sociologism, or psychologism). Under the pretext of a conversion to a proper interest in man and a proper openness to the world, the Church runs the risk of dissolving herself in them, which would be betraying her mission. For the Church does not exist only for the world. She exists for God. It is the overflow of her love for God which carries her towards the world, so that the world may live in God, and God in all men, and all things be summed up in Jesus Christ (Eph 1). All the other dangers can be reduced to the fundamental danger of forgetting this.

2. There is a tendency to make man the measure and criterion of the initiatives of God. God is so completely adapted to the

26. K. Rahner, "Reflexions théologiques sur le problème de la secularisation," in: *La théologie du Renouveau* (2 vols., Toronto and Paris, 1968), vol. 2: 257-279; English translation, *Theology for Renewal* (New York, 1965); E. Schillebeeckx, "Foi chrétienne et attente terrestre," in: K. Rahner and collaborators, *Gaudium et Spes. L'Église dans le monde de ce temps* (Paris, 1967), pp. 117-158; J. B. Metz, "L'Église et le monde," in *Théologie d'aujourd'hui et de demain* (Paris, 1967), pp. 139-155; C. Duquoc, "L'Église et le monde," *Lumière et Vie*, 75 (1965): 47-78.

human outlook that there is no longer any room for his free intervention in human history. Consequently miracle, Incarnation, resurrection, redemption, salvation are emptied of their content. God is reduced to the meaning man wants to give him, in his understanding of himself and his relations with others. In this way one arrives at the encyclopedists' notion of a *Deus otiosus*, an inert and distant Deity, who is no trouble or encumbrance, and above all gives no scandal to anyone.

3. There is a danger, in an effort to bring men together, of reducing Christ to *inter-subjectivity*: Christ is *the other*, and in the end the other becomes the reality of which Christ is only the symbol. Love for God becomes a mere symbol of human solidarity. The first commandment is swallowed up in the second. First Christ disappears, and then, soon afterwards, Jesus of Nazareth himself.

4. There is a danger of reducing religion to ethics, of making Christ a professor of humanism and levelling down his message in order to eliminate the scandal of the cross and all forms of renunciation. In short there is a danger of arriving at a diluted Christianity, a Christianity which has been flattened out, so that nothing in it stands out in contrast to its surroundings, in order to make it an easy religion, acceptable to everybody, a religion everyone can manage at no great cost, in the spirit of liberal Protestantism.

5. There is a danger of changing from a hierarchical Church to a democratic Church, in which functions or ministries would be based on representation of those to be served and the delegation by them of authority and power. In reality the Church's structure transcends both the autocratic model and the democratic model. For it is Christ who founds, constructs, sanctifies and governs his Body; and all power comes from him through the mission entrusted to the apostles and their successors. The democratic model could not therefore be applied completely to the Church.[27]

27. P. Eyt, "Vers une Église démocratique?" NRT 91 (1969): 597-613.

6. Finally there is a danger of a *generalized relativism,* a danger, for instance, of attaching little importance to the dogmatic expression of revelation, provided that an inner attitude continues to subsist—a relationship with God, salvation through faith. In the same way, there may be, in practice, an indifference with regard to the historical reality underlying the biblical narratives (of the resurrection for example, or other miracles): what matters, it may be said, is the *meaning* given to them. Again, it may be said that it does not matter very much which Church one adopts; for all are valid. By continually insisting on the universal grace of salvation, one may come to ask oneself: why the Church at all? Why the gospel? Why the sacraments? Why the missions?

The Church's manner of engaging in the world which is being shaped today is still too ill-defined for us to speak with certainty of whether these dangers are deep or lasting. There is no question therefore of taking up a uselessly alarmist attitude, but rather of recognizing in a clear-headed fashion that these dangers are real, solidly attested and a cause of anxiety in many different countries. The Church of the Second Vatican Council is trying to regain her hold on man in the twentieth century, but she is still in search of new forms of presence and dialogue, of engagement and action.[28]

9. Conclusion

So, distant from the world, but engaged in it, engaged in human history in order to save human beings, the Church cannot avoid the risks of being involved in time. The problem of

---

28. The dangers indicated have been denounced on occasion with vehemence. See for instance: H. U. Von Balthasar, *Cordula ou l'épreuve décisive* (Paris, 1968); L. Bouyer, *La décomposition du catholicisme* (Paris, 1968), trans., *The Decomposition of Catholicism* (New York, no date); A. Manaranche, *Je crois en Jésus-Christ aujourd'hui* (Paris, 1968), pp. 9-36; *Ibid., Quel salut?* (Paris, 1969); H. de Lubac, *L'Église dans la crise actuelle* (Paris, 1969); *Ibid., L'Éternel féminin* (Paris, 1968), chapter "La Crise"; Y. Congar, *Au milieu des orages* (Paris, 1969); K. Rahner, *Faith Today* (London, 1967).

maintaining a balance between too much insertion in history and too little, is beyond all doubt one of the most exacting problems that she has to solve. And if no satisfactory solution has so far been found, it is no doubt because none exists. The Church lives and must live in a constant state of tension, which is part of her nature as a society at once human and divine, incarnate in time and affected by the limitations of man's spatio-temporal condition.

At this point another remark seems called for. To acknowledge that the Church has, for two thousand years, been constantly *engaging and disengaging herself* is *ipso facto* to acknowledge that each epoch she has passed through has left traces in the Church. When she passes from one age to another, from one type of society to another, there is inevitably something still left in her of previous adaptations. These vestiges of her former experience give the appearance of a persistence in anachronism. There are some, weary of the slow weight of institutions, who want to abolish them, to shatter structures altogether. But is this not to dream of an ideal Church, a Church in the abstract, deprived of her human constitution, without any real link with the history of mankind? In the Church, as in all earthly societies, each age leaves its traces in the age which follows. History shows that even a Council is subject to this law of temporality. The Second Vatican Council is, without doubt, the greatest reforming operation ever accomplished in the Church. And yet the real meaning of the Council will not be apparent for several decades. The Church is moving from a past which has not yet disappeared to a future which is only just beginning. The Council of Trent gave its name to a period of more than four hundred years; and the present Council marks a much deeper change than the Council of Trent. We should not, therefore, be surprised at the slowness of the transition, given the scope of the operation involved. There is room, rather, for surprise at the important results already accomplished, in the spheres of ecumenism, liturgy, ecclesiology and pastoral life, as also at the even more decisive level of attitude—in dialogue, service, participation, religious liberty, inwardness and so on. The history of the Church witnesses also that if it is true that the renewal of structures or the creation of more adequate structures is of great importance in order that the Church may continue to advance according to the human rhythms of each new age, it is still more true that the essentials of reform lie in a reform of mentalities and hearts, which puts man once again under the guidance of the Spirit. The authentic reformers are those who have given the Church the only thing she really needs—saints.

This acknowledged, how are we to explain the permanence of the Church in spite of all these dangers from temporality with which she is surrounded, and in spite of all that makes for decadence and death? Even if, at each point in history, we can or could find a coherent and plausible explanation in the context of the time, how are we to explain that circumstances always favor the Church and allow her to survive? If one appeals to chance, how is one to explain that chance always works in her favor? "The Church, considered at each stage in her history, appears as an improbable phenomenon, a failing, vulnerable thing, antique and prophetic, a heap of ruins out of which seeds sprout, always engaged in dying and being reborn." [29] The Church remains a riddle. She should have been dead long ago. And yet she is still here. Like Israel, which thanks to her prophets survived in the midst of foreign occupation, in spite of the dangers of nationalism within and the pressure of nature worship without, the Church survives. But hers is a survival in a more proper sense than that of Jewish religion, which has never been able to disentangle itself from its racial, institutional and ritual conditioning; for the Church constantly engages and disengages herself. She is not afraid, in each new age, to re-engage in an unknown, formidable world, which threatens her with assimilation and the risk of being involved in its own ruin.

Inserted, bogged down in the political structures of the

---

29. J. Guitton, *L'Évangile et l'Église*, pp. 389-390; trans., *The Church and the Gospel*.

Roman Empire, of feudalism, of medieval Christendom and of the modern nation states, the Church should have shared their danger and their death. In recent centuries, on the other hand, more and more at liberty as far as the State is concerned, but more and more absent from the world, the Church, like some *grande dame,* very aristocratic but very antique, should have succumbed to a seclusion worse than death. But the astonishing thing, the paradox, is that she did neither, that she always subsists, and always finds the strength to live anew and be young again. Twenty centuries have not been able to exhaust her unity or her vitality. In human history as we know it, such permanence within the conditions of temporality constitutes a *riddle.* To be sure, we know through faith, that the Church will not die. She will live, indestructible in duration, unchanging in stability, because her permanence, her stability, her unity, are not of man but of God and the Spirit of God. Nevertheless, the, as it were, historical outcrop of this action of the Spirit may perhaps arrest the attention of the believer, and even of the unbeliever, and awaken him to the presence of the Mystery. For anyone aware of all that there is of fragility and decay in human history will be amazed that an institution so *inserted* into, so *involved* in this history, and submitted to such *tensions* for twenty centuries, should have succeeded in preserving its identity, its consistency, and its dynamism. The *phenomenon* seems to open upon a *mystery.*

The Paradox of Sin and Holiness In the Church

The problem and ways of approach to it

The third and greatest paradox of the Church is that of the co-existence in her of sin and holiness. This is the paradox, too, which gives rise to most questioning, even among believers; for to many it is a stumbling block, a scandal, pure non-sense. And the way we should present this paradox is an excellent example of the mutual support there should be between pastoral studies and theology proper.

To assess the dimensions of the paradox and perceive the elements which go to make it up, there is no better course than to set out the statements of the magisterium on the subject. We are faced with a double series of texts.

1. *The declarations of the magisterium*

Holy is the first adjective which was applied to the word *Church*. In the baptismal creed of Jerusalem, about 348, the believer declared his faith εἰς μίαν ἁγίαν καθολικὴν ἐκκλησίαν (DS 41). The creed of Epiphanius, in 374, equally declared the Church to be holy (DS 42). The Nicaeno-Constantinopolitan creed, in 381, repeated: "Credimus ... unam, *sanctam* catholicam et apostolicam Ecclesiam" (DS 150).

Nearer to our own time, the Second Vatican Council has several texts in which it declares that the Church is *holy*. For

instance: it was the Father's will "to call together all those
who believe in Christ to form a *holy* Church" (LG 2); "the
mystery of the *holy* Church is manifested in her foundation"
(LG 5); "Christ, the only Mediator, creates and sustains unceasingly on earth his *holy* Church" (LG 8); "The baptized
are consecrated as a *holy* priesthood" (LG 10); "the *holy* People
of God share also in the prophetic function of Christ" (LG 12);
"the Church on earth is already distinguished by a *holiness* which
though imperfect is real" (LG 48).

Side by side with these solid affirmations of the holiness of
the Church, there are many texts on the sinful members of the
Church, and on a Church in need of repentance. There are,
first of all, the condemnations by the magisterium of those
who wanted to reduce the Church to the righteous, to those in
grace, to her holy members alone. Clement XI, in 1713, rejected
the proposition of Paschase Quesnel that "the Church, that is
to say the total Christ, has as head the Incarnate Word and as
members all the saints." [1] The synod of Pistoia, under Pius
VI, in 1794, condemned as heretical the proposition that "only
the faithful who are perfect adorers in spirit and in truth belong to the body of the Church." [2] The Council of Constance,
in 1415, condemned the proposition of John Huss, which wanted
to reduce the Church to those predestined alone: "the holy universal Church is one, constituted by all the predestined." [3] Finally,
Pius XII's encyclical, *Mystici Corporis,* in 1943, declared that
sinners remained members of the Church, "for it is not every sin,
even if it be a grave sin, that of its nature—as is the case with
schism or heresy or apostasy—separates a man from the body
of the Church." [4]

---

1. "Ecclesia sive integer Christus Incarnatum Verbum habet ut caput,
omnes vero sanctos ut membra" (DS 2474).
2. "Ecclesia ... intellecta hoc sensu, ut ad corpus Ecclesiae non per-
tineant nisi fideles, qui sunt perfecti adoratores in spiritu et veritate"
(DS 2615).
3. "Unica est sancta universalis Ecclesia, quae est praedestinatorum
universitas" (DS 1201).
4. "Siquidem non omne admissum etsi grave scelus ejusmodi est, ut —
sicut schisma vel haeresis vel apostasia faciunt—suapte natura hominem

On the subject of sin in the Church and her sinful members, the Second Vatican Council makes the following declarations.

"While Christ, holy, blameless and unstained (Heb 7:26), knew no sin (2 Cor 5:21), . . . the Church, who includes sinners within her, is at once holy and always in need of purification, and constantly pursues her efforts at penitence and renewal." [5]

"As she advances through temptations and tribulations, the Church is strengthened by the power of God's grace, which was promised to her so that she should not fail in the perfection of her faithfulness through the weakness of the flesh, but should remain a Bride worthy of her Lord, ceaselessly renewing herself through the action of the Holy Spirit, until she attains by means of the cross to the light of that Sun which has no setting." [6]

"Mother Church does not cease to hope and pray and work for this, exhorting her children to penitence and renewal, so that the sign of Christ may shine more brightly in the face of his Church." [7]

Christ has communicated his own power to his disciples "so that they may, through their renunciation and holiness of life, overcome the power of sin in themselves." [8] Christ's faithful people "strive to grow in holiness through overcoming sin." [9]

---

ab Ecclesiae corpore separet" (DS 3803).

5. "Dum vero Christus, sanctus, innocens, impollutus (Heb 7:26), peccatum non novit (2 Cor 5:21), Ecclesia in proprio sinu peccatores complectens, sancta simul et semper purificanda, poenitentiam et renovationem continuo prosequitur" (LG 8).

6. "Per tentationes vero et tribulationes procedens Ecclesia virtute gratiae Dei sibi a Domino promissae confortatur, ut in infirmitate carnis a perfecta fidelitate non deficiat, sed Domini sui digna Sponsa remaneat, et sub actione Spiritus Sancti, seipsam renovare non desinat, donec per crucem perveniat ad lucem quae nescit occasum" (LG 9).

7. "Ecclesia Mater precari, sperare et agere non desinit, filiosque ad purificationem et renovationem exhortatur, ut signum Christi super faciem Ecclesiae clarius effulgeat" (LG 15: see also GS 43).

8. "Quam potestatem discipulis communicavit, ut et illi in regali libertate constituantur et sui abnegatione vitaque sancta regnum peccati in seipsis devincant" (LG 36).

9. "Christifideles adhuc nituntur, ut devincentes peccatum in sanctitate crescant" (LG 65).

Christian division "is a source of scandal to the world, and an obstacle to the most holy of all causes, the preaching of the gospel to every creature." [10]

The Second Vatican Council makes, then, a double series of statements. On the one hand the Church is holy; on the other, she is a pilgrim Church whose members are sinners, vulnerable, weak, assailed by temptations, constantly in need of repentance and reform. She has been a source of scandal, and by her division she has hindered the spreading of the gospel. If the Church is constantly in need of purification and renewal, and if sinners, although they are sinners, remain members of the Church, are we to conclude that the Church herself is sinful? The Council nowhere deals systematically with the disturbing question of the co-existence of sin and holiness in the Church. Nevertheless, it never uses the expression *sinful Church*. The question remains open, left to the research and discussion of theologians.

2. *The nature and dimensions of the paradox*

It is obvious that Catholicism takes the Church's holiness seriously. On the one hand, the Church is holy: we have here a constant declaration on the part of the magisterium, which we cannot reject. But in the face of this declaration, there arises another, no less radical: the Church needs constantly to purify and reform herself.

We must avoid here, of course, confusing sin and what is simply historical error, human clumsiness, lack of foresight, the results of the fact that the Church has, in successive ages, involved herself in human history, and the defects and limitations of national temperaments—Jewish ritualism and formalism for instance, Greek intellectualism and conceptualism, Roman conservatism and juridicism, Germanic subjectivism and mysticism in its more misty sense, the particularism of the Western

---

10. "Quae sane divisio et aperte voluntati Christi contradicit et scandalo est mundo atque sanctissimae causae praedicandi Evangelium omni creaturae affert detrimentum" (UR 1).

Church.[11] It is true that men are more sensitive in the twentieth century than they were formerly to these historical errors or exhibitions of awkwardness, which one cannot, properly speaking, call sins.

But side by side with these non-culpable weaknesses, and the onus of history, there are faults and real sins. And often, beneath the historical failings, passions and real vices are hidden. There are in the Church not merely mistakes attributable to human history in general; there is also a history of the sins of the Church.

St. Paul's letters already witness to the fact that there were in the communities of the early Church, instances of a lack of faith and charity, of envy, of lying, of greed, of unchastity. In every one of the Apostle's letters there are to be found exhortations against sin: exhortations not to go back to former habits, not to go on building up the body of sin, exhortations to lead a life worthy of those who are dead to sin. It is impossible to escape the conclusion: short of conceiving the Church as an idealized hypostasis, separate from Christians themselves, we must, it would seem, speak of a "sinful" Church. The Church is an organic society of the baptized, of the members of Christ. The actions of Christians are the actions of the members of Christ. The sins of the members of the Church are the sins of the People of God. And because these sinners remain members of the Church it must be said that the sins of Christians affect the Church herself. They sully, they defile the mysterious and holy Body of Christ.

The Church is thus a communion of sinners and a communion of saints. In spite of her sin, the Church is called *holy*, and although she is holy, she is stained with *sin*. In the words of the evocative and pregnant antithesis used by the Fathers of the Church and taken up again by Von Balthasar, the Church is a *casta meretrix, a* "chaste prostitute." [12] Such is the paradox.

11. H. Küng, *L'Église* (2 vols., Paris, 1967), vol. 2: 450-451; English translations, *The Church* (New York, 1968; London, 1969).

12. H. U. Von Balthasar, "Casta Meretrix," in: *Sponsa Verbi* (Einsiedeln, 1960), pp. 203-205.

How are we to reconcile these two affirmations, the affirmation that the Church is holy, and at the same time, the affirmation that she is sinful? Have both these affirmations the same weight? Are they both true for the same reason? Which is the decisive, the definitive note of the Church, her sin or her holiness? And what is the relation of one to the other? In what sense exactly is it true to speak of a "sinful" Church?

There are two different ways of looking at this paradox: from the dogmatic point of view and from the apologetic point of view. Looked at from inside, that is in the light of revelation and faith, the paradox is more easily resolved. Yet, even with this illumination, it remains difficult in its depths to understand. Looked at from outside, from the point of view of the unbeliever, the paradox of a Church at once holy and sinful poses an acute problem for theology. How indeed, in a secularized, self-sufficient world, can the Church be a sign of a transcendent reality necessary for the fulfillment of human life? And above all, how can a tarnished Church still be an *expressive sign* of the salvation she proclaims? How can she call herself a sign lifted up before the nations? Is she not rather a counter-sign, a witness-against? How can the Church, in her concrete reality still *give-a-sign* to those outside her, to pagans, that she is the place of salvation, the "universal sacrament of salvation" willed by God? Here, even more than in the two paradoxes we examined earlier, a complementary vision, dogmatic and apologetic, seems indispensable.

3. *Ways of approach*

To throw light on the paradox of sin and holiness in the Church, one can, I think, make use of a three-fold way of approach. The first way consists in considering the biblical concept of *holiness,* so that one may have a notion of it which conforms to that of revelation itself; the second way consists in studying the great biblical images which express the mystery of the Church, especially those of the People of God, the Bride, and the Body of Christ; the third and last way consists in interrogating the theologians, and examining the solutions they have proposed. These three ways, as we shall see, converge, and lead us in the same direction.

The first way of approach: the biblical conception of holiness

The origins of the word ἅγιος are biblical. It is therefore scripture we must interrogate if we are to understand the idea of holiness aright.[13] In the Old Testament, as in the New, holiness is first of all something proper to God. To say *God* is to say *holiness;* it is all one. God's holiness designates, quite simply, the mystery of his life. Holy, holy, holy, is Yahweh (Is 6:3). In Amos 4:2, God swears by his holiness, that is, by his inmost essence, which distinguishes him from all which is created, and *a fortiori,* from all which is sinful. Yahweh's *name* is holy like his person, since the name, according to Semitic ways of thought is itself the person. Holiness, then, is identical with divinity. In prophetic theology especially, holiness connotes the absolute moral transcendence of God as compared with man. While man is sinful and unfaithful, God is love and charity. "I will not return to destroy Ephraim; for I am God and not man: in the midst of thee I am the Holy one, and it is not my will to destroy" (Hos 11:9). In Hosea, God's holiness is an inexhaustible source of love for his people. Holiness in the Old Testament, then, designates above all what is innermost in God, the core of the divine life.

In the New Testament, in the same way, holiness takes its reference from God, and designates his inmost essence (Rev 4:8). If Christ is holy, it is precisely because he is the very

---

13. On the biblical conception of holiness: see: O. Procksch and G. Kuhn, article ἅγιος, TWZNT, 1: 87-115; P. Van Imschoot, *Théologie de l'Ancien Testament* (2 vols., Paris-Tournai-Rome, 1954-1956); L. Cerfaux, *La théologie de l'Église suivant S. Paul* (Paris, 1948), pp. 89-110; E. Pax, "Heilig," in: J. B. Bauer, ed., *Bibeltheologisches Wörterbuch,* 1: 606-612; Y. Congar, "L'Église est sainte," *Angelicum,* 42 (1965): 273-279; W. Dommershausen, "Heiligkeit, ein Altestamentliches Sozialprinzip." *Tübinger Theologische Quartalschrift,* 148 (1968): 153-166.

reality of God among us, the Word of God made flesh and dwelling among us (Jn 1:14), the only Son, who is in the innermost depths of the Father (Jn 1:18). As holy, Christ has the attributes of God (Rev 6:10). *Holy* designates Christ's divinity.

We can, therefore, distinguish in the biblical concept of holiness a three-fold sense.

1. *The first sense* — God alone being holy, a reality is called holy in so far as it has reference to God, either because it comes from God, or because it is consecrated to him, and therefore belongs to him.

So, in the Old Testament, the People of God is a holy People (Ex 19:6; 24:4-8): it comes from God, drawn out of the nothing of servitude, literally created by him; and it belongs to God, united and consecrated to him in a deep covenant. There are many texts on this subject: "Thou art a people *holy* to the Lord thy God: the Lord thy God has chosen thee to be his own people, out of all the peoples that are on the face of the earth" (Dt 7:6; 14:2; 26:19; Is 62:12; 63:18; Jer 2:3; Am 3:2). In the same way the commandments are holy (Jer 23:9), the earth is holy (Ex 3:5), Jerusalem is holy (Is 56:7), priests are holy (Ps 132:9 and 16), because they are *from* God and *for* God.

Again, in the New Testament, individual Christians and the whole People together constitute a holy temple (Eph 2:21), a holy priesthood (I P 2:5), a holy nation (I P 2:9), in virtue of their election and covenant in Jesus Christ. Paul, like the author of *Acts* and the author of *Revelation*, calls the Christians of his own time *saints.* Applied first to the community at Jerusalem (1 Cor 16:1; 2 Cor 8:4; 9:1 and 12; Rm 15:25 and 31), that is to say, to Jewish Christians, the expression was then extended to non-Jewish Christians (Rm 16:2; Eph 1:1; Phil 1:1; Col 1:2), since Jews and Gentiles alike had been called by God to the obedience of faith, and by baptism consecrated to Christ. *Saints* came in the end to designate the whole body of Christians as such.

The Church is holy, then, because she is consecrated to God, by election, vocation and covenant, like the old Israel. From all eternity she has been chosen by God, set apart to fulfill "the mystery of his will, the purpose to unite all things in Christ" (Eph 1:9). The primordial holiness of the Church is a holiness of being chosen and set apart. Destined to be the *locus* of God's worship and the instrument of his salvation, she is not one secular form of life among others, but the life, the being, which is consecrated and set apart. She belongs to Christ, who has gained her with his own blood, who has purified her from her sin in his own passion and death, and who does not cease to sanctify her through his own Spirit (Eph 5:26-27). The Church belongs to the Lord; she is vowed to his service.

2. *The second sense* — This holiness of election, of vocation, of belonging, calls for the ethical expression of a holy life. Israel is the People of God: it belongs to God; it is consecrated to him. This holiness of belonging demands a moral holiness: "Be holy as I am holy" (Lev 19:2). God invites his people to *communion* with him. But how is such a union conceivable unless Israel adopts a *style of life* which conforms to this alliance with a holy God? The law of Israel, or the decalogue, simply expresses the character of that *commercium* which should exist between God and his people. Because God is holy, he desires a people set apart, united to him, holy as he is holy. The observance of the decalogue signifies that Israel is really God's people, really belongs to God. Jeremiah sums up the whole situation when he says, "Listen to my voice, and I will be your God, and you shall be my people" (Jer 7:23).[14]

The same sort of thing holds true in the New Testament. The Christian is essentially someone called by God, in Jesus Christ, to a communion of life with the divine persons. For St. Paul, the corollary of this vocation in Christ is a *holy life*, a *filial life*, after the example of Christ, who in all things does, in the Spirit of love, the Father's will (Phil 2:6-11). Just as, formerly, Yahweh's covenant with Israel involved the obligation to holiness of life, so in the same way, vocation in Christ should

14. E. Hamel, *Les Dix Paroles* (Brussels-Paris-Montreal, 1969), pp. 11-40.

be accompanied by faithfulness to the precepts which express God's will in terms of the life of the individual. Christians are holy if they observe the commandments of a holy God (Jn 14:15). The Church must be not only the assembly of those who are called to holiness, but also the assembly of those who try faithfully to live their calling, their belonging, through baptism, to Christ, to God.

3. *The third sense* — Lastly, a reality can be said to be holy when it sanctifies. God is holy, Christ and his Spirit are holy, because they sanctify, because they are the source of sanctification and holiness. The Church is holy in this sense, since she is the source of sanctification through the gifts which she has received from Christ: the gospel, the ministry, the sacraments.

Already, from this brief semantic study, an initial conclusion emerges. Holiness in the biblical sense has, as it were, two sides. (1) God alone is holy, and all holiness comes from God. The People of God is holy, the Church is holy, because chosen, called by God, consecrated to God and to Christ in baptism. (2) This holiness which proceeds from God's initiative, from grace, calls for a holiness in response, on man's part, that is, an ethical holiness. This distinction already throws light on the paradox of sin and holiness in the Church. It puts us into a context of personal relationships, of gratuitous love on the part of God, of free and loving response on the part of man.

The second way of approach: the great images of the Church

The mystery of the Church is inexhaustible. No expression, no image, can express the whole of it. The biblical authors, therefore, had to make use of many different ways of approach to the one mystery, each symbol serving to illuminate a single aspect, each image serving to complement or correct another.[15] Following the example of revelation itself, the Second Vatican Council has, in attempting to express the reality of the Church,

---

15. H. de Lubac, *Paradoxe et Mystère de l'Église* (Paris, 1967), p. 44; trans., *The Church: Paradox and Mystery* (Alba House, New York, 1970).

made use of these many ways. It speaks of the fold (*ovile*), of God's field (*ager Dei*), of God's house (*aedificatio Dei*), of the People of God, the Bride of Christ, the Body of Christ, the new Jerusalem (LG 6-7). All these images have their roots in the Old Testament and develop in the New. Let us deal with those among them which, of their nature, can illuminate for us the paradox of sin and holiness in the Church. I think that as we go from one to another, the mystery of the union between God and his Church will grow deeper and deeper.

The People of God

It is common knowledge that the Council, after some hesitation, adopted the image of the People of God [16] as its fundamental way of presenting the Church. We can, therefore, eliminate at the outset all conception of an hypostasized Church, a sort of meta-historical, supra-personal institution, separate from the human beings who go to make it up, preserved from the contamination of every sin. The image of the People of God underlines the fact that the Church does not exist without human beings. It throws into high relief several essential aspects of the Church, not so well expressed by the images of the Body, the Temple and the Bride. It stresses particularly the following aspects.

1. *The communal aspect.* In this connection, the idea behind the image of the People of God is more fundamental, more primitive, than that behind the image of the Body of Christ.

---

16. On the image of the people of God, see: L. Cerfaux, "Les images symboliques de l'Église dans le Nouveau Testament," in: G. Baraúna, ed., *L'Église de Vatican II* (2 vols., Paris, 1966), vol. 2, pp. 243ff.; G. Langevin, "L'Église, Peuple de Dieu," in: *La foi et le temps* (Bruges and Paris, 1969), pp. 44-55; L. Cerfaux, *La théologie de l'Église suivant S. Paul* (Paris, 1948), pp. 31-57; Y. Congar, "The People of God," *Concilium*, n. 1 (1955): 7-16; H. Küng, *L'Église*, 1: 154-185; English translations, *The Church*. Fr. Congar's article has been reissued in: Y. Congar, *Cette Église que j'aime* (Paris, 1968); English translation, *This Church that I love* (New York, 1969).

The People of God is the community of slaves set free, formed and united by the covenant. In the New Testament it is the community of the baptized. The expression stresses the fundamental equality of all the members of the Church in the "belongingness" constituted by baptism. The People of God precedes the hierarchy. All the members of the People of God are chosen and holy; they are all disciples and brethren. It is important, from the ecumenical point of view, to put in the foreground of our vision of the Church, not the hierarchy, but the community of those baptized into Christ.

2. *The aspect of the divine initiative.* The bond between God and his people is based on the free and loving intervention of God in this People's history. Israel exists only in virtue of God's gracious initiative, by which it is constituted. It is born out of nothingness and formed of those to whom God has given *grace.* Election, salvation, covenant are all pure *gifts.* The same is true of the Church, the new People whom Christ has gained by his blood and his death. It is God who chooses, who calls and calls together, who saves and sanctifies.

3. *The aspect of historical continuity in the sphere of salvation.* To speak of the People of God is to suggest the whole history of salvation, from its beginnings to its final fulfillment. It is to suggest all the stages in the life of this People: its infidelities and God's faithfulness. Israel and the Church are one continuous People of God. And this People appears to be constantly unfaithful, in contrast to the faithfulness of God. After the breaking of the old covenant, God promised a new and final covenant, with new gifts. Once more he would intervene, would have mercy, would forgive and save. Yahweh would raise up a new People with a new spirit and a new heart. The Church is the historical fulfillment of this promise of final salvation. She is the new People of God. But in contrast to the old People, this new People will be formed of both Jews and Gentiles.

4. *The dynamic and missionary aspect* of a Church laboring to bring all peoples together again. For the Church could not be

the universal sacrament of salvation without visibly manifesting what is a very exigence of her nature and calling.

5. *The eschatological aspect.* The Church is essentially a pilgrim People, a caravan. She could not finally establish herself here in this world. She could not "settle down." On the march towards the eschatological kingdom, she traverses the centuries, her eyes turned constantly towards new horizons. The Church is *in transit.* And because this People is *en route,* it is subject to the vicissitudes of time: it is weak and sinful; it is constantly in need of repentance and reform, of mercy and forgiveness. After the Exodus, the People of God murmured and was unfaithful. But this eschatological aspect stresses also that the Church journeys towards an *end,* which will be her rest and joy. It is a dialectic of *now* and *not yet.*

The bride of Yahweh and the Bride of Christ

The theme of the covenant between God and his people deepens in the image of the Bridegroom and the Bride, especially in the New Testament. For it is in order to espouse mankind, to make himself one flesh with men that the Son of God became the Son of man and was incarnate; in the Eucharist he makes himself the food of his Bride, who becomes the flesh of his flesh.

In the Old Testament, the People which broke the covenant was an adulterous and prostitute Bride. It is Hosea who inaugurates this theme, taken up again afterwards by the prophetic tradition, and often stressed by the Fathers of the Church. Ezekiel, especially, in chapters sixteen and twenty-three, developed in two vast allegories this theme of the faithlessness and prostitution of Israel, the Bride of Yahweh. In Ephesians 5:24-27, St. Paul presents Christ as the Bridegroom who purifies and sanctifies the sinful Bride, who makes her chaste and beautiful. This new image has certain aspects which throw light on the paradox of sin and holiness in the Church.

1. The image stresses *the initiative of God*: it is he who first loved and chose his Bride. He found her wounded and forsaken, covered with her own blood. He dressed her wounds, and healed her; he purified and adorned her. He remains faithful to her in spite of her infidelities. The Fathers of the Church insisted constantly on this change brought about by Christ. Before, the Church was a *meretrix,* a prostitute; Christ made her a chaste virgin. The Bride must never forget what once she was.

2. The image stresses the *interpersonal character* of the relationship between God and his Church, more than the image of the People-community does, and more than the image of the Body and its members, who are parts of an organic whole. It stresses the character of freedom in love, and reciprocity in gift. It stresses the free response of the Bride to the Bridegroom's love. The Church's love must answer the initial love of God; for what kind of love-making would it be where there was no response, no reciprocity?

3. Lastly, the image stresses the *permanent gifts* which the Bridegroom makes to the Bride: the gospel, the sacraments, and above all his Spirit, In the Old Testament, the gift of the Spirit was transient. In the New Testament, it is permanent. "The Church is faithful, thanks to the Spirit of God who gives her life... it is Christ glorified who has loved and continues to love her, without possibility of failure, either on his part or on the part of his Bride" (L. Cerfaux). The Church in this world will need ceaselessly to be purified, but she will never wholly betray her Bridegroom.

The Body of Christ

Although it can suggest a great deal, the image of the People of God cannot express the depths of the mystery of the Church. It could be said of this primitive image that it establishes the generic element which serves to express the continuity between the two covenants. But the Church's mode of association under the new covenant is expressed by the image of *the Body of Christ*. As a consequence of the union of the divine nature with human nature through the Incarnation of the Son, and of the resurrection of Christ, the Church is the Body of Christ. When the design for salvation in the People of God was realized in Christ, this People became the Body of Christ. The image of the Body expresses the Christological element in the Church of the New Testament, that is to say, what is specific in the mystery of the Church, as compared with the generic element expressed by the People of God.[17]

This third image connotes several aspects, whose order of importance it is important to respect.

1. First of all, the image stresses the inseparable union of Christ and the Church, of the Head and the members (Rm 12: 5; 1 Cor 12:12-27): this is a union even deeper than that in the earlier images: one same life circulates within the Head and the members of this unique organism. Through baptism and the Eucharist, we are incorporated into Christ: we become one with him. As children of the Father we have the right to the same inheritance as Christ (Eph 2:6; Col 3:1-4). We form a single Body of which Christ is the Head, and of which the Spirit is the life-giving and sanctifying principle (Eph 4:2-7). The Spirit of Christ is given to the Church, not merely because she is the People of God, but because she is the Body of Christ, because it is the same Spirit who gives life to the whole Body, to the Head and the members. *Lumen gentium* rightly says that Christ "shared with us his Spirit, who, being one and the same in the Head and the members, gives life to the whole Body, unites it and moves it, so that his action was compared by the Fathers to the function which is fulfilled in the human body by the principle of its life, the soul." [18]

---

17. A. Antón, "Hacia una síntesis de las nociones Cuerpo de Cristo y Pueblo de Dios en la eclesiología," *Estudios Eclesiasticos*, 44 (1969): 161-203.

18. "Ut autem in Illo incessanter renovemur (cf. Eph. 4, 23), dedit

Because Christ loves his Bride, the Church, as his own Body, she is indissolubly united to him. The Bride and the Bridegroom are no longer separate. Some members of the Church may of their own will withdraw from the life-giving and sanctifying influence of Christ and the Spirit, just as sickness may affect a member of the human body, but nothing could separate the Bridegroom from the Bride. Nothing could dry up or contaminate the source which ceaselessly gives life to the Body of Christ; for this source is God himself.

2. The image of the Body of Christ illustrates, in the second place, the organic *diversity* of members and functions in the same Body (Rm 12:4-5 and 1 Cor). And lastly it illustrates the Church's position in relationship to Christ who is her Head, and to the Spirit who is the life-giving principle of her Body.

Two conclusions may be drawn from consideration of these images of the Church.

1. When we speak of the Church, we speak of the whole People of God, not merely of the clergy, but of these and the rest of the faithful at the same time, of all the baptized, of all the members of Christ. This People is, in the New Testament, the Body of Christ. The Church includes then a *horizontal* element, that is, believing and baptized human beings, and *vertical* elements, that is Christ, the Head of the Body, the Shepherd of the People, and the Spirit of Christ, who does not cease to give life to the whole Body, and to sanctify it. To forget these vertical elements and reduce the Church simply to our

nobis de Spirito suo, qui unus et idem in Capite et in membris exsistens, totum corpus ita vivificat, unificat et movet, ut Ejus officium a sanctis Patribus comparari potuerit cum munere, quod principium vitae seu anima in corpore humano adimplet" (LG 7). On the image of the Church as the Body of Christ, see: L. Cerfaux, *La théologie de l'Église suivant S. Paul* (Paris, 1948), pp. 201-218; H. Küng, *L'Église*, 1: 310-332; English translations, *The Church*; A. Antón, "Hacia una síntesis de las nociones Cuerpo de Cristo y Pueblo de Dios en la ecclesiología," *Estudios Eclesiasticos*, 44 (1969): 161-203; H. Mühlen, *Una Mystica Persona* (Paderborn, 1967²).

human selves would be to empty the Church of her specific element, and reduce her to a purely human and natural society. The Church, to be sure, is we ourselves, poor sinners that we are, but with Christ, our Head, and his Spirit, the source and principle of holiness and supernatural life.

2. In each image studied we shall notice an aspect of an initiative taken, a vocation given, an appeal addressed, a sanctifying action coming from God; and on the other hand an aspect of free response to this initiative and appeal. The People of God is asked to be faithful to God who is holy, and to his covenant. The Bride is asked to respond to the Bridegroom's love. The Christian, says St. Paul, must not sully in its members the Body of Christ, or profane the Temple of the Spirit. The initial holiness, which comes from God, calls for a holiness in response, an ethical holiness. Union and communion with God, who is holy, demands a style of life which is in conformity with such a union and communion.

3. *The third way of approach: the reflection of theologians*

Theological reflection has been slow in giving consideration to the paradox of sin and holiness in the Church. To tell the truth, most articles bearing upon the subject have been written within the last ten years. There is nothing astonishing in this delay; for the theology of the Counter-Reformation practically eliminated the problem by its very conception of the Church. It is therefore thanks to the renewal in ecclesiology that the paradox has aroused new interest among those engaged in research. Brief as it is, the history of theological reflection on the subject is nonetheless revealing.[19]

1. *Early heresies*: The segregation of "holy" members. Gnostics, Novatians, Donatists, Montanists, Cathars, and later Paschase Quesnel and John Huss wanted to exclude sinful members from

---

19. On this subject see especially an article by P. McGoldrick, "Sin and the Holy Church," *The Irish Theological Quarterly*, 32 (1965): 3-27.

the Church and keep within her only the pure and sinless, the "saints," the "elect." The early Councils, as we have seen, took their stand against this conception.

2. *St. Augustine.* For St. Augustine, the Church was an inextricable mixture of wheat and tares: of good and bad (PL 36, 539), of the upright and the sinful (PL 35, 1763). If the Church is *holy*, this can be so only through her upright members (PL 43, 195 and 241:42, 291), who are animated by the Spirit and live the life of charity. This Church, which is the real Church, is therefore hidden in this world within the visible community. The Church of which St. Paul speaks, perfectly pure and holy (Eph 5:26-27), belongs to eschatology.

3. *The Middle Ages.* Medieval theological reflection was relatively hesitant about the ecclesial status of the sinner. On the one hand, he was recognized as a member of the Church in so far as the Church is the community of the faithful constituted by belief and baptism. On the other hand, he could not be a member of the real Church, since he did not belong to the *communio sanctorum*, which was composed of the upright, living the life of the Holy Spirit. The Middle Ages, then, like Augustine, distinguished a double sense of belonging to the Church, an *exterior* belonging, without merit, which was the way the sinful belonged, and an *interior*, meritorious belonging, which was that of the upright, and the only valid belonging. For how could the spirit animate a dead member? The Middle Ages seem, therefore, to share the ambiguity of the Augustinian conception of the holy Church hidden within the visible community. It needed the errors of Wiclif and John Huss for the magisterium to reaffirm that the sinful really belonged to the Church.[20]

---

20. G. Dejaifve, "L'Église catholique peut-elle entrer dans la repentance oecuménique?" NRT 84 (1962): 231-232; Landgraf, "Sünde und Gliedschaft am geheimnisvollen Leib," in *Dogmengeschichte der Frühscholastik*, IV, 2, pp. 48-99.

4. *Luther.* As a consequence of his doctrine of justification, according to which man is *simul peccator et justus,* that is intrinsically a sinner, but extrinsically "accounted" just, Luther conceived the Church in the same way: *simul sancta et peccatrix.*

5. *The Counter-Reformation.* In reaction against the Reformation, and also against the pessimistic tendencies of St. Augustine, post-Tridentine theology had a tendency to reduce the Church to the functioning of the hierarchy, and to conceive the Church as a sort of hypostasis, a subsistent reality placed before the eyes of the People of God as its guide and master, and never touched by sin. This Church bears no resemblance to the People of God journeying in the midst of temptations and tribulations. Theology practically eliminated the paradox of sin and holiness in the Church by distinguishing between objective and subjective holiness, *objective* or institutional holiness having its source in the gospel, the ministry and the sacraments, and *subjective* holiness being variable, with, in particular, a great mass of sinners.[21] In short the Church was *holy;* it was its members who were sinful. This distinction fits ill with reality, since there is no Church without the People of God, and this People is sinful.

6. *C. Journet.* In order to be understood Msgr. Journet's position has to be put into the more general context of his ecclesiology.[22] He distinguishes in the Church a sociological aspect and a theological aspect, only the latter having the value of a formal element and composing the soul and the body of the Church. The

---

21. For instance, J. Salaverri, *De Ecclesia Christi* (Madrid, 1962), pp. 1182-1192; 1204-1208; 1228-1240; 1254-1263.

22. Msgr. Journet has returned several times, in both books and articles, to the theme of sin and holiness in the Church. See particularly: C. Journet, "Remarques sur la sainteté de l'Église militante," *Nova et Vetera,* 9 (1934): 299-323; *Ibid.,* "Du probleme de la sainteté de l'Église au problème de la nature de l'Église," *Nova et Vetera,* 9 (1934): 27-32; *Ibid., L'Église du Verbe incarné* (3 vols., Bruges and Paris, 1955, 1962, 1969).

soul of the Church is both uncreated (the Holy Spirit) and created (charity). The Holy Spirit is the supreme cause of the Church's activities, and it is to him that we must attribute the preservation of her unity and charity.[23] Charity, or the created soul of the Church, resides chiefly in the upright. In the sinful, it acts "instrumentally and by extension," in giving them the power to perform certain actions through which spiritual life is expressed (teaching and dispensing the sacraments for instance), just as corporal life allows even paralyzed members of the body to execute certain movements.[24] The body of the Church is not so much the material congregation of Christians as the spatio-temporal sphere of the Church's activity.[25] The purpose of the body, that is, is to make visible in time and space (through the activities of the faithful and the exercise of hierarchical powers) the uncreated soul and the created soul of the Church.[26] The body, consequently, "is not made up of all the activity of baptized human beings, but of that part of their exterior activity which is informed by the created soul of the Church (charity), and aims immediately at the spiritual ends of the Church."[27]

Hence it is understandable that Msgr. Journet defends intransigently the idea of a pure and holy Church without spot or wrinkle; for since sin is an act which is not animated by charity, it is foreign to both the soul and the body of the Church. His fundamental thesis is expressed thus: "The Church theologically considered is without sin."[28] "The Church is not without sinners," but "she is without sin."[29] As such, she has, formally, no need of purification: she is immaculate. If she does penance, it is not for any sins which she has committed, but because she cares for her sinful children and takes upon herself the

---

23. C. Journet, *L'Église du Verbe incarné*, 2: 472-474, 534-536.
24. *Ibid.*, 2: 577, 694, 702.
25. *Ibid.*, 2: 873.
26. *Ibid.*, 2: 871.
27. *Ibid.*, 2: 873.
28. *Ibid.*, 2: 904.
29. *Ibid.*, 2: 904-905.

responsibility for their penance.[30] Msgr. Journet makes his position still more precise: "I am saying that the Church includes all that is holy even in her sinful members, and that she excludes whatever is impure even in her righteous members." [31] Charity, that is, which is the soul of the Church, leaves traces of virtue even in sinners, which the holiness of the Church retrieves and appropriates.[32] The Church takes on body and is incarnate "through and in the being and exterior behavior of her righteous children, but also through and in what remains pure and holy in the being and exterior behavior of her sinful children, that is, through and in all that, in spite of their sins, is the result of a supernatural gift . . . her real and proper frontiers enclose all that is pure and good in her members, both just and sinful, leaving outside all that is impure, even in the just." [33] "The total Christ, Head and Body, is holy in all his members, both righteous and sinful, drawing to himself all holiness, even in his sinful members, and rejecting every impurity, even in the just." [34]

Msgr. Journet's position, as is to be seen, is consistent with his ecclesiology. But this ecclesiology, although it is well defended, still seems to me that of an abstract Church, not of a real Church, a People of God, a community of human beings. This fissure, moreover, this vertical split which is introduced into the depths of every member of the Church (dividing what is holy from what is impure), seems highly artificial; for it is the entire People of God, and the entire individual Christian who is holy and sinful: the person as such is indivisible. One last point is that in stressing the mystery of holiness in the Church, Msgr. Journet does not face the apologetic problem (which is both ecumenical and pastoral, and very serious) of a Church who presents to the world a sinful face.[35]

---

30. *Ibid.*, 2: 907.
31. *Ibid.*, 2: 911.
32. *Ibid.*, 2: 898-899, 610-611.
33. *Ibid.*, 2: 914.
34. *Ibid.*, 2: 915.
35. *Fr. Malmberg* tackles the problem from a different point of view, that is, from that of the Church as the mystical Body of Christ, but he takes up a position similar to Msgr. Journet's: the Church is essentially holy,

7. A. *de Bovis.* Fr. de Bovis envisages the paradox of sin and holiness in the Church in a biblical perspective.[36] From this point of view he distinguishes a holiness of belonging and a holiness of resemblance. The holiness of belonging is a holiness of consecration, for the sake of God's saving purpose. The Church is set apart, consecrated to God by Christ who has, so to speak, acquired her at the price of his own blood (Eph 5:26). In giving himself up for her, Christ has made her forever his Bride and his Body. This initial holiness of belonging and consecration is given by baptism, which, in a real sense, makes each baptized person holy. It constitutes at the same time a call to a holiness of resemblance or transformation. To be holy means not only to belong to Christ, but also to receive his Spirit and live the life of his Spirit (Gal 3:8). Christ's taking possession of us in our consecration implies the obligation to follow him along the various ways he leads us. This holiness of resemblance consists in expressing the Spirit of Christ, in allowing Christ to enter and penetrate our whole existence, to shape our thoughts, our actions, our desires: it consists in living and dying as Christ did. This holiness of resemblance could never be totally lacking in the Church; for the sacramental system "constitutes for the Church as a whole, if not for each individual baptized person, an infallible guarantee, a guarantee that the Church will always have within her saints in the most exacting sense of the term, that is to say, human beings configured to Christ, souls transfigured into the image of the Son of God, liv-

---

and the expression "sinful Church" cannot be admitted. (F. Malmberg, *Ein Leib, ein Geist* (Freiburg, 1960, pp. 295-298). More recently, *Fr. J. Stöhr,* after criticizing Fr. Rahner's position with respect to "the sinful Church," adheres to Msgr. Journet's opinion. (J. Stöhr, "Heilige Kirche — sündige Kirche," *Münchener Theologische Zeitschrift,* 18 [1967]: 119-142). *Fr. G. Philips* concedes that one may talk of a Church "for sinners," that is to say, working for the sanctification of sinners, but not of *"a sinful Church,"* or *"a Church of sinners."* (G. Philips, *L'Église et son mystère au deuxième concile du Vatican* (2 vols. Paris, 1967-1968, vol. 1: 124ff.).

36. A. De Bovis, "Credo sanctam Ecclesiam," *Christus,* n. 22 (April 1959), pp. 163-181.

ing for God in Jesus Christ." [37] And again: "For the Church as a whole, and for the time of the Church, consecration is the promise of transfiguration, belonging is the guarantee of resemblance." [38]

When it comes to personal holiness, this varies according to the generosity of each individual. The Church knows that many of her members do not answer the call to sanctity, and there is nothing triumphant about her holiness. [39] The sin of her members dims the visible light of the Church's sanctity and casts doubts upon her divine origin. Nevertheless this sin could not destroy the holiness of vocation and consecration which exists in the Church. [40]

The solution offered by Fr. de Bovis is an improvement on that of Msgr. Journet. Whatever else may be said about it, it does put the problem of sin and holiness in the Church into its proper perspective. It very rightly distinguishes between ecclesial sanctity (the sanctity of the Church as a whole) and personal sanctity. It recognizes that sinners diminish the Church's splendor and therefore her power to attract. But the binaries "belonging-resemblance," "consecration-transfiguration" could be expressed in more dynamic terms.

8. *C. Dejaifve.* The question Fr. Dejaifve asks himself is whether one can talk of a *sinful* Church. [41] Obviously the Church is not a personal subject, susceptible of moral acts. The Church, the Bride of Christ, distinct from him, exists only in her members and acts only through them. It is persons who act morally: it is persons who are responsible. But if the Church is a social body acting through responsible members, it cannot be denied that the sins of the members affect the community. If the ecclesial

---

37. *Ibid.,* p. 172.

38. *Ibid.,* p. 174.

39. A. De Bovis, *L'Église et son mystère* (Paris, 1961), p. 118; trans., *The Church* (London, 1961).

40. *Ibid.,* p. 109.

41. G. Dejaifve, "L'Église catholique peut-elle entrer dans la repentance oecuménique?" NRT 84 (1962): 225-239.

community is not destroyed by the sins committed by her members, she does, in a way, assume responsibility for them.[42] In the liturgy it is the whole Church, as a community, who says the *Pater* and the *Confiteor,* and who is asked to lament the sins of her members and repent.

It is possible then, in a certain sense, to talk of a sinful Church. "The expression can be given an acceptable meaning, in so far as what is designated by Church is the community of her members." [43] This vision of the Church, however, leaves in the shade Christ and his life-giving influence. On the other hand, the sins of the community do dim the splendor of the Church and consequently obscure "the sign lifted up among the nations." If the Church "is sure of never lacking Christ's grace, she knows also that she can always, by her faults, limit its fruitfulness, and that the sins of her members are a wound in the Body of Christ and weaken the radiance of his glory in the world." [44]

9. *Y. Congar.* Fr. Congar takes a middle course between Msgr. Journet's and Fr. Rahner's positions. He sets out from the biblical notion of holiness: in so far as she comes from God and belongs to God the Church is holy.[45] It is proper, then, to distinguish between the Church as an institution (the Church *congregans*) and the Church as a community (the Church *congregata*).[46] As an institution, the Church precedes the community of her members, and depends directly on God, in his free act of will and in Christ who "pre-contains" the Church, and also in the means established by Christ to reunite and sanctify mankind.[47] The Church is holy in virtue of the *gifts* she has received from God: the deposit of faith, the sacraments, the ministry.

---

42. *Ibid.,* pp. 226-227.

43. *Ibid.,* p. 236.

44. *Ibid.,* pp. 238-239.

45. Y. Congar, "L'Eglise est sainte," *Angelicum,* 42 (1965): 273-298; *Ibid., Vraie et fausse Réforme dans l'Église* (Paris, 1950), pp. 78-80.

46. Y. Congar, *Vraie et fausse Réforme dans l'Église,* p. 94.

47. *Ibid.,* pp. 95-96; see also Y. Congar, "L'Église est sainte," *Angelicum,* 42 (1965): 280.

"These realities are holy in themselves, since they come from God, and they are directed towards holiness. They are, in themselves, instruments by means of which God sanctifies. They can be said to have an objective holiness." [48] This holiness which comes from God cannot be lost. In spite of the sins of her members, the Church, "as an institution for salvation, ceaselessly accomplishes the work of holiness in the Church . . . as the community of the faithful, the people of God." [49] Through her origin and principle the Church never ceases to produce saints. The Holy Spirit "has never left her and will never leave her." [50] And in the darkest hours of her history she has given birth to saints. She is therefore holy, not only because she uses the means of sanctification she has received (an objective sanctity, of the Church *congregans*), but also because she is composed of saints and of those who try to be saints (a subjective sanctity, of the Church *congregata*, the Church as a community). In those of her members who welcome God's gifts, the Church is holy but imperfectly so: it is a dialectic of *already* and *not yet*. Fr. Congar refuses simply to call the Church "sinful," because only a person can be called so. But he attributes to the Church collectively historical mistakes which often have their source in the moral faults of individual persons. He prefers in this case to talk of collective responsibility rather than of culpability, in the same way as one talks of the collective responsibility of nations.[51] This is why the ecclesial community must repent and be reformed. In 1961, in commenting on the relationship of his own views to those of Msgr. Journet, Fr. Congar wrote: "I should as a whole, subscribe to Msgr. Journet's formula (the Church is holy although made up of sinners), but complete it by a consideration of that order of wretched historical mistakes, on which, moreover, questioning and sometimes scandal bear more particularly today." [52]

---

48. *Ibid.*, pp. 282-283.
49. Y. Congar, *Vraie et fausse Réforme dans l'Église*, p. 112.
50. *Ibid.*, p. 107.
51. *Ibid.*, pp. 592-595.
52. Y. Congar, *Sainte Église* (Paris, 1961), p. 147.

If Fr. Congar's position has some resemblance to Msgr. Jour-net's, let us be precise about noticing that it avoids the artificial division which Msgr. Journet introduces into the innermost depths of the person. Fr. Congar looks at the Church from above (objective holiness, the holiness of the institution), and from below (subjective holiness, the holiness of the community). In this way he preserves the holiness of the Church from the sins of her members. Sinners remain united to the institution by faith. The Church as an institution labors to purify them, and thus to realize her holiness as a community. But we are left with the fact that the division established between the Church as an institution and the Church as a community resolves only imperfectly the paradox of sin and holiness, since the institution itself exists only *in* and *through* the community: there is no Church except as realized in human beings and their history. And there are, moreover, in the ecclesial community, more than historical errors; there are also, I think, in local communities, real conspiracies of sin.[53]

10. *K. Rahner.* Fr. Rahner considers that an ecclesiology which wishes to be serious and complete must face the question of the *sinful* Church—the more so in that the solution of this problem impinges at depth on the ecumenical problem, especially among Protestants, who accuse Catholics of developing a triumphant ecclesiology, and paying only absent-minded attention to the fact of sin in the Church.[54]

In spite of the traditional position, which stresses above all the objective holiness of the Church and is reluctant to speak of the sin of the Church, Fr. Rahner does not hesitate to talk about a Church subjectively sinful. In effect, he says, if the Church is not an abstraction, but the People of God, and if this People is composed of sinners, who remain members of the com-

---

53. This problem is touched on in the following chapter.
54. On this, see especially: K. Rahner, "Sündige Kirche nach den Dekreten des zweiten Vatikanischen Konzils," in: *Schriften zur Theologie* (vol. VI, Einsiedeln, 1965), pp. 321-347; *Ibid.*, "Kirche der Sünder," *Ibid.*, pp. 301-320.

munity in spite of their sins, we are bound to say that the sins of Christians have a real effect on the Church and affect her character: they sully the Body of Christ, and make the Church, in her concrete reality, sinful.[55]

If it is true, moreover, as *Lumen gentium* (LG 8) and the decree on ecumenism (UR 4 and 6) affirm, that the Church is constantly in need of purification, renewal, reform and repentance, and if she should devote herself constantly to overcoming the empire of sin in herself, it follows that the Church, *in a certain sense,* is affected by sin, subject to sin, and therefore "sinful." [56]

Fr. Rahner does not pretend that sinfulness can be attributed to the Church in the same sense as it can be attributed morally to a person, but his intention is to stress that the sins of persons have their influence upon the ecclesial community: they disfigure the Church and make her unrecognizable by those outside her.[57] If the Church does not recognize herself as sinful, how can reforms bear fruit?

Nonetheless, it does not follow that sin and holiness are of the same order, and have the same weight in the definition of the Church. The Church is both objectively and subjectively holy, and, more than that, it is not sin, but holiness, which is the decisive note of the Church. Sin is the contradiction of the Church,[58] and though the sinner remains a member of the Church, he deprives his membership of its meaning and efficaciousness: it is like a sacrament which is valid but bears no

---

55. K. Rahner, "Kirche der Sünder," *Schriften zur Theologie,* vol. VI: 308-310. H. U. Von Balthasar expresses himself in the same terms in "Casta Meretrix," in *Sponsa Verbi* (Einsiedeln, 1960), pp. 203-305.

56. K. Rahner, "Sündige Kirche nach den Dekreten des zweiten Vatikanischen Konzils," *Schriften zur Theologie,* vol. VI: 336; *Ibid.,* "Kirche der Sünder," *ibid.,* p. 312.

57. K. Rahner, "Vergessene Wahrheiten über das Bussakrament," in: *Schriften zur Theologie* (Vol. II, Einsiedeln, 1958²), pp. 144-148; English translation, *Theological Investigations II* (London, 1963, and New York, 1964).

58. K. Rahner, "Kirche der Sünder," *Schriften zur Theologie,* vol. VI: 312-313.

fruit.[59] The holiness of the Church is always of more weight than
her sin, since it depends on the action of God who gives it to
her. Christ, by his passion and death and resurrection, has overcome sin, and merited for the Church as a whole the prevenient
and efficacious grace of unfailing faithfulness to her Bridegroom. Properly understood, this charism is the equivalent on
the moral plane of the charism of infallibility on the doctrinal
plane. Holiness is the expression of what the Church *is*, in
essence, that is to say, it is the efficacious sign of the active,
continuous, victorious and irrevocable presence of God's saving
grace in the world, in Jesus Christ.[60] That is why sanctity cannot
cease to flower in the Church and to be perceptible in the
saints as a sign of her divine origin.[61] The historical holiness of
the Church is the expression of what she is and remains till
the end of time: the presence of grace in the world.[62]

Exception may be taken to Fr. Rahner's terminology.[63] But
I think that his approach has the merit of showing the inade-
quacy of approaches which practically refuse to recognize the
presence of sin in the Church. Fr. Rahner does, besides, remind
Christians of their responsibility, as a community, for the
face that the Church presents to the world, and therefore for the
witness she gives for or against Christ whose Sign she is.[64]

59. *Ibid.*, pp. 307-308.
60. K. Rahner, "Sündige Kirche nach den Dekreten des zweiten
Vatikanischen Konzils," *Schriften zur Theologie*, vol. VI: 343-344.
61. K. Rahner, "Die Kirche der Heiligen" in: *Schriften zur Theologie*
(vol. III, Einsiedeln, 1957²), pp. 111-126; English translation, *Theological
Investigations III* (London and New York, 1967).
62. *Ibid.*, pp. 114-117.
63. J. Stöhr ("Heilige Kirche — Sündige Kirche," *Münchener Theologische Zeitschrift*, 118 [1967]: 119-142) declares that the expression
"sinful Church" is theologically false.
64. *Fr. Ratzinger*, like Fr. Rahner, thinks that the Church on earth
is a sinful Church, but he stresses that the tension between sin and
holiness, characteristic of the Church on earth, is definitive witness to the
victory of grace over sin. Cf. J. Ratzinger, "Free expression and obedience
in the Church," in *The Church, Readings in Theology* (New York,
1963), pp. 194-217.

11. *G. Martelet.* Fr. Martelet values the paradox of sin and holiness in the Church.[65] If the Church is something real she is *ipso facto* sinful, since her members are sinful and remain her members, in spite of their sinfulness. In consequence the Church is at the same time holy and always in need of purification. These two characteristics, however, are not proper to the Church in the same way. The Church is holy with the inalienable holiness which Christ confers upon his Bride, and it is through this holiness that the Church is the Church, and not through the sins of her members. What makes the Church sinful comes not from Christ but from us. The Church, moreover, is never wholly subject to sin; she never ceases to be the instrument of salvation in the world. Even in the depths of her poverty and wretchedness she remains a sign of holiness, and in this sense participates in *sacramentality.* It is with the Church as with the sacraments, where the value of holiness is not attributable either to the value of those who receive them, or to the value of those who administer them, but to the value of Christ, who founded them and does not cease to offer himself by their means. In virtue of the presence of Christ and his Spirit, the Church gives always, in her source, a holiness which she uses ill. "The sacramentality of the Church expresses the inalienable character of a holiness which, notwithstanding, sin always corrupts." [66]

In *Sainteté de l'Église et vie religieuse,* Fr. Martelet distinguishes between a holiness of gift and a holiness of response.[67] The holiness of gift (the holiness of institution, objective holiness) is assured to the Church by the presence of Christ in her and of his unfailing faithfulness.[68] The holiness

---

65. G. Martelet, *Les Idées maîtresses de Vatican II* (Bruges and Paris, 1967), pp. 82-101.

66. *Ibid.,* p. 101.

67. G. Martelet, *Sainteté de l'Église et vie religieuse* (Toulouse, 1964), p. 15.

68. *Ibid.,* p. 17. Fr. Martelet allies himself here with Fr. Congar's position.

of response or subjective holiness will never be wholly lacking in the Church; for the holiness of institution "unfailingly guaranteed, is oriented towards a holiness of result, unfailingly obtained." [69]

12. *H. Küng.* Fr. Küng's position matches Fr. Rahner's. The Church, he stresses, is, in the concrete, the People of God. "It is not God, not the Lord, not the Spirit, but human beings who make up the Church," which is at once a community of sinners and a community of saints.[70] But if men can become saints it is in so far as God sanctifies them through Jesus Christ (1 Cor 6:11) in the Holy Spirit (Rm 15:16; 1:4), and in so far as they respond to God's action. "The Church is holy in so far as she has been *called* by God in Christ as the communion of those who believe, and has put herself at his service, because she has been separated from the world and finds herself at the same time enveloped and carried by the grace of God." [71] It is God who sets the Church apart and it is God who sanctifies her through his Spirit. Within this People, apparently so like other peoples, dwells the Spirit of God, who does not cease to give it life and make it holy.[72] By themselves, men form the communion of sinners. They are constantly in need of justification and sanctification. The Church will be without spot or wrinkle only at the end of time. Nevertheless, in spite of the infidelities, and impurities and manifold unworthiness of her members, "the power of sin will not go so far as making an end of her"; for God maintains her life. In spite of her sin, the Church will not betray her trust, will not be wholly unfaithful; for Christ sustains her with his Spirit.[73] She will always remain the Holy Church. On the other hand it is undeniable that sin pervades the Church, darkens her and soils her. Like

---

69. *Ibid.*, p. 19.

70. H. Küng, *L'Église* (2 vols., Bruges and Paris, 1968), vol. 2: 453. On the problem in general, pp. 448-482; English translations, *The Church* (New York, 1968, London, 1969).

71. *Ibid.*, 2: 457.

72. *Ibid.*, 2: 457-458.

73. *Ibid.*, 2: 479.

Fr. Rahner, Fr. Küng is of the opinion that the sinful members of the Church affect the quality of the Church and make her in a certain sense "sinful." But he prefers the expression "Church of sinners"; for simply to talk of a "sinful" Church leaves in the air a grave ambiguity as to the real nature of the Church. What is deepest, most inward, in the Church, that is, Christ, his Spirit, his grace, cannot become sinful. The Church's Head, her Principle of life, her sacraments are holy. The truth is that the two expressions complement and correct each other. "*The Church of sinners* indicates that there is no sin in the Head or in the Spirit, or in the divine institution and constitution of the Church; *the sinful Church* brings out the fact that sin in the Church concerns the Church herself, involves her in responsibility, wounds her, disfigures her." [74]

In these theological reflections on the subject there are to be found, in spite of divergencies of perspective, a certain number of points on which agreement becomes more and more marked. (a) Short of conceiving the Church as an unreal hypostasis, we are obliged to talk about her as the People of God, and therefore as both an assembly of the holy and an assembly of the sinful. (b) Nevertheless, the decisive note of the Church is not sin but holiness, and this is in virtue of the election, vocation and action of God, who, through Christ and his Spirit brings the Church into being and never ceases to give her life. (c) The Church as a whole is subjectively holy by reason of the unfailing faithfulness that Christ has merited for her, in uniting her for ever to himself as his Bride and his Body. (d) The Church shares in the general mystery of sacramentality in the Christian economy: in spite of her poverty and wretchedness the Church remains always, in her source, the instrument for the salvation of the world. (e) In her members, ethical holiness depends on their more or less generous response. (f) The completely pure and completely holy Church will be realized only at the end of time.

74. H. Küng, *Concile et retour a l'unité* (Paris, 1951), pp. 29-30; English translations, *The Council and Reunion* (London, no date); *The Council, Reform and Reunion* (New York, 1957).

Finally, it is noticeable that recent theologians (Fr. Rahner and Fr. Küng for instance), because they approach the mystery of holiness and sin in the Church in the light of an ecclesiology more conversant with the positions of other Christian communities, are looking for a language and a solution which, without abandoning any point of Catholic doctrine, will be more consistent with the reality of the Church—as both Mystery and Phenomenon.

CHAPTER VIII

The Paradox of Sin and Holiness In the Church

Theological reflection

I. *The dogmatic point of view*

Let us go on from the threefold approach just outlined (the biblical idea of sanctity, the images of the Church, the account of theological positions taken up), and try to resume the valid elements to be found there in a theological synthesis, adding the necessary precisions.

To be faithful to the scriptural perspective will be to distinguish in the Church a holiness of God's initiative or holiness of vocation, and a holiness of response.

The holiness of God's initiative

1. *The Church as the means of sanctification and salvation designed by God* — Let us briefly remind ourselves of the Church's place in God's purpose. God willed through Christ to introduce mankind into the communion of the Trinitarian life, into the mystery of love which is the life of the divine Persons. He willed to make of all mankind a single People of God, a single body, the Body of Christ, and he willed that the element of unity and cohesion in this People and this Body should be the very Spirit himself through whom the Father and the Son love each other and give themselves to each other. In short God willed to extend to mankind the life of the Trinity itself: in each of us he willed to give birth again to his Son and *inspire* his Spirit.

According to this purpose, the Church was constituted to be

"the instrument of all men's redemption" (LG 9). The plenitude of means has been entrusted to her so that she may bring about the salvation of all men. As an institution for salvation, conceived and willed by God, the Church depends directly on God and on his wholly gratuitous initiative. She is holy in the first place in virtue of this personal initiative of God, who gives her existence as the instrument of salvation. This holiness comes from God and is inalienable: it cannot be lost.

2. *The Church as the People of God, "called" to holiness by the gospel, consecrated and sanctified by baptism* — What is meant by the Church here is not an abstraction, a subsistent entity, but a real People, the People of the new covenant, the People of the baptized.

This people is first called together by the word of God: "It is I," says St. Paul to the Corinthians, "who, through the gospel, have given birth to you in Christ Jesus" (1 Cor 4:15). Christians are *called* by the gospel of Christ (Rm 1:6), "called to be saints" (1 Cor 1:2), "chosen in Jesus Christ before the creation of the world, to be holy and without blame in his presence" (Eph 1:4). Before it is a baptismal and Eucharistic community, the Church is a community *called together* by the word of God. As Israel was once "called" by Moses and the prophets, the Christian is called by the word of salvation to a communion of life with a God who is holy.

More than that, this People is *consecrated* to God by baptism. Those who receive baptism are introduced into the life of a consecrated People: they become in their turn consecrated beings, dedicated to the work of salvation. They belong to Christ and receive the imprint of this consecration, a consecration which, as the very act of Christ, is imperishable and indelible. It is the seal of belonging to "the Holy One of God" (Mk 1:24): it is what we call the sacramental *character*, the sign of God who is faithful and "without repentance" in his gifts. In the same way as the priest is consecrated to God for ever (even if his personal life does not always correspond to this consecration), so the whole Christian People is indefectibly consecrated to God. This is the original fact of holiness.

Through baptism this People is really *made holy,* and not only called holy or designated as holy. On this matter *Lumen gentium* says clearly: "*Called* by God, not according to their works but according to his purpose and grace, justified in Jesus our Lord, Christ's disciples are, in the baptism of faith *made* really children of God and sharers in the divine nature, and therefore *really* holy. This sanctification which they have received they ought then, with God's grace, to make living and perfect in their lives. They are reminded by the Apostle that they should live 'as befits those who are holy' (Eph 5:3) . . . bearing the fruits of the Spirit in their sanctification." [1]

Baptism, therefore, really purifies and sanctifies (1 Cor 6: 19). Each member of the People of God, which is the Church, has, in turn, in the course of the centuries, been immersed in the blood of Christ, and shared in his death and resurrection. Each member of the Church has been truly purified, justified and sanctified; each has become, in baptism, the holy member of a holy People of a holy God. Fr. Schlier interprets Ephesians 5:24-27 in a continuous present. In a perpetual today Christ is purifying and sanctifying each of the members of his Body and so constituting a holy People.

3. *The Church as constantly sanctified by Christ and his Spirit*—The Church, as has been said, must be envisaged in her totality, that is in her *horizontal* elements (the community of believers) and her *vertical* elements (Christ and his Spirit). The unity which binds Christians together in a single Body does not come from themselves. The principle and source of the

---

1. "Christi asseclae a Deo non secundum opera sua, sed secundum propositum et gratiam Ejus vocati atque in Jesu Domino justificati, in fidei baptismate vere filii Dei et consortes divinae naturae, ideoque reapse sancti effecti sunt. Eos proinde oportet sanctificationem quam acceperunt, Deo dante, vivendo tenere atque perficere. Ab Apostolo monentur, ut vivant 'sicut decet sanctos' (Eph 5:3), . . . fructusque Spiritus habeant in sanctificationem" (LG 40).

unity which constitutes the Church as such, that is, as a society of grace and salvation (and if she is not so she does not differ from other human societies), is of a divine order. It is Christ, through baptism in his death, who makes men members of his mystical Body and it is he, through his Spirit, who actuates them and gives them life, and makes them capable of fulfilling their prophetic and priestly and royal mission. There is, in the Church, something more than her members: there is their *communion* itself, and the means of establishing and assuring it. And all this comes from Christ and his Spirit. When we talk of the Church then, we must include this *permanent* and *divine* influx of life, which the whole community of the baptized, clergy and the rest of the faithful together, receive from Christ and his Spirit. The Holy Spirit has been sent "to sanctify the Church perpetually . . . He is the Spirit of life, the well of water springing up into life everlasting . . . He makes the Church young again and ceaselessly new." [2] This inpouring of sanctifying life, which comes from Christ and his Spirit, and which is of itself the vital principle of the Church, can never perish or become corrupt: it belongs to the essence of the Church. That is why holiness, not sin, is the definitive element in the Church. What characterizes her as such is this inexhaustible life which springs from Christ and his Spirit. Through sin, some members may voluntarily withdraw from this inflowing of divine life, but they could not dry it up or contaminate its source. Sin and holiness have not then, as we shall see, the same relation to the Church.

The holiness of response

To the holiness of the Church which comes from the loving initiative of God (vocation, baptism, Christ and his Spirit) must correspond on the part of man a holiness of response. For what would a call be which has no answer, no response?

---

2. "Missus est Spiritus Sanctus die Pentecostes, ut Ecclesiam jugiter sanctificaret . . . Ipse est Spiritus vitae seu fons aquae salientis in vitam aeternam . . . Virtute Evangelii juvenescere facit Ecclesiam eamque perpetuo renovat" (LG 4).

1. *The faithfulness of the Church taken as a whole* — Christ's covenant with the Church, his Bride, his Body, is definitive, indefectible, indissoluble. "For Christ, the Son of God, who with the Father and the Spirit, is proclaimed as alone holy, has loved the Church as his Bride and delivered himself up to make her holy (cf. Eph 5:25-26): he has united her to himself as his own Body, and crowned her with the gift of the Holy Spirit, to the glory of God." [3]

We are concerned here with the mystery of grace, on the plane of the ecclesial community. If men were alone in constituting the Church, the sin of her members would, like a cancer, end by penetrating the whole organism and destroying it. But Christ, through his passion and death and resurrection, has merited for the Church that she should never wholly abandon her Bridegroom. The Spirit has been given to her as a *lasting gift,* and this influx of the divine life prevents the ecclesial community from being wholly unfaithful to Christ her Bridegroom, or to the mission with which he has entrusted her. Fr. Rahner says that the Church has received from Christ a prevenient and efficacious grace to the end that sin should never have over her, as a *whole,* a final victory—even if it accomplishes partial victories. Because Christ's victory over sin is final, and because the Church is forever the Bride and Body of Christ, her faithfulness is a *gift* which will never be withdrawn. The gates of hell shall not prevail against her.

This grace of *faithfulness* is analogous, in the ethical sphere, to the charism of infallibility in the doctrinal sphere. Just as Christ preserves his Church from wandering doctrinally a very great way from his word, so he preserves her from total infidelity. Individuals may make mistakes, but God protects the community against error. Individuals may sin, but God protects his People from total faithlessness. Again it can be said that if

---

3. "Christus enim, Dei Filius, qui cum Patre et Spiritu solus sanctus celebratur, Ecclesiam tamquam sponsam suam dilexit, Seipsum tradens pro ea, ut illam sanctificaret (cf. Eph 5, 25-26), eamque sibi ut corpus suum conjunxit atque Spiritus Sancti dono cumulavit, ad gloriam Dei" (LG 39).

truth and error, like sin and holiness, co-exist in the Church, it is truth and holiness which are the distinctive marks of the Church. For the same Spirit of truth who witnesses to Christ and prevents the Church from betraying his word, prevents her from betraying his love. The paradox is the same. And this means, too, in the concrete, that the Church will never cease to bear the fruit of holiness, and that there will never be a total apostasy.

2. *The holiness of the converted and forgiven* — The Church could never exhibit a triumphant holiness; for she is a People purified from its sin in the waters of baptism. She is called to perfection, but she knows that she is not always faithful to this call. This People constantly sanctified by Christ and his Spirit falls back into sin; it has constant need of forgiveness. That is why the Church does not cease to say the *Pater,* the *Miserere* and the *Confiteor.* The Church, in the very avowal of her weaknesses, appears better than her sins. Her holiness is not the holiness of the discreet and well-behaved; it is not a stoic holiness, not a holiness of the perfect, or irreproachable or pure, not a holiness of the Pharisees. What is best in the members of the Church is this acknowledgment that they are not holy. Like Israel, the Church is the communion of those who have been forgiven and do not forget their sins. She is the "prostitute" who remembers her old slavery. The sacrament of penance is the concrete existential expression of a Church who recognizes the perpetual need for *metanoia.* It reveals the inner attitude of a Church *broken* by contrition, like David, or Peter or Mary Magdalene.

3. *A holiness in state of tension* — The Church's holiness is a dialectic of *already* and *not yet.* The Second Vatican Council speaks of a holiness which is real but imperfect (LG 48). Though holy, the Church always needs to be purified (LG 8). In baptism she is consecrated to God, but like Israel, also consecrated to God, she has to live this fundamental holiness which

comes to her as a pure gift from God. There is therefore a tension between what has been given and received and what must be conserved and realized. The conversion of baptism, says the decree *Ad gentes*, is an "initial" conversion, which needs to become mature (AG 13). Ethical holiness, or the holiness of response, should tend constantly towards becoming commensurate with the holiness of vocation and consecration received in baptism. The Church is called to live always more fully and more perfectly her fundamental holiness. Even in great saints, there is a considerable time-lag between the holiness of vocation and the holiness of response.

It could be said that the Church (the whole People and each of its members) is *born* holy, but that this holiness, inasmuch as the Church is on a journey, is threatened, attacked, subject to temptations and to sin, that it has, in consequence, constantly to be protected, developed or regained. It is because she *is* holy (born holy) that the Church must *be* holy. The indicative demands the imperative: "the Church is at the same time holy and called to purify herself."[4] Holiness is a mystery of cross and resurrection. It is not impeccability, but struggle and conquest, a perpetual death to sin, a painful and penitential sanctity, where victories alternate with defeats.

The holiness of the Church is not so much something accomplished, as a long patience, made of failure and recovery, of giving way and starting afresh, with a few rare moments of rising sheer like an arrow and halting upon the mountain tops. It is revealed not so much in the splendor of ecstasies and raptures as in the patience of daily life. At most junctures and for most of the time, sanctity is much more like Nazareth than like Tabor.

This vision of a holiness which is a perpetual gift from God, always needing to be preserved and recovered, should protect the Church against all temptation to self-sufficiency and triumphalism. And yet on the other hand, it should sustain her in

---

4. "Ecclesia, . . . sancta simul et semper purificanda" (LG 8).

confidence and hope; for Christ has overcome sin and death, and won efficaciously for his Church the possibility of holiness.

4. *A holiness partially achieved* — It is true that the absolutely pure Church belongs to eschatology. Nevertheless the Church is already authentically holy in some of her members. It is said in Revelation 19:7-9, that the Bride of the Lamb has made herself ready, that she is clothed in dazzling white linen, which is made of the good deeds of the saints, the fruit of grace and their free co-operation with grace. The holiness of the Bride is a holiness to be acquired during her earthly pilgrimage.

The Church is holy precisely in virtue of all those who have responded to their call to holiness, and who are fully incorporated into Christ (LG 14). No doubt the Church is composed of sinners, but above all and more obviously she is composed of God's friends, of the just, the temples of the Holy Spirit, the holy members of the Body of Christ, who, even if they sin venially, live in a state of friendship and communion with God. Because of this holiness, ordinary or heroic, the Church is holy with an ethical and personal holiness, which is already a partial but real actualization of the absolute holiness of the heavenly Jerusalem. Already, on earth, the Church is authentically holy in some of her members.

5. *Eschatological or final holiness* — God has been faithful to his promise. The Church, in those of her members who have finished their course and won their recompense, constitutes a Bride whose holiness is fulfilled, who has responded completely to the Bridegroom's call. It is from this that the cult of the saints derives all its meaning. It reminds us of God's faithfulness to his promises. He has really given us his Spirit; he has really changed man's rebellious heart into a filial and obedient heart; he has really made men holy. The saints are the witness, before the Church militant, that the salvation announced has in fact been accomplished, that the Bride has been faithful to the Bridegroom, that God has been faithful to his promise and that his grace is efficacious. Christ's blood has not

been shed in vain. He has given us his Spirit, a Spirit able to create in man a free response to the infinite love of God. The Spirit of love has made our world holy.

In what sense can the Church be called "sinful"?

To answer this question in a way which avoids ambiguity, it is important to look at the Church, first from the inside (from the dogmatic point of view), and then from the outside, in the *image* which she presents to the world.

The Mystery of the Church

1. If by *the Church* we mean the *human members* of the People of God, we are obliged to acknowledge that they are all of them sinners—in the sense that though they have been justified in baptism, all commit venial sins, many commit grave sins and a considerable number live habitually in a state of sin. And yet sinners remain members of the Church. Since the Church, as the People of God, is composed of men who are sinners in one sense or another, and since she is in constant need of forgiveness and penitence, we can say that she is sinful.

2. Nevertheless, when we speak in this way, we risk putting into parentheses the vertical elements of the Church, as if Christ and his Spirit were outside the Church. If there is no Church without man, no more is there a Church without Christ the Head, or without the Holy Spirit. For it is God who constitutes his People, who incorporates each one of his members through baptism in Christ, and who gives life to each through the Spirit. What distinguishes the Church as a supernatural institution is her principle of life. And sin could not destroy this principle. In spite of the infidelities of her members, the Church remains the sacrament of salvation, that is, the inexhaustible source of sanctification. Her holiness must be attributed to the principle of her life. When someone sins, he freely withdraws from the life-giving action of the Church and of this principle within her.

Holiness and sin have not therefore an identical relation to the Church. While holiness belongs to the essence of the Church, sin is her *un-essence* (Küng). Sin is a foreign body which the Church is at work to eliminate, in order to become what she really is.

3. The state of those who are fully incorporated into Christ and the Church, and who live by his Spirit, is a state of holiness. Now there is no doubt that the Church is to be defined in terms of those who live authentically and fully by the principle of her life—just as human life takes its character not from the state of madness but from the *reasonable* activity of those who live a fully human life. Holiness, therefore, is the definitive element in the Church.

4. Properly speaking, sin is attributable to *persons,* and not to the collectivity as such. It is persons who sin, are judged, are in bliss or are condemned. One cannot, therefore, in the full rigor of the term, talk about the culpability of the Church as a universal ecclesial community. Nevertheless the Church cannot detach herself from the evil done by her members: she has, if not culpability, at least in a certain sense, responsibility for it.

5. More than that, it seems legitimate, in certain cases, to speak of the ecclesial community as really sinful. When a monastic community, for instance, is unfaithful to its obligations and sinks into immorality, or when a local Church, in a sort of conspiracy, voluntarily adopts an attitude contrary to that of the gospel (it would be easy to give examples), this community deserves to be called sinful, as a community and not only as persons. It certainly seems that St. Paul (1 Cor 5) and Revelation allude to cases of this kind.

6. From the dogmatic point of view, as holiness and sin have not the same relationship to the Church, it is better not to talk simply about the *sinful Church,* or *the Church of sinners,* since this is to leave out the definitive note of the Church, recognized

by all theologians, that is, the holiness which comes to her from Christ and his Spirit, and it is also to pass over in silence the actual holiness which has been realized, whether ordinary or heroic. Perhaps it is better to talk about *the holy Church of sinners.*

The image of the Church

On the other hand, it is undeniable that the Church is a visible community, whose witness takes not merely a personal but a communal form. The quality of the members of this community affects the quality of the community itself, and the character of the image which it presents to the world. If the community lives according to the gospel, it *ipso facto* affirms the hold which the gospel, recognized as the supreme value, has upon it. When all or most of its members live so, the result is a faithful *image* of Christ and his Spirit. The witness given by each member is then nourished by the witness each receives, and there arises, as it were, a constant flux and reflux of witness and life, from the individual to the community and from the community to the individual. There is established among the members of the community, as it were, a network of interpersonal relationships, made up of justice and charity and peace, of purity and kindness, gentleness and serenity and mercy and all the human virtues. The communal witness is a *resultant,* and not merely a simple addition or juxtaposition of individual witnesses.

The witness given in a community by its holy members constitutes a holy community, which radiates, among those who come in contact with it, the Spirit of Christ. Sin, on the other hand, establishes among members of a community a network of sinful interpersonal relationships. A community whose members are divided, egotistical, full of hatred, cruel, sexually immoral, liars or thieves, is rightly described as sinful. And colloquial language is not wrong. Such a community presents to those outside it a face and body of sin. If, then, the ecclesial community, among too great a number of its members diffuses a spirit of sin, its image is that of a sinful Church. It constitutes a counter-sign of salvation; for it contradicts the gospel which it proclaims.

One cannot pass over this aspect of the Church in silence or minimize its importance. For, in the end, it is the image which the Church presents to the world which makes her either an expressive and infectious sign of the salvation she preaches or a sign which negates. This image of the Church which results from the witness of the community does not, to be sure, prejudice in any way the personal holiness of a certain number of the members of the Church. But at the level of ecumenical and missionary influence, the image of a sinful Church paralyzes and destroys the action of the gospel. It is important to stress before the Christian conscience the responsibility which members of the Church have in forming the image which she presents to the world. For if it is true that she is holy in Christ, her Head, and in the Spirit, who is the principle of her life, it is no less true that it is in the ecclesial community and in the local communities that the men of every time meet Christ and salvation. In the sphere of apologetics, therefore, it is legitimate to speak of a sinful Church, making clear that it is a question of *the image of the Church* which results from the witness of the community.[5]

2. *The Church as an observable reality*

In considering the paradox of sin and holiness in the Church, we must remember that *observable* holiness is not the holiness of the Church triumphant, but of the Church militant, *en route* and on probation. Nor does the Church claim that she has a monopoly of holiness, as if it did not exist outside her—among the Orthodox, or among Protestants or Hindus for instance. If we have any doubts about that, the Second Vatican Council, in the constitution on the Church and in the decree on ecumenism, gives us a useful reminder that there do exist, outside

---

5. Paul VI has publicly asked forgiveness for the Church's faults. Cf. AAS 55 (1963): 853 and 879.

the visible limits of the Catholic Church many astonishing examples of holiness which are the fruits of the Spirit of holiness himself (LG 8 and UR 3). The Church, then, does not set herself up, either as an unmitigated light, or as the only light in a world which would otherwise be nothing but darkness and sin. The world is full of the active presence of God, of Christ and of his Spirit.

The Church's holiness is a supernatural holiness, but at the same time it is a human holiness, pursued by means of human behavior and human acts, in the midst of institutions regulated and administered by human beings. It is through the mediation of Christ's flesh, and through the mediation of churchmen that the kingdom of God grows. If all the members of the Church are called to holiness, and have through the sacraments the possibility of reaching it, only a certain number fully respond to their vocation. The rest slow down and hinder the development of the Church. Even the saints are rather disconcerting. They retain faults of temperament and weaknesses of judgment. Sanctity attracts, astonishes and sometimes irritates.

This said, what are the *facts*, observable even by those "outside," by unbelievers, which can cause wonder and give rise to the question, "If there were salvation in the world, would it not be in this community which says it was founded by Christ to save mankind?" In other words, what are the visible manifestations in the Church of a holiness which, in spite of sin, can attract the attention even of the unbeliever? It is obvious that looking at the Church from his point of view will lead to a shallower, less complete vision of the paradox of sin and holiness. But here are some of the observable facts.

1. *The Church does not cease to preach the gospel of salvation and the means of salvation* — The preaching of the gospel of Christ is one of the major characteristics of the Catholic Church. "Woe to me if I do not preach the gospel," said St. Paul (1 Cor 9:16). "I was not sent to baptize but to preach" (1 Cor 1:17)—not that the sacraments are unnecessary, but that the sacramental order itself depends on the preaching of the

gospel. If Christ is to be known and the Father glorified there must be tongues to preach the gospel; for "how are men to call upon him in whom they have not believed? And how are they to believe in him of whom they have not heard? And how are they to hear without a preacher?" (Rm 10:14-17). Preaching the news of salvation in Jesus Christ has always been regarded by the Church as an absolutely necessary task, and it would seem that no Christian communion can rival her in her missionary effort to spread the gospel.[6] But we need above all to notice the special characteristics of her preaching of the gospel.

First of all, there is an extraordinary anxiety to be faithful to the gospel of Christ. The Church speaks not of herself, but of Christ, whose Witness she is. Her message is not her own, but that of him who has sent her (cf. Jn 8:28; 14, 24). Her preaching is an invitation to share her faith in Christ.[7] St. Paul recognized no gospel but the gospel of Christ, and condemned those who abandoned it or perverted it (Gal 1:6-10). The same desire to be faithful is expressed throughout the documents of the magisterium. It is always a matter of "conserving the gospel in its purity" (DS 1501), of "faithfully preserving and setting forth the word of God" (DS 3000), of "being the servant of the word of God" (DV 10).

The second characteristic of the Church's preaching is that she pursues it in spite of the opposition she encounters. The gospel that she preaches, salvation through the cross, is disconcerting to the wisdom of this world: it is a stumbling block (Rm 9:32), a scandal and a folly (1 Cor 1:23). Salvation through a God made flesh, visible and palpable, scourged and crucified, seems unintelligible and unacceptable to many of our contemporaries.[8] And in consequence the preaching of the gos-

---

6. W. J. Richardson, ed., *The Church as Sign* (New York, 1968).

7. A. Dulles, *Revelation and the Quest for Unity* (Washington-Cleveland, 1968), pp. 102-114.

8. "The Church," observes A. Manaranche, "galls men not so much because of her defects as because of the very *effect* she pursues, the signifying to the world that its efforts are in vain unless it consents to go through the straight gate of reconciliation in Jesus Christ" (*Je crois en Jésus-Christ aujourd'hui*, Paris, 1968, p. 184).

pel meets often with opposition, contradiction, persecution and even martyrdom. Yet the Church continues her mission, out of faithfulness to Christ.

2. *The Church does not cease trying to raise the moral level of mankind* — She does not cease to "encourage unity and charity among men."[9] She acts in human society as a moral and spiritual leaven which continually renews it, constantly inspiring it with a sense of peace and justice, a moral sense and a sense of love. Let it suffice to remember in this connection the Church's countless appeals for peace since the beginning of the twentieth century. And she continues this effort in spite of the enormous pressures which are brought to bear upon her.

She protects man against himself, and preserves him from degradation. In this respect the constitution *Gaudium et spes* records a new grasp of the Church's responsibilities, and a new defense of the rights and dignity of the human person.

"The Council emphasizes the reverence due to the human person: it stresses that each should regard his neighbor, without any exception, as another self . . . . All that is opposed to life as such, every sort of homicide for instance—like genocide, abortion, euthanasia or deliberate suicide itself; all that constitutes a violation of the integrity of the human person, like mutilation, physical or mental torture or psychological constraint; all that is an offense against the dignity of man, like sub-human living conditions, arbitrary imprisonment, deportation, slavery, prostitution, commercial traffic in women or young people, and degrading conditions of work, which reduce the workers to the level of mere instruments of profit without regard for their personality as free and responsible human beings; all these practices and others like them are infamous: they corrupt civilization, dishonoring those who instigate them more than those who suffer them, and they are a grave insult also to the honor of the Creator."[10]

---

9. Declaration on non-Christian religions (*Nostra aetate*, 1).

10. "Concilium reverentiam inculcat erga hominem, ita ut singuli proximum, nullo excepto, tamquam alterum seipsum considerare debeant . . .

If the Church is undertaking in this way the defense of human dignity, it is because she takes for granted the gospel, which speaks of man created in the image of God and destined to share his life; it is also because she is aware that no society, let alone the Church, can subsist without this respect for the human person. It is not easy to find in the world another religion which concerns itself to this degree with the moral and spiritual values of mankind as such. On many points it would be easy for the Church to give in for the sake of peace, or at least for the sake of popularity among the masses of men. It is important to stress also, that those who have, during the course of history, maintained these moral and spiritual demands, have not always been saints, but sometimes notorious sinners. And yet, in spite of the temptation to reduce their principles to the level of their practice, they have remained faithful to the gospel.

3. *The Church welcomes sinners* — The Church does not cease to preach the ideal life of the gospel, but she is full of mercy for those who sin. While she makes the most demanding appeal for holiness, she sympathizes at the same time with man's human poverty and distress. We tend instinctively as human beings to be hard on those who have sinned against the law, and much more yielding in matters of principle. The Church, on the contrary, following the example of Christ, is firm in matters of principle, but almost indulgent towards sinners. There is in her heart, as in the heart of Christ, a secret weakness, a loving

Quaecumque insuper ipsi vitae adversantur, ut cujusvis generis homicidia, genocidia, abortus, euthanasia et ipsum voluntarium suicidium; quaecumque humanae personae integritatem violant, ut mutilationes, tormenta corpori mentive inflicta, conatus ipsos animos coercendi; quaecumque humanam dignitatem offendunt, ut infrahumanae vivendi conditiones, arbitrariae incarcerationes, deportationes, servitus, prostitutio, mercatus mulierum et juvenum; conditiones quoque laboris ignominiosae, quibus operarii ut mera quaestus instrumenta, non ut liberae et responsabiles personae tractantur: haec omnia et alia hujusmodi probra quidem sunt, ac dum civilisationem humanam inficiunt, magis eos inquinant qui sic se gerunt, quam eos qui injuriam patiuntur et Creatoris honori maxime contradicunt" (GS 27).

predilection for those who are obviously sinners in the eyes
of the world, who were the first to benefit from the passion and
death of Christ. The Church objects to sin, but not to sinners.
They may dim the splendor of her holiness, but she does not
seize a broom to sweep them out in the wake of their sins.
She treats them with the utmost tenderness, going on endlessly
forgiving them. If they leave her, she prays for their return.
When they come back, she weeps for joy with them, like the
father of the prodigal son. For when they sin they are still her
children, and, more than that, she knows that one act of love
transforms a sinner into one of God's friends. It should be added
that the Church's attitude towards the sinner has become,
even in externals, considerably more flexible. More conscious
of the dignity of the human person, even when he is culpable,
she treats him with much more consideration and respect than
she once did.

4. *The Eucharistic assembly* — It is in the Eucharist that
the Church attains the greatest degree of actuality, visibility
and intensity. In essence, the Church is the presence through
the centuries of the Word made flesh. She is the concretization
throughout history of the saving will of God which became
a fact in Christ. Hence she reaches the maximum of her palpabil-
ity and intensity when Christ himself, in the Consecration of
the Mass, is present within the community of his faithful people,
dispensing to them his salvation. The celebration of the Eucharist is the most intense way for the Church to make herself
present at a particular point in time and space. It makes visible
and tangible the unity of Christians with Christ and their unity
in charity with one another.

The Eucharistic celebration is therefore an *epiphany* of
the mystery of the Church in its deepest sense. For God's People
appear assembled there in the unity of charity, in the confession
of their faults, in the hearing of the word, in the kiss of peace, in
the Communion of the sacrifice of Christ; they appear there as, at
the same time, active and passive, immolating and immolated,
sinful and holy, each individually and yet a community, each

recollected in himself and yet open to others, desiring to be made holy in himself and to give glory to God. The Church's whole mystery of unity and charity is concentrated here: the union of the baptized with Christ in the Communion of his Body and Blood; the union of the baptized with one another in the Communion of the same Body and Blood. If the Church must, in virtue of the gospel and of baptism, be an *assembly*, she must, in virtue of the Eucharist, be and remain, in spite of her weaknesses, a *communion*. If baptism is the sign of faith, and of obedience to the word of God, the Eucharist is the sign of love responding to love. Those who share in the Body of Christ become one Body with him, and with one another (1 Cor 10:16-17). In the Eucharistic assembly, then, it appears visibly, as nowhere else, that the faithful are one, and only one, in love. The meaning of this assembly and celebration are, moreover, attested and proclaimed in the words of the priest.[11]

5. *The Church does not cease to offer the ideal of evangelical perfection,* inviting those of her children who desire to do so, to live completely, even in this world, their full life as the adopted children of God, wholly consecrated to God and to the service of men, wholly vowed in the Spirit to the service and imitation of Christ. The religious life does not pretend to be an exhaustive means of the Church's holiness, but it symbolizes in a concentrated form the vocation of the whole Church—on the condition obviously that it is a really significant and unambiguous manifestation of life according to Christ.[12] It is

---

11. That the Eucharistic assembly can act as an appeal to those outside it is proved by the testimony of many converts, who attribute to the sign of the Eucharist the fact that they returned to or entered the Church.

12. "Religious should direct the whole force of their being towards the end that through them the Church may manifest Christ more and more perfectly, both to *Christians* and to *non-Christians*" (LG 46). "The religious tries to imitate more closely, and represent continually in the Church, that form of life which the Son of God embraced when he came into the world to do the Father's will, and which he proposed to the disciples who followed him" (LG 44).

in this sense that *Lumen gentium* observes that the religious life
is inseparable from the life and holiness of the Church (LG
44 and 40).

In poverty and detachment from worldly goods, religious
life shows that the blessedness to come is already present in the
world. In chastity, it anticipates, through a deep, exclusive
and immediate union of the heart with Christ, our eschatological
condition.[13] In obedience, it is in conformity with Christ, who
came on earth to fulfill the Father's will, even to the point of
death on the cross. Poverty, chastity and obedience express one
and the same unique preference, "the preference of Christ to all
the goods which the world has to offer, in the sacrifice of which
he is seen as the one thing necessary; the preference of Christ
to physical procreation, and more than that to conjugal love,
in the sacrifice of which he is seen as the supreme Love; the
preference of Christ to our own individual liberty, in the sacrifice of which he is seen as the only Lord." [14]

Far from disappearing, this ideal of the religious life, even
if it is at present being tried in the crucible of many defections,
is tending to spread to conditions of life where it would once
have been a stranger. The creation of *secular institutes*, for
instance, consecrates men and women living in the world by
means of a true profession of the evangelical counsels. Since
the religious life is to such a degree bound up with the holiness of the Church, it is easy to understand, as Pastor Schutz
of Taizé points out, how Luther, in rejecting monasticism as

---

13. On the meaning of the vows see: the decree on the religious
life (n. 12); the decree on the ministry of priests (n. 16). Pastor Roger
Schutz of Taizé writes apropos of chastity, "we have discovered at Taizé
that committing ourselves to chastity in the sense of celibacy is closely
bound up with the waiting of contemplation. If not, how are we to make
authentic the sign of a love for God which wishes to be undivided?"
(*Dynamique du provisoire* [Taizé, 1965], p. 163); trans., *The Power of the
Provisional* (London, 1969).

14. G. Martelet, *Sainteté de l'Église et vie religieuse* (Toulouse, 1964),
p. 62.

a form of religious life, has put the authenticity of his Reformation seriously in question.[15]

6. *The witness of heroic sanctity* — The Church does not content herself with proposing evangelical perfection and holiness as an ideal. For what would be the value of preaching an ideal of life which was never realized? She not only brings to bear the means of holiness (the gospel and the sacraments), but she also gives birth to saints. If she must carry the weight of many sinners, she counts also among her members a not inconsiderable number in whom an ordinary degree of holiness is to be found. But more than that, she can count in her ranks in every epoch, those of all ages and all social circumstances who have arrived at an heroic sanctity, contemplative, apostolic or reparative. Every man can encounter this holiness if not in the course of his personal experience, at least in the report of history; for St. Paul, St. Ignatius of Antioch, St. Basil, St. Gregory, St. Athanasius, St. Augustine, St. Ambrose, St. Bernard, St. Bruno, St. Benedict, St. Clare, St. Monica, St. Francis of Assisi, St. Dominic, St. Louis, St. Edward, St. Henry, St. Thomas Aquinas, St. Bonaventure, St. Joan of Arc, St. Ignatius of Loyola, St. Francis Xavier, St. Vincent de Paul, St. John Vianney, St. John Bosco, St. John of the Cross, St. Alphonsus Liguori, St. Francis de Sales, St. Philip Neri, St. Charles Borromeo, St. Teresa of Avila, St. Thérèse of Lisieux, St. Peter Canisius, St. Robert Bellarmine, St. Jean de Brebeuf, St. Isaac Jogues, St. Peter Claver ... all these and a great many others belong to universal history. There is no one of even an elementary degree of culture who has not heard of these human beings who have shaped history, and there is no one who cannot grasp the intensity, the completeness and the constancy of the charity which is manifested in their lives.

7. *The periodic reformation of the Church* — The Church, as we have noticed, includes, as well as these instances of heroic sanctity, a great mass of sinners. She needs constantly, therefore,

---

15. R. Schutz, *Dynamique du provisoire* (Taizé, 1965), pp. 164-165; trans., *The Power of the Provisional*.

in her whole body as in her members, to reform herself. The
Second Vatican Council has expressed this duty of the Church
to renew and purify herself with a unanimity and force which
have never been so urgent before.[16] Not only has the Council recognized the Church's need of constant reform, but, setting the
example, it has itself proceeded to a vast examination of conscience. It has acknowledged on the part of the Church omissions and negligences in adapting the message of the gospel
to different countries and peoples, harshness and lack of understanding in dealing with those who have gone astray, attitudes which showed little discernment and so on. It has rec-
ommended a return to simplicity, in worship, in preaching and
in faith. It has inculcated upon those in authority the care they
should take to be humbly and charitably at the service of those
over whom they are set. It has continually stressed the tension
which exists between the painful situation of a Church composed of sinners and the vocation to holiness to which all are
called.[17]

The Church is constantly in need of reform and she is aware
of it. History is our witness indeed that she is not only *reforman-
da* but *reformata*.[18] In order to be faithful to the gospel, which
demands a constant *metanoia*, the Church has periodically proceeded to renew herself through a succession of reforms. *The
Cluniac reform*, for instance, was extended to the clergy in
general and to the whole of the Church, thanks to Henry III,
Leo IX, Gregory VII, and Innocent III, and thanks to the Cistercians of St. Bernard, the Canons Regular of St. Augustine,
the Premonstratentians, the hospital and military orders of the
twelfth century and the Franciscans and Dominicans of the
thirteenth. The Tridentine reform of the sixteenth century, with
the reform of the papacy and the curia and the immense move-

---

16. See, for example: LG 8, 9, 15, 65; GS 43; UR 6.
17. A. Grillmeier, "Esprit, position fondamentale et caractère propre
de la Constitution," in: G. Baraúna, ed., *L'Église de Vatican II*, 2: 167-
173.
18. H. Küng, *L'Église*, 2: 474-476; English translations, *The Church*
(New York, 1968; London, 1969).

ment of Catholic restoration was prolonged by St. Ignatius and
the Company of Jesus, by St. Charles Borromeo, St. Francis de
Sales, St. Vincent de Paul and many more. *The present reform
of the Second Vatican Council* is a veritable revolution in the
Church's order, whose repercussions cannot be foreseen.

Even in her poverty and distress the Church remains a
paradox. It is she herself who judges and reforms—and in the
depths of disaster finds the strength to recover. The paradox
is that men so weak and contemptible should have the strength
to raise their eyes, and look to the future. The paradox is that
the Church, in spite of her weakness, regularly produces saints,
great and faithful enough to be offered as models for the imitation of all. Yet this paradox is only one of the many paradoxes
which constitute the sign of the Church.

CHAPTER IX

Discerning the Sign of the Church

Up to this point we have been concerned simply with a description of the many and various paradoxes and tensions which go to make up the Church as a Phenomenon. Let us return now to the question posed at the beginning: how can the Church as an observable reality make even unbelievers understand that she is in fact and not merely in name the *locus* of salvation in Jesus Christ? How can *the Church as a Phenomenon* attract men's attention and awaken them to the presence of the *Mystery* which lives within her and explains her? To answer this question entails examining the dialectic of the sign of the Church, and trying to envisage the position of those confronted by it.

1. *The dialectic of the sign*

This discussion takes for granted from the outset that in all the reflections which follow, one should bear constantly in mind what has been said in preceding chapters about paradoxes and tensions in the Church. It is indeed *all these characteristics*, taken together and qualitatively, contrasting, multiple, multiform and complex, which go to make up what theology calls the sign of the Church. Only faith, we know, perceives beneath appearances the profound and mysterious provenance of the ecclesial reality. But it would seem that there is enough light in the Church, despite the faults which obsure her face, to attract the attention of men of good will and arouse them to positive questioning about the *meaning* of her presence in the world. The importance of a phenomenology of the Church, as a basis for an authentic semiology, has already been stressed; for only reflection founded on facts can do justice to the dynamism and originality proper to each of the signs.

It seems to me that if we ask ourselves precisely how the sign of the Church acts, by what process it is able to lead man today to question himself about the Church and conclude that she is the place of salvation, we shall find that it operates according to a process analogous to that which leads us to recognize in Christ the sign of God.

In the dialectical movement through which we pass from the sign to the thing signified, it is convenient to distinguish on the one hand the *spontaneous* discernment of the man who, at a given moment in his life and religious experience, finds himself confronted by the sign of the Church and discovers salvation there, and, on the other hand, the *scientific* discernment of the theologian, who seeks to make explicit in methodical discourse the elements of which the intuitive and synthetic process of spontaneous discernment is composed. This scientific discernment is not better than spontaneous discernment: they are at two different levels.

Discourse itself, whether it is spontaneous or scientific, may have two different orientations. If one takes up the position which was that of the nineteenth century, the sign of the Church appears dominantly as a phenomenon indicative of transcendence, a moral transcendence comparable, in its own order, to the physical transcendence of miracle. It will be a matter then, according to this perspective, of showing that only the power of God could account for the facts observed (unity, stability, holiness, fruitfulness), that only a divine cause explains an effect of this dimension. This is the point of view of the First Vatican Council.

Without denying the validity of this approach, I think that the Second Vatican Council, as has already been stressed, gives us a slightly different orientation, more in accordance with the phenomenological data, and with the mentality of man today. From this new point of view, the Church appears as a sign of *Presence,* and, more precisely, as a sign of an enigmatic Presence.

Like Christ himself, the Church appears as a particularly intense focus of holiness and salvation. It is true that the Church has to carry a heavy weight of sin and sinners. And yet there is in the very acknowledgment of her *lack of holiness* and of her divisions, in her daily assembly round the altar to celebrate the death of Christ (the witness to the love of God the Savior come to bring men together again in unity), in her mysterious survival through history, in her perpetual renewal and capacity to start afresh, in the dynamism which leads her to offer the word of salvation to all races and peoples, and above all in the perpetual spring of heroic sanctity, a Sign of a Presence within her, personal, active and sanctifying. In her, salvation seems to be concentrated and operative.

The question arises then, "If there were salvation in the world, would it not be in this active *Presence?* Is not the Church that light in the darkness which men look for and which a secret instinct makes them anticipate? The exterior Presence of the Church, moreover, meets in man's heart with the hidden connaturality of grace. The question arises all the more in that this Presence of the Church acts on the mind, through its paradoxical characteristics, as a sort of provocation, a demand to be understood. For it does not surrender itself at once, like something evidential. It appears rather as a *riddle* to be solved, or better a mystery to be explored. The paradoxical presence of the Church matches that other paradox in whom she claims her origin, Christ himself. As Christ appears as a *theophany,* so the Church appears as a *Christophany.*

Confronted by the Church, man finds himself then in the presence of a Plenitude of holiness and salvation which refers itself to Christ as the source and explanation of its existence. The enigmatic presence of this Plenitude of salvation among men is an invitation to seek the answer to the riddle, to come nearer in order to understand the mystery. It may be that the appeal which the sign makes will remain unanswered; it may also be that the appeal will reach the inner citadel of the soul only after long resistance, followed by reflection and a process of inner ripening; but it may be, again, that the process of discerning the sign will be sudden and headlong, and that under the action of grace a man will pass directly from the plenitude observed to its source, and identify the Church as the place of salvation where God wills to bring all men together in the unity of love.

This intuitive and synthetic approach which characterizes spontaneous discernment can be analyzed in scientific discernment to yield the following elements.

We find ourselves in the presence of a religious society apparently like the many other religious societies dispersed throughout the world. And yet this apparent *identity* masks a profound *difference*. The Church as a visible organism, with her members, her doctrine, her clergy, her rites, her institutions, the whole of her existence and history, provides the external structure of the sign. It is the phenomenological analysis of this structure, with all its elements, which allows us to lay bare the real meaning of the phenomenon (what the sign signifies). The dialectic of the sign is aimed precisely at leading us from the signifier to the thing signified, from the Phenomenon to the meaning of the Phenomenon, the reality at depth, the absolute hidden in the appearances.

The expressiveness of a sign is variable. In Christ sign attains its maximum expressiveness. For in Jesus-Christ-as-a Phenomenon, what is apparently identical with the phenomenon, that is, the man, "the Jesus of history," expresses the wholly-Other, that is, God himself in Person. Jesus is sign *par excellence*, sign carrying in itself the highest degree of signification, sign which is identified with its own meaning in the single unique Person of the Son of God. In the case of the Church, *the-Church-as-a-Phenomenon*, which appears as a purely human totality (apparently identical with the phenomenon), is revealed on analysis as something profoundly different. The *meaning* of the sign is that the Church is the community of salvation in Jesus Christ, instituted and willed by God.

But how is the mind projected in this way beyond appearances, beyond the Phenomenon itself, and challenged *to look for meaning*, that is to say, the meaning of the mystery hidden in the Phenomenon? It is through attentive and detailed analysis of the Phenomenon, and in particular through consideration of the paradoxes and tensions in the Church. The rôle of paradox is to draw attention and to arouse curiosity.

The Church, as we have seen, presents to the view of the observer, even the unbelieving observer, a *tout ensemble* of paradoxical characteristics, themselves constituted of many-sided tensions, each with sufficient explosive potentiality to shatter the Church. It is not, as we have seen, a matter of theoretical threats, over which one might split hairs as over so many innocent algebraic possibilities, but of historical realities which have all but engulfed the Church. The Church-as-a-Phenomenon provides, in totality, a problem which demands explanation, which demands a sufficient and commensurate cause. The Phenomenon refers us to something else, to Another. For we need to discover the principle of intelligibility which underlies the great antinomies of the Church: unity and catholicity, permanence and temporality, sin and holiness. What then is the key to the riddle?

If one allows that historicity is a constitutive element in man, in so far as man is consciousness, it already follows that history is the place for a contingent manifestation of God, and that man should interrogate history to find at what time and place it has perhaps been touched by salvation. If one allows, besides, that man is essentially both person and society, one should be on the look-out for some great, privileged social entity, an institution in which salvation is as it were concentrated and fulfilled. But one should expect also to find in this society all the marks of weakness which affect an institution made up of human beings. Now the Church, in all that she is and in all that she says about herself, certainly seems to be this great privileged society.[1]

For the Church offers as an explanation of herself, that all that she is and does proceeds from a special intervention of God in Jesus Christ. Like Mary, she attests that of herself she is nothing, that all her cohesive and expansive force, all her power to save and sanctify come from God in Jesus Christ, the epiphany of the Father. What is apparently identical with the phenomenon is thus revealed as totally different. The real meaning of the-Church-as-a-Phenomenon is the actuating presence within her of Christ, the Son of God, and of his Spirit, the source of unity and charity.

Such an explanation is not to be rejected without examination, since it certainly seems the only one adequate to explain the facts observed. If it is admitted, everything becomes lucid, coherent, intelligible. If not, it is vain to persist in the pursuit of "natural" explanations: the Church, with all her paradoxes and tensions and her twenty centuries of history, remains a riddle which cannot be read. In the face of the character and importance of the facts observed, it is rationally safe to recognize as veracious the Church's testimony to herself—that she is, in the midst of mankind, the community of salvation in Jesus Christ, willed by God.

This conclusion is the more reasonable in that there is an astonishing harmony between the facts observed and the message of Christ, to which the Church refers herself. For the gospel proclaims that Christ is the Son of God, come among men to set up the kingdom of God on earth, that is, to transform men's hearts into filial hearts and to unite all mankind in one People of God, so that they may be one Body, the Body of Christ, given life by the Spirit of love who unites the Father and the Son. And the Church appears in our world as the visible Presence, at least inchoatively, of the transformation proclaimed.

1. K. Rahner, L'homme a l'écoute du Verbe (Paris, 1968), pp. 309-312; English translation, Hearers of the Word (New York, 1969).

Wherever the Church is, the sanctifying power of Christ and his Spirit is at work, and does not cease to purify, to give life, to make holy. In the *saint*, particularly, a new type of humanity appears, a child of God, who lives and acts under the influence of the Spirit. "In the lives of our fellow human beings most perfectly transformed into the image of Christ (cf. 2 Cor 3:18), God reveals vividly to men his presence and his countenance. In them God himself speaks to us, gives us a sign of his kingdom and draws us powerfully towards it, so great is the cloud of witnesses who surround us (cf. Heb 12:1), and so great is their testimony to the truth of the gospel." [2] In the *Church*, a new type of society appears, where, as well as indications of her human and earthly condition, there is, as it were, a transparency, through which shine *incunabula* of the heavenly Jerusalem. There is already to be seen in her, in outline, the face of mankind assembled in unity and charity, in the image of the Trinity's communion of life. From this consistency between the gospel of Christ and the paradoxical characteristics of the Church, we may legitimately infer that the Church is really, as she declares, the sign of the advent of God among men, the place where the Presence of salvation in Jesus Christ is to be found. The *paradox* cloaks the *Mystery*.

Let us go back to the method used. It proceeds by way of internal intelligibility, of search for meaning. It sets out not from the glorious and absolute attributes of the Church, but from the paradoxes which she constitutes. It seeks to understand these paradoxes, in themselves, in their mutual relationships, and in connection with the explanation which the Church offers of herself and her relation to Christ. The consistency of the explanation offered and its ability to account for the phenomena observed (for their nature, their scope and their paradoxical

---

2. "In vita eorum qui, humanitatis nostrae consortes, ad imaginem tamen Christi perfectius transformantur (cf. 2 Cor 3, 18), Deus praesentiam vultumque suum hominibus vivide manifestat. In eis Ipse nos alloquitur, signumque nobis praebet Regni sui, ad quod tantam habentes impositam nubem testium (cf. Heb 12, 1), talemque contestationem veritatis Evangelii, potenter attrahimur" (LG 50).

character) lead us to think that the Church's testimony is truthful, that she is really in the midst of mankind, "the universal sacrament of salvation" in Jesus Christ. The explanation of the *Phenomenon* resides in the *Mystery attested*. We do not set out from the moral miracle: we end in it. This approach does not, any more than others do, lead to an evidential certainty, but to a moral certainty, sufficient to provide a motive for a rational decision. In order to open ourselves to the presence of the mystery which is hidden in the flesh of the Phenomenon and the fragility of the institutional Church, we must be ready to lose ourselves and to be carried by the Spirit who speaks in the innermost depths of our being.

2. *Men confronted by the Sign*

We are limited in any comments we may make on this confrontation by the very specificness of the sign itself.

1. Let us remind ourselves, first of all, that we are dealing with a sign, not a blow from a blunt instrument. We are dealing with a sign which indicates a Presence to be recognized, a riddle to be solved. This presence is revealed gradually as a plenitude of sanctification and salvation. This is not to say that the sign in itself lacks consistency, that it is deficient and consequently unfit to fulfill its *rôle* as a sign. In the sign of the Church, as in every other sign, we have to distinguish an objective pole (the sign in itself) and a subjective pole (the man confronted by the sign). More so than miracle or prophecy, the sign of the Church, a polyvalent sign, is inexhaustible in intelligibility. But it does not follow that it acts *ex opere operato*, or that all human beings are equally prepared to grasp it in its entirety. Christ was sign *par excellence*: many saw and heard him, and yet how many identified him? "The Church," says Fr. Rahner, "appears to unprejudiced eyes which have taken in the whole panorama of history, as being the holy Church. An inexhaustible source of holiness, she is an intelligible sign lifted up before the nations (Is 11:10), constituting in herself a

living witness to God's action in her." [3] The value of the sign
is real, its dynamism is real; nevertheless its discernment is
bound up, even more than that of the sign of Christ, with the
circumstances and dispositions of the human subject.

2. The sign of the Church, as we have seen, is *complex, paradoxical, enigmatic*. Because it is so, it presupposes, on the part
of the observer, a certain ability to grasp values in terms of
wholes, and to judge them in relation to other wholes of a like
nature and quality. Exclusive attention, for instance, to the
detail of the sign and an incapacity to grasp it in its many-
sided totality, robs it of all its dynamism. In the same way, insufficient knowledge, and, *a fortiori*, ignorance of the life of
the Church throughout the ages, deprives the sign of one of
its most evocative paradoxes; for the Church is not simply, as
it were, a single incision in the line of time, but a movement,
a history which is prepared and accomplished, and *lasts*. The
action of the sign, therefore, depends, in great part, on the
knowledge a man has of the Church and her history. Even
among Catholics themselves, who live in the midst of the
Church, is there not a very great diversity in their knowledge
of her and consequently in their appreciation of her value as a
sign?

This is still more true when it is a question of those who see
the Church only from the outside. The discernment of the sign
and its values is more than ever bound up with whatever experience they may have of the Church. How many have never
met the Church? How many more are acquainted only with her
less important manifestations: her monuments, her pilgrimages,
her customs, her folklore? They have never had any real contact with the *life* of the Church. How could the Church then
be a sign to them?

Lastly we must take account of the extremely varied circumstances in which even those who do so effectively make con-

---

3. K. Rahner, *Est-il possible aujourd'hui de croire?* (Paris, 1966),
p. 41; English translation, *Faith Today* (London, 1967).

tact with the Church. They may approach her from the point
of view of the historiographer, the sociologist or the aesthetic
critic: they may experience before her art, her doctrine and her
institutions the same sort of curiosity, esteem and even ad-
miration which one experiences before the Roman Empire or
before Buddhism. They may write superbly about her, like
Macauley,[4] but their religious life is nonetheless unchanged. The
look which rests on the Church remains a *profane* look.

There are, on the other hand, those who approach the
Church humbly and sincerely seeking for the truth. This is a
religious attitude, the attitude of one who already belongs to
Christ in his openness to grace, who asks in his heart whether
the Church is not the door to salvation he is looking and hoping
for. If this search is pursued in solitude, without help from the
Church herself, it may be long and painful. It may stop half-
way, in a communion which is certainly Christian, but not in the
full sense of the Catholic communion. But it may happen—as I
think it most often does—that those who seek the truth, are in
their journey towards faith, helped by the Church herself, in

---

4. Fr. Latourelle gives here part of the famous passage from Macaulay,
as quoted, in a French translation, by Karl Adam in *Le Vrai visage du
Catholicisme* (Paris, 1934), pp. 20-21. The quotation is from Macaulay's
review in 1840 of Von Ranke's *History of the Popes,* in print today in
Macaulay's *Critical and Historical Essays,* vol. II, p. 38 (London, 1967).
The original text is as follows:

"There is not, and there never was on this earth, a work of human
policy so well deserving of examination as the Roman Catholic Church.
The history of that Church joins together the two great ages of human
civilization. No other institution is left standing which carries the mind
back to the times when the smoke of sacrifice rose from the Pantheon,
and when camelopards and tigers bounded in the Flavian amphitheatre.
The proudest royal houses are but of yesterday, when compared with the
line of the Supreme Pontiffs. That line we trace back in an unbroken
series, from the Pope who crowned Napoleon in the nineteenth century
to the Pope who crowned Pepin in the eighth.... The republic of
Venice came next in antiquity. But the republic of Venice was modern when
compared with the Papacy; and the Republic of Venice is gone, and
the Papacy remains. The Papacy remains, not in decay, not a mere

one of her members or communities, and that thus helped and sustained in their search, they grasp more quickly and more completely the real meaning at depth of the Church-as-a-Pheno-menon.

Reflection on the discernment of the sign of the Church must then take account of this infinite variety of human sit-uations and dispositions. To tell the truth, it is only after entering the Church and experiencing her life that the neophyte will discover the full meaning of the sign of the Church. For—it needs to be stressed again—the *fullness* of intelligibility in a sign such as this (as also in the sign of Christ) is possessed by the Church as a social Body, since no individual could exhaust the depth and breadth of intelligibility in a sign as complex as these. Christians share in the awareness of the community, each according to his intelligence, his cultivation and his experience of the Church.

3. The Church is a *vulnerable,* a fragile sign, to be distin-guished, in this respect, from the sign of Christ. Christ's holi-ness could not, it is true, avoid the scandal of God's epiphany in the flesh. In becoming incarnate, God exposed himself to the risk of hearing that he was blaspheming or that he was dead. But Christ was without sin, and the same cannot be

---

antique, but full of life and youthful vigour. The Catholic Church is still sending forth to the farthest ends of the world missionaries as zealous as those who landed in Kent with Augustin, and still confronting hostile kings with the same spirit with which she confronted Attila . . . . Nor do we see any sign which indicates that the term of her long dominion is approaching. She saw the commencement of all the governments and of all the ecclesiastical establishments that now exist in the world; and we feel no assurance that she is not destined to see the end of them all. She was great and respected before the Saxon had set foot on Britain, before the Frank had passed the Rhine, when Grecian eloquence still flourished in Antioch, when idols were still worshipped in the temple of Mecca. And she may still exist in undiminished vigour, when some traveller from New Zealand shall, in the midst of a vast solitude, take his stand on a broken arch of London Bridge to sketch the ruins of St. Paul's."

said for the Church. In her, Christ's Spirit has come down upon sinful men. The *kenosis* of the Spirit, if one may put it so, is deeper even than that of the incarnate Word.[5] That is why the sign of the Church can easily become a stumbling-block. The sign, objectively speaking, is given, and it is striking enough for the man of good will to be able to discern in the Church the action of Christ and his Spirit. But this discerning of the sign is conditioned by two factors: the good will of the observer, and the sufficiently striking witness of the Catholic community.

On the part of the observer, the sign of the Church, in that it is ambiguous and vulnerable, takes for granted a certain magnanimity. The mean in soul will not be able to see the true greatness of the Church. They will see only her ugliness and her sin, like a visitor to a bombed cathedral who notices only the broken glass of the windows and is insensible to the prayer which rises from the ordered columns and the vault above. The sign of the Church is not inconsiderable, but the mean-minded will always find reasons for thinking it insufficient, and will always be able to justify their reasons.

4. The *impact*, that is, of the sign of the Church is, in contrast to the sign of Christ, bound up with the variable life of the members of the Church. Whether the sign is more or less operative, depends not only on the observer but on *what is observed*, that is to say, on Catholics themselves. Many outside the Church are asking themselves whether the Church is not their home, the place of salvation. The Church is like a star in the night, or a lighthouse shining across the dark sea; the brightness of the light and therefore the scope of its radiance depend on us. It depends on Catholics themselves whether the Church makes more and more manifest the holiness which comes from God's initiative, which she has received from Christ; for it is difficult to proclaim the gospel of salvation when life has already refuted the gospel. To proclaim the gospel, or

---

5. H. Mühlen, *Una Persona Mystica* (Rome, 1968), p. 456.

salvation through the Son of God, is to propose the Church as a living reality, carrying within her the operative and transforming Presence of the God she preaches. The Church cannot proclaim the gospel to the world unless she lives it in the world. She cannot proclaim Christ unless she derives her own life from him.

Jesus' contemporaries encountered salvation in Christ. Since then, from Pentecost to the parousia, it is in the Church (in pastors and people) that the men of every time must meet Christ and salvation. The encounter with the ecclesial community living in unity and charity, must become the sacrament of encounter with God. "Charity incarnate, or the transposition of our love for God into the realm of our relations with our fellow-men is the great and irresistible motive for the credibility of the Christian faith. By means of this transposition men are confronted with the reality of salvation appearing in the midst of their own lives. They meet grace visibly present on the very path along which they walk; they cannot escape, and are obliged to take up some position in regard to it." [6]

They will be drawn to it, however, only if the unity in charity which Christ has brought is really visible to them as men of their own time; for it is above all in the visible *contemporaneousness* of what is given, received and lived (that is, unity in charity), that the attraction of the Church consists. If many pass the Church by, without even registering the fact that she exists, is it not because her visibility is too poor, her light too dim? The sign of the Church cannot operate unless, in the Catholic community, the Church appears as a force which transforms life. If the Church lives the life of Christ and his Spirit, then, and then only, will she become the sign of the authenticity of the salvation she proclaims. And having met salvation in the Church, men will desire to share it.

In the end, the Church is sign in so far as she tends to approximate to the *Res* or *Reality* which she images, that is,

---

6. E. Schillebeeckx, *Le Christ sacrement de la rencontre de Dieu* (Paris, 1960), p. 248; trans., *Christ: the Sacrament of the Encounter with God* (London and New York, 1963).

Christ in his universal love. The more faithfully she reflects Christ, like a clear glass, the more the holiness of the Bride tends to reproduce that of the Bridegroom, the more she *signifies* and *attracts*. As Christ was the epiphany of the Father for the Jews of his time, so the Church must be the epiphany of Christ for the men of today. It is from this point of view, of a Church which needs to be the authentic sign of Christ, that the Second Vatican Council has stressed with an insistence almost amounting to obsession the necessity of the witness of holiness of life. The Church, in each of her members and in all the communities which go to make her up, must be the living witness to Christ through the ages. As she is the communion of men with one another and with God, the more visible and striking this communion is, the more the sign will attract.

5. In the eyes of the Second Vatican Council, then, the great sign of the coming of salvation in Jesus Christ is the life of unity in charity lived by the Church and her members as individuals. It is in the *visibility* of this charity that the Church presents herself to men as a sign among the nations of the love of God revealed in Jesus Christ. It is not, however, without importance here, to specify precisely under what conditions this life of charity can become for the men of our time, the sign of the coming of God.

The witness of charity assumes, in the world today, a greater importance than ever before; but, to be efficacious, it must take new forms, assume modalities which are concrete and even specific.

(a) *The importance of respect for human values* — Man is more sensitive today than he used to be to respect on the part of the Christian for the human values recognized in secular society—professional competence, for instance, efficiency in work done, respect for truth and care to speak it, honesty and humility in scientific research, frankness and sincerity in human relationships, consistency between what is said and what is done, respect for promises, for the word given, respect for freedom of conscience, respect for the well-being of others, a sense of public service.[7] Contemporary man has a respect for anyone who is engaged in his own particular task (whether he be a religious, a cleric or a layman), and who is fulfilling it faithfully according to his conscience. He inclines towards the man who knows how to share the sorrows and sufferings as well as the joys of those in his own *milieu,* who tries to improve the social institutions of his own country.

If, on the contrary, the Christian shows no respect, or shows too little respect, for these values recognized by the secular world, his profession of Christian faith, however open and vehement it may be, is apt to fall on deaf ears. Contemporary man demands of the Christian who refers himself to the gospel, that he should respect human values, which are, besides, assumed in their entirety by the gospel. He does not think that the Christian is to be taken seriously when he talks about holiness, if he is a liar or a thief, or lazy or incompetent.

Witness is not bound up with any particular profession or *métier,* but with the human subject who witnesses. It is in the measure in which the Catholic, the Christian, submits to the demands of his profession or *métier* that he is already a focus of light (AG 12).

(b) *Witness in a pluralist society* — In other times, in a homogeneous Christendom, or in the midst of wholly Catholic nations, charity had to operate only among Catholics, missionaries alone assuming the responsibility of carrying the gospel beyond the visible frontiers of the Church. It is quite another matter today. In a world *now* becoming more and more unified, walls of separation no longer exist: all the spiritual families

---

7. It is with this in mind that the decree *Presbyterorum Ordinis* insists on respect for human values. Since priests must be witnesses in the world, "certain qualities play a great part, those which are rightly appreciated in human relationships — like kindness, sincerity, moral courage, perseverance, a passion for justice, tact and consideration, and many others."

(Protestants, Jews, Muslims, Hindus and so on), all forms of belief and unbelief, live side by side, associate with one another, mix, fuse.

It is at the heart of this new humanity (where the closed compartments of Christendom no longer exist) that the members of the Church have to witness to the charity of Christ. Each must become, in the very beautiful words of Charles de Foucauld, *"le frère universel."* It follows that "the charity of Christians will have to witness to the coming of the God of light and love in their daily encounters with the most diverse spiritual families."[8] Pastor Schutz, addressing Catholics, writes in the same vein: "Give us existential evidence that you believe in God, that he is indeed your security. Show us that you live the gospel in its primal freshness, in the spirit of poverty, in solidarity with all, and not only with your own confessional family."[9]

(c) *Witness inside the Church* — On the other hand, if witness to charity has to become more universal, more ecumenical and more missionary than before, it has also to become more intense among Catholics themselves. The Church in her local communities and as a world-wide community should stand out among other communities as a communion, whose members have a special love for one another in the Spirit. She should become more and more what she is—messianic and divine, giving to the world through the radiance of her love an effective sign that the love of God has come among men. "For a Catholic," to quote Pastor Schutz again, "to show solidarity with all the baptized means first of all to show solidarity *inside his own Church*, with all the spiritual families who are the inspiration of Catholicism. At this juncture of history, we do not expect

---

8. H.-M. Féret, "L'amour fraternel vécu en Église et le signe de la venue de Dieu," *Concilium*, n. 29 (1967): 29: translated in English edition.

9. R. Schutz, *Dynamique du provisoire* (Taizé, 1965), pp. 44-45; trans., *The Power of the Provisional* (London, 1969).

Catholics to jib at one another. If the different cross-currents which are being revealed were to hinder dialogue, it would put ecumenism to an unparalleled test." [10]

(d) *The witness of belonging to the Church* — Lastly, it needs to be emphasized, the witness of Catholics must be inseparably a witness of belonging to the Church. For how is one to witness to a Church one blushes to belong to, to a Church one is always attacking and accusing of betraying Jesus Christ? What sort of Christ is it who could be perpetually set up in opposition to his own Body? And what sort of member is it which is always in revolt against the body of which it is a part? It is incomprehensible that a Catholic should dissociate himself from the Church out of anxiety to be faithful to Christ. For by very reason of his faith, he confesses that Christ and the Church are united as Bridegroom and Bride, as Head and Body. We do not have to go outside the Church to bind ourselves afresh to Christ and the gospel. After all, the Catholic belongs to that small remnant which believes that the only real unity will be accomplished in Christ and the Church. If he refuses to identify himself with the Church his witness is deceptive and vain.

6. The place where, *par excellence,* there is to be found that unity in charity to which the ecclesial community and the local communities must witness, if they are to be really a sign of the advent of salvation, is the Eucharist, as *assembly* and as *sacrifice.* [11] For the Eucharistic celebration gathers up all the moments in the life of Christ and all the moments in the life of the Church.

The Eucharist brings together all the temporal modes of *Christ's Presence:* (a) it presupposes his Presence among men at the time of his mortal life and reminds us of this in the reading of the gospel; (b) it manifests his personal and spiritual

---

10. *Ibid.,* p. 109.
11. *The decree on the ministry of priests,* 5.

Presence in his Church, since it is in virtue of this actuating Presence that the community is assembled in faith, made capable of pronouncing efficaciously, in the person of the priest, the words of Consecration, and made spiritually ready for the Communion; and lastly (c) it reproduces, through the real Presence of Christ in the Sacrament in which he gives himself as our food, the synthesis of the personal and spiritual Presence of Christ in glory with Christ the Word incarnate in history.[12]

The Eucharist brings together also all the temporal modes in *the life of the Church*. It is the meal of remembrance, the memorial of the saving passion and death of Christ, who gave birth to the Church. In the present it is the communion of all his faithful people with the living Christ in glory, and at the same time their communion in charity with one another. And lastly, as the meal of hope, it images and anticipates the eschatological banquet, where all the elect are united at the table of the Lord.

What is accomplished in the Eucharist is *already*, then, a bringing together in the unity of love, but it is at the same time a call to extend this unity to the whole of mankind. For the Eucharistic celebration represents not only the real and actual unity of members of the same Body, but also the actuating dynamism of union, which is orientated towards bringing together mankind as such, in order to constitute the mystical Body of Christ. In giving himself as food, Christ brings together in unity those who receive him, and at the same time fosters the growth of his mystical Body. Through those to whom he gives life and nourishment, he actuates and operates this growth, so that the mystical Body, present intensively in the liturgical assembly, tends by its internal dynamism to coincide with the whole of mankind.

In the Eucharistic assembly, the unity of the Church in charity is at once symbolized and accomplished. The Eucharistic community *images* and *realizes* the community of those who live the life of Christ and his Spirit. If it is true that the

---

12. E. Pousset, "L'Eucharistie, sacrement et existence," NRT 88 (1966), 946.

Church is the sign of the communion of love which the Trinity seeks to establish among men, we must say that it is in the Eucharistic assembly that this sign reaches its highest and most concentrated expressiveness.[13]

3. *Conclusion*

In the end, therefore, the more the ecclesial community lives to the full the sacramental life which culminates and is concentrated in the Eucharist, the more significant it becomes— the more *expressive* of the Mystery of the Church, which is the Mystery of unity in charity. The more the Church is *an authentic sacrament*, that is to say, the more she unfurls in history her power to represent and realize salvation, the more also she will become a source of light, making visibly manifest that the salvation she preaches is really accomplished. The more the members of the Church live the Mystery of communion that she essentially is, the more this communion itself will become a sign, expressing the salvation which she proclaims as the decisive event in history.

There is no doubt, because of the theandric nature of the Church, that there will always be an inevitable tension between the sign and what is signified. But the consistency and harmony between them can always grow and develop. And it is precisely in the measure in which the Church lives to the full her reality as a sacrament, an efficacious sign, that she will become at the same time for those outside her, the sign of the coming of salvation into the world. At this point the sacra-

---

13. On this subject Pastor Schutz has said, "The Eucharist, at once the means and the manifestation of unity, is alone able to give us the supernatural strength and power to accomplish here on earth our unity as baptized Christians. In the Eucharist we have existential truth. The Sacrament of unity, it is offered us to dissolve, in ourselves and about us, all the ferments of separation . . . . The wave of ecumenism will fall back unless the day soon comes which will unite at the same table all who, though separated confessionally, believe in the real Presence of Christ in the Eucharist" (*Dynamique du provisoire*, p. 134; trans., *The Power of the Provisional*).

mental economy and the economy of the signs of revelation meet and tend to coincide. The salvation accomplished is a sign of the salvation announced. "That they all may be one. As thou Father art in me and I in thee, that they also may be one in us: *that the world may believe that thou hast sent me*" (Jn 17:21). When the members of the Church are united in Christ and through him among themselves, they make men, even unbelievers, understand that salvation has come into our world, and that the Spirit of Christ, the source of unification and unity, is at work among men. *The Spirit of Christ* is then revealed historically in the visible Church. Definitively speaking, it is he who makes the visible Church the universal sign of salvation.[14]

---

14. H. Mühlen, *Una Persona Mystica* (Rome, 1968), pp. 516, 517, 523.

CHAPTER X

The Witness of Life

"Man today listens more readily to witnesses than to masters";[1] and if he listens to masters it is because he finds in them witnesses. The only thing that matters in his eyes is truth incarnate in a decision, and in the whole of a life. What he demands, if he is to "give himself," is a total commitment, without reservations, accepting all the risks. As a corollary to this, he has a deep-seated revulsion against all that can be described as mystification, camouflage, political jobbery or compromise.

In this context, it is easy to understand the importance of the witness of a life which is authentically holy. The saint is precisely the person who bears witness to Christ and the gospel as to an Absolute. Whether he is prophet, apostle, martyr or confessor, he is someone who stakes his life on the gospel, recognizing in it the *meaning* of his life and of all human life. And the man who meets a saint, even if it be only in the pages of a book, can no longer look at human beings through the same eyes. For he has had a revelation of another sort of human being. He has discovered Someone. In the saint the lineaments of Christ gradually take form before him, and human existence takes on a divine meaning. He is aware that he himself is being invited, even urged, to become also a son of the Father.

Up to now, a great deal of study has been made of miracle, the sign of power, but very little of the sign of holiness. Pius IX's encyclical *Qui pluribus* declares that the Christian faith is confirmed by the constancy of its martyrs and the glory of

---

1. E. Barbotin, *Le témoignage spirituel* (Paris, 1964), p. 7.

its saints (DS 2779). The First Vatican Council speaks of
the "eminent holiness" of the Church as a motive of credibility.
Above all the Second Vatican Council strongly stresses the need
for all Christians to witness to their faith in the gospel by a life
in accordance with the gospel.² The declarations of the magisterium are clear, but they do not elaborate. The theology of
the sign of holiness is itself still very undeveloped.³ Generally
it is content to apply to the moral miracle what has been
said of the physical miracle, regarding it as something which
goes beyond voluntary powers and demands as its ultimate
explanation a special intervention of God. In this way the
physical miracle absorbs all the energies of theology and becomes the typical sign, the model which is used to explain all
the rest. This is a regrettable simplification; for in the witness
of Christ himself, men's coming to faith is bound up with the
sign of charity: "By this shall all men know that you are my
disciples, if you have love one for another" (Jn 13; 35; 17:22-23).
It is to be remembered also that the sign of charity is the most
"speaking" sign in the eyes of our contemporaries, and in itself
the most impelling sign.

1. *The contemporary appeal of the sign of holiness*

The action of the signs in the course of history is partly
connected with the varying situation in which man finds himself. Now, if it is true that those who witness to God have
always been credited not only for their miracles but for the
holiness of their lives, this sign of holiness has become for our

---

2. See Chapter I.
3. "It is remarkable that authors who make use in practice of the
moral miracle scarcely take the trouble to produce a theory of it," cf.
P.-A. Liégé, "Réflexions pour une apologétique du miracle," *Revue des
Sciences philosophiques et théologiques*, 35 (1951): 253. One of the rare
articles on the moral miracle is that of E. Gutwenger, "Zum Begriff des
moralischen Wunders," *Zeitschrift für theologische Theologie*, 71 (1949):
90-97.

contemporaries the most decisive of all the signs. God's right to upset the laws of the universe (which is regarded as an area reserved for human action) is disputed, sometimes with acrimony, but it is more readily accepted that God may act within man, to convert him and transform him.

There is no doubt at all that holiness interests our contemporaries.[4] What is it that is described in the works of Mauriac, Malègue, Julian Green, Van der Meersch, Estang, Bernanos, Ghéon, Merton, Coccioli, Graham Greene, Bésus, Cesbron, Stuart, or Cronin, if it is not the battle between man and grace, the struggle of human love at grips with divine love? Often the heroes of these works are saints. We have sanctity too in the cinema. Think of the films *Dieu a besoin des hommes, Journal d'un curé de compagne, Le défroqué, The Prisoner,* or of the films on Bernadette, Vincent de Paul, Joan of Arc, Maria Goretti, the Curé d'Ars, Ignatius of Loyola, Francis of Assisi, John Bosco, Father Damien. We have sanctity in the theater, with Claudel, Ghéon, Hochwälder, T. S. Eliot, Bernanos, Lavery, Julian Green and so on. Interest in the mystery of holiness is manifest again in what might be described as the hagiographical renewal (Brodrick, Hugo Rahner, Martindale, Bernoville, Goyan, Auclair, Chesterton, Papini, Dudon, Daniel-Rops, Trochu, Timmermans, Farrow, Talbot, Michael de la Bedoyere), in the proliferation of spiritual reviews, and of series and dictionaries devoted to spiritual problems,[5] and in the creation of institutes of spiritual theology. If the voice of John XXIII met with so deep a response in the hearts of twentieth century men of all races and all religious denominations, it was

---

4. P. Blanchard, *Sainteté aujourd'hui* (Paris, 1953), pp. 11-32; P. Molinari, *I Santi e il loro Culto* (Rome, 1962).

5. For example: the series *Christus;* the series *Études Carmélitaines;* the *Dictionnaire de spiritualité;* the series *Problèmes de la religieuse d'aujourd'hui;* and among the reviews: *Christus; Manresa; Geist und Leben; Revista de Espiritualidad; La Vie spirituelle, Supplement; Revue d'ascétique et de mystique; Cross and Crown; The Way; Rivista di ascetica e mistica,* etc.

because it revealed an immense love, because it spoke with the charity of the Good Shepherd.[6] This attraction towards holiness in twentieth century man has various causes, principally, it would seem, the following.

1. In the very measure in which twentieth century man dominates the material world, subjugates it and does violence to it to an extent which evokes anticipations of the apocalypse, he experiences the weight and scope of interior solitude. For though he is the ruler of a mechanized world which is obedient to his whims, this world can never be a *person* with whom he can communicate. The more he pushes back the limits of the universe, the more he deepens his own solitude. The saint has dealings with another mystery, more unfathomable than that of matter, but a mystery which is a person who invites him to friendship, a mystery at once *transcendent* and *near*. This mystery is a mystery of love, and its dimensions, infinite in all directions, are those of love. Twentieth century man, isolated in spite of appearances, desires to experience this personal fulfillment which matter denies him.

2. The man of the twentieth century knows better than any of his predecessors how *fragile* man is. He knows this painfully from his own experience; he knows that man can be degraded in concentration camps, where his freedom is destroyed and his personality disintegrated by drugs, in order to wrest from him disturbing confessions in a state of subhuman unconsciousness.

He knows from the experiments of psychology, psychoanalysis and psychiatry how unstable the human equilibrium is. He is more aware than men used to be of the hidden motives, sometimes unpleasant, which inspire human behavior. And that is why he is more sensitive than men used to be to the extra-

---

6. Add to this that the ecumenical movement is not unconnected with the attraction exercised by holiness in the world today. If Christ made unity in charity the sign by which his true disciples were to be recognized, it is to be expected that with the strengthening of unity, there should be a correspondingly greater attraction exerted by the Church on the world.

ordinary achievement represented by holiness, to its serenity and balance, its peace and joy, its unfathomable love for God and men. He can assess better than his predecessors the difference between the saint and the ordinary man.

3. In different and even contradictory contexts, men like Péguy, Bloy, Nietzsche, Saint-Exupéry, Psichari and Dostoievsky have denounced pharisaism in all its forms—in the bourgeois notion of propriety, which is pre-occupied with security before everything else, in a hypocritical legalism, in the merely indolent preservation of the *status quo*, in a replete and self-sufficient intellectualism, entrenched in ready-made solutions.[7] Twentieth century man, especially post-war man, craves for sincerity, for truth, authenticity, faithfulness. He is frank to the point of brutality; his capacity to be true to himself extends from Marxism to sanctity, from suicide to martyrdom. His preference is for extreme solutions, that is, for those where tension is stretched to the uttermost. How then should he not be interested in holiness? For the saint is precisely the man who does not wear a mask: he is transparent to God and men. He is not, as Péguy would say, an "habitué"; perpetually young, he goes from one renewal to another, from spring to spring, like grace. For him there is no ease, self-satisfaction or hardening of the spiritual arteries; for grace is always inciting him to new ways of surpassing himself. He is engaged in the uncompromising experiment of holiness, of total consecration to God and men. That is why sanctity, as experience of life in a limit-situation, attracts the man of today.

4. Lastly, twentieth century man poses to himself with a lucidity which is sometimes a rather sick lucidity, the problem of the *meaning* of man and human life. Has life any sense at all? Can it justify itself, and how? What is the meaning of freedom, of power, of action, of suffering, of "the others," of death? And in this obscurity, the witness to Christ, the man who lives according to the gospel, looks like someone who

---

7. P. Blanchard, *Sainteté aujourd'hui,* p. 29.

has found *a meaning to life*. He knows what he is doing. He knows where he is going. He has found in his love for God a fulfillment, a perfection which is in striking contrast to all that the anthropocentric systems offer. Christ's message is mysterious, it is true, but it is a source of light, of meaning.

There is no doubt that witness of life attracts contemporary man. But it must be added that he suffers from not meeting it more often in the world about him. The Jews of Pilate's and Caesar's time met salvation in the person and preaching and signs of Christ. For twentieth century men this contact with Christ and salvation is normally made through encountering the Church (both priests and people); and the credibility of the gospel, which was once manifest in the power and holiness of Christ, must now be manifested in the holiness of the Church and her members. It is through charity in the flesh that the men of our time need to be confronted by the reality of salvation: so the holiness of the Church must be *perceptible* to them, as the visible presence of grace and salvation. And in spite of the appearance and development of new forms of the apostolate, in spite of the employment of more and more precise techniques, it would seem that holiness, in the twentieth century, does not always shine enough, that it does not strike the eyes of our contemporaries with a brilliance which would force them to attend to it. "Men have had enough of our preaching," observes Fr. Schillebeeckx. "They are looking for a meaning which will give a force to their lives. The only way to make higher values and a higher power appreciated is to make them present in action. Christians must show that Christianity is a force which transforms human life." [8] "It is not dogmas," he says later, "that we have to present to men crying out in their distress. Our dogmatic value is the personal value of our lives given for our fellow-men; our lives themselves must be incarnate dogma." [9] "It is your task to publish the gospel from the house-tops not

8. E. H. Schillebeeckx, *Le Christ sacrement de la rencontre de Dieu* (Paris, 1969), pp. 248-249; trans., *Christ: the Sacrament of the Encounter with God* (London and New York, 1963).

9. *Ibid.*, p. 251.

in your words but in your life," Charles de Foucauld used to say to himself.[10] What men ask for is not preachers, but silent *witnesses* to the love of Christ, men in whom dogma can be seen in practice as a living value which draws them towards it. How many men are swept along in the current of life without ever meeting in their surroundings anyone whose holiness puts them in the presence of a better world? If they did meet someone like this it would awake deep within them the desire for salvation, and make faith possible. "What can be of decisive importance in any *milieu*," Fr. de Montcheuil emphasizes, "is that there is in it no witness to the Christian mystery capable of striking eyes which are too weak to see it where it merely subsists."[11]

2. *The testimony of twentieth century converts*

The testimony of twentieth century converts throws light on the contemporary relevance of the sign of holiness. Conversion, it is true, is a complex phenomenon. It may involve a whole set of psychological and moral processes, a whole series of motivations, intellectual and affective. It admits of positive antecedents which prepare the way for it, opening the mind and spirit to certain values, and, on the other hand, of negative antecedents, like deceptions, wrongs and trials, which prepare for it by helping the spirit to outgrow certain paralyzing attitudes, which hinder the way to God. It allows of stages, of withdrawals or retreats, of recoveries or renewals. Again there are many different types of conversion: conversions where intellectual motives are dominant; conversions where the dominant motive is the desire to realize a moral ideal of purity and liberation from sin (conversions from paganism to Christianity); conversions of an emotional type (particularly in the case of col-

---

10. J.-F. Six, *Vie de Charles de Foucauld* (Paris, 1962), p. 72; trans., *Witness in the Desert: the Life of Charles de Foucauld* (New York, 1965).

11. Y. De Montcheuil, *Problèmes de vie spirituelle* (Paris, 1947³), p. 45.

lective evangelization). There are slow conversions, like St.
Augustine's, and others which are sudden and stark like St.
Paul's. There are individual conversions, and collective conversions (as in Billy Graham's meetings or the appeal of the
great popular missions of Blessed Julien Maunoir and of St.
Francis of Geronimo).[12] But whatever the rhythm and duration
of these inner transformations, it is often, not to say always,
noticeable, that conversion is occasioned or produced, begun
or accelerated by an initial shock. In their accounts, converts
themselves refer to this first shock which opened their eyes to
a hope of *salvation*, involving their life as such and putting it in
question. And this shock, this first sign, is very often that of
Christian witness—whether it is a matter of ordinary holiness
or heroic sanctity, of a person or of a live and enthusiastic
community. Under one form or another they were confronted
with the witness of holiness of life, and this encounter was
decisive. Fr. John O'Brien, after comparing the testimonies of
hundreds of converts, estimated that, with most of them, the
dominant motive for believing in Christianity had been the
witness of a devoted Christian life, or the encounter with authentic sanctity.[13] "Christian living, the fact that we meet saints
in our own neighborhood, this is the concrete apologetic argument for our faith."[14]

Charles de Foucauld attests that he was brought to Christ by
the witness of his cousin Marie de Bondy, "by her silence, her
gentleness, her kindness, her perfection." Later he would himself ask of his disciples that they should be simply present
among men, silent witnesses to the love of Jesus Christ.[15] M.
Gabriel Marcel speaks of the profound influence exerted over

12. G. Bardy, *La conversion au christianisme durant les premiers siècles*
(Paris, 1947), pp. 117-161; Y. Congar, *Sacerdoce et laïcat* (Paris, 1962),
pp. 23-49.

13. J. A. O'Brien, ed., *Bringing Souls to Christ* (New York, 1955),
pp. 75 and 104; *Ibid., Roads to Rome* (London, 1955), p. 228.

14. E. H. Schillebeeckx, *Le Christ sacrement de la recontre de Dieu*,
p. 247; trans., *Christ: the Sacrament of the Encounter with God*.

15. J.-F. Six, *Vie de Charles de Foucauld*, pp. 30-31; trans., *Witness
in the Desert: the Life of Charles de Foucauld*.

him by his meetings with sincere and devoted Catholics. "These meetings," he says, "played a dominant rôle in my life ... I came to know human beings in whom I was aware so vividly of the reality of Christ that I could no longer doubt it." [16] Daniel-Rops attributes his return to God to meeting a religious "made of the stuff that saints are made of." "There is nothing more decisive than seeing with one's own eyes what Christianity lived and incarnate is." [17] G. K. Chesterton acknowledged that the example of his friends Ronald Knox and Maurice Baring, who had preceded him into the Church, helped him to follow in their footsteps.[18] The socialist René Leyvraz was converted by the witness of Léon Bloy: "Léon Bloy revealed to me what Christian love of the poor is like. It was through love of the poor that he introduced me to the love of God. Léon Bloy's heart was an unfathomable depth of love, burning with charity. He loved with a vehemence and passion to be found to the same degree in none of his contemporaries. His violence is the violence of love, of consuming love." [19] Raïssa Maritain recounts how she and Jacques were drawn to Catholicism by reading Léon Bloy's *La femme pauvre,* and then by following his advice and reading the lives of the saints. In the saints and mystics they met Christian humility and charity; they were won by the combined encounter with holiness and with the sublimity of the Christian message itself.[20] Ernest Psichari confesses in his turn that in the last phase of his conversion, the influence of Jacques Maritain was decisive: "Your persuasive words, the still more persuasive example of your life, so magnanimous, so purged of impurities by grace, your brotherly affection...." [21] Karl Stern was also

---

16. F. Lelotte, ed., *Convertis du XXe siècle,* vol. III (Paris-Brussels, 1955), p. 52.

17. *Ibid.,* pp. 107-108.

18. F. Lelotte, ed., *Convertis du XXe siècle,* vol. IV (Paris-Brussels, 1958), p. 81.

19. *Ibid.,* p. 111.

20. J. A. O'Brien, ed., *The Road to Damascus* (London, 1949), pp. 253, 269, 275.

21. C. Poulet, *La sainteté française contemporaine,* vol. II (Paris, 1952), p. 154.

influenced by meeting Jacques Maritain.[22] Henri Ghéon considered that the onset of his conversion dated from the day he
came to know Pierre-Dominique Dupouey, a naval officer,
whose absolute clarity of soul and personal sanctity threw him
into confusion and overcame him.[23] The Japanese general, Ig-
natius-Paul Suganami, who became a Catholic at the age of
fifty-three, declared that "the example of the humility of Fr.
Okaschi (who instructed him) was the best part of his instruction. "This humility," said the general, "was the key, for
me, to the knowledge of God, and led me to accept the supernatural and divine."[24] Thomas Merton speaks of the deep influence over him, at the age of twelve, of a Catholic family,
the Privats: "They were saints in that most effective and telling
way: sanctified by leading ordinary lives in a completely supernatural manner."[25]

The witness of holiness of life is even more powerful when
it has a sociological dimension, when it emanates from a *community*. The sight of a group of Christians living together as
one family in prayer and charity is almost irresistible. A convert
relates that what produced in her the initial shock which led
to conversion was meeting a group of real Christians. "The reunion began. I shall never forget that moment. They began to
say the *Our Father* together with such warmth that before the
end of the prayer there were tears in my eyes, as I made the
second great discovery of my life. I had discovered a *really
Christian community*, quickened by love of Christ...I had
never seen anything like it, never thought that such a thing
could exist."[26] Another convert says the same sort of thing:

22. F. Lelotte, ed., *Convertis du XXe siecle*, vol. II (Paris-Brussels, 1954), p. 36.
23. H. Ghéon, *L'homme né de la guerre* (Paris, 1923).
24. B. Schafer, *Pourchassés de la grâce* (Montreal, 1955), p. 199.
25. T. Merton, *The Seven-Storey Mountain*, New York, 1948; in the New American Library, 1952, p. 73; *Elected Silence* (London, 1954), pp. 49-50.
26. M. Nédoncelle and R. Girault, *J'ai rencontré le Dieu vivant* (Paris, 1952), p. 350; trans., *God's Encounter with Man* (New York, 1964).

"To want to be a Christian, one needs to see Christianity incarnate, to see it as evidence. For myself, I could not become
a Catholic until after I had seen the Catholic religion realized
in people's lives." [27] "For the first time in my life," says Dr.
Paul Van K. Thomson, "I found myself in contact with the
Catholic Church, and saw this religion lived by the priests
and lay people who shared my own life. I found in them the
evident proof of the unity, the inner peace, the warmth of
affection which binds together children of the same Father." [28]
Dr. Cornelia J. de Vogel said, after long study of the Church's
history, that for her the whole question was: "Who was wrong
then, the centuries-old Church, the Church of Athanasius and
Augustine, the Church which built the cathedrals of the Middle
Ages, and still today bears the fruit of extraordinary holiness—or
those who, in the sixteenth century, separated themselves from
this Church to found another tradition?" [29]

Holiness awakens in those who have seen it the desire for
communion in its world of love. Papini, after reading the
philosophers without being given any answers, began to read
the gospels "to look for Christ there." He read Augustine, Pascal,
the *Fioretti, The Introduction to the Devout Life*, the *Spiritual
Exercises*. He read them doubtless from curiosity, from a desire
for information, but "there was also," he says, "a leaven of
the will to believe, a humble desire to share in this great religious
experience which had, since the time of Jesus, given to the
world so many masterpieces in art and life." [30] Paul Claudel,
touched by grace as he listened to the chanting of the *Magnificat*
in *Notre-Dame de Paris*, was drawn irresistibly by God's holiness
and by Christian blessedness. "I was suddenly torn by an
awareness of innocence, of the everlasting childhood of God,
a revelation too great for words." [31] Sigrid Undset writes: "In

27. *Ibid.*, p. 303.
28. B. Schafer, *Pourchassés de la grâce*, p. 35.
29. M. Nédoncelle and R. Girault, *J'ai rencontré le Dieu vivant*,
p. 103; trans., *God's Encounter with Man.*
30. F. Lelotte, ed., *Convertis du XXe siècle*, vol. II, p. 161.
31. *Ibid.*, p. 10.

the saints there suddenly bursts upon us a realization of what
God meant us to be, when, in the words of the offertory of the
Mass, he 'marvellously created our nature and more marvellously
still created it anew.' Only the saints allow us to satisfy our
need for hero-worship without having to exalt anything in our
nature which it would be cowardly or degrading to honor." [32]
Edith Stein tells us, "One day I picked up by chance a rather
important book, *The Life of St. Theresa written by herself*. I began to read; I was fascinated and did not put the book down
until I had finished it. As I shut it I said, 'This is the truth.'" [33]
Dr. Reinhard Frauenfelder, a Swiss archivist, says that he was
"fascinated by men who suffered a total and sudden interior
change—St. Paul, St. Augustine, St. Francis of Assisi and so
many others." [34] Another convert felt irresistibly attracted by the
example of a fellow-workman: "As I was feeling that I was on
the edge of a slippery slope and realizing all that that meant,
I wished desperately that I was like him, and as I knew he was
a Christian, I supposed it must be his religion which made
him so much better than the rest of us." [35]

This is the conclusion that converts often draw from the
sight of sanctity: there is a mysterious Presence at work in
the Christian and the saint, which raises him above the level
of common mediocrity. Denise Aimé, a convert from Judaism,
attributes her conversion to meeting a well-known historian,
whom she saw suffering in hospital, but with a super-human
joy; "One day I went to see him at the clinic. He was on a
board, suffering atrociously and radiant with joy. I have forgotten what he talked about, about grace, no doubt, or sacrifice . . .
perhaps even he talked about nothing at all. What is certain
is that I saw in him the presence of a power greater than him-

32. M. Nédoncelle and R. Girault, *J'ai rencontré le Dieu vivant*,
p. 134; trans., *God's Encounter with Man*.
33. F. Lelotte, ed., *Convertis du XXe siècle*, vol. I, (Paris-Brussels,
1953), p. 43.
34. B. Schafer, *Pourchassés de la grâce*, p. 189.
35. M. Nédoncelle and R. Girault, *J'ai rencontré le Dieu vivant*, pp.
245-246; trans., *God's Encounter with Man*.

self. Almost at the same moment I was aware of this power
in myself, and then at once I knew its name: Jesus. I left the
clinic converted.... The *Confessions* of St. Augustine, the
Interior Castle of St. Teresa of Avila completed what was already begun, the opening of my inner being to Christian
spirituality." [36] St. Benedict, too, taught me the plenitude of
love." [37] The great Chinese convert John Wu was led to Christ
and the Church by the life of St. Thérèse of Lisieux, in whom he
saw the harmonious and sublime synthesis of apparently opposite
virtues, the synthesis of Buddha, Confucius and Lao-Tse. After
reading this book, "I understood clearly," he says, "that nature
alone is incapable of explaining so angelic a personality, and
that such perfection could be only the fruit of divine grace.
I realized that mysticism and humanism were in harmony within
her, because she was united to Christ, who is true God and
true man. I remembered the words of Christ: 'Such things are
impossible with men, but not with God, for with God all things
are possible.' " [38]

These accounts, restricted as they are in number, could
not, obviously, represent all the ways in which holiness has
influenced and acted upon converts. But they are soundings
of the situation, and they authorize certain conclusions. Christianity, in the eyes of the convert, comes above all as the discovery
of good news which concerns *him*, and which involves the whole
of his life. In the breach in nature made by frailty and sin, he
has caught sight of *salvation*. He has discovered this salvation,
sometimes in scripture, sometimes in the preaching of the
Church, but most often in *a Christian life as lived*. What is
finally decisive for him is his meeting the evidence of a life
rooted in Christ, which is sometimes reinforced by a verbal
declaration of the gospel, but which is often unaccompanied
by any comment, by any intellectual statement. In seeing a
really Christian life, in seeing a *community* living a life of

---

36. *Ibid.*, 172-173.
37. *Ibid.*, 176.
38. J. A. O'Brien, *Roads to Rome*, pp. 164-165.

prayer and charity, he has seen salvation. He did not conclude to the existence of salvation at the end of an intellectual process: he saw it in operation.[39]

This meeting with a fullness and perfect coincidence of truth and life exercises over the convert an invincible attraction. Holiness appears to him as a value he wants to share.[40] At the same time, it makes him aware of a Presence within man, more than man, able to raise man and transform him into a new creature, no longer dominated by egotism, but by a consuming love. And this Presence seems to be continuous and personal, an inexhaustible source of energy and inner renewal. From the negative point of view, it appears also from what converts say that the greatest obstacle to their coming into the Church, after their own past, was the spectacle of bad Christians. These elements are not always explicitly formulated, but they are frequent enough to constitute *constants*.

3. *Holiness from the point of view of faith*

Holiness can be envisaged from a dogmatic point of view and from an apologetic point of view. Dogmatics looks at holiness as a mystery of grace, and asks in the light of faith the secret of this mystery, while apologetics, looking at holiness first

---

39. "In every case," writes Girault, "what is decisive in conversion is meeting a message which is alive, meeting Christ in his words or in one of the elements which go to make up his mystical Body, which is the Church. Most often there will be words and witness at the same time, or else a swift connection of one with the other in terms of actual living, but it is of little importance, in the end, whether the point of departure is a written or spoken word, or the witness of a life; we are in a domain here where the distinction between words and deeds is secondary, both being elements in the experience of a deep reality beneath, which alone is our concern" (M. Nédoncelle and R. Girault, *J'ai rencontré le Dieu vivant*, p. 357; trans., *God's Encounter with Man*).

40. The holiness with which we are concerned in the examples given is not always holiness in its heroic degree. Most often, as we have seen, it is a matter of a constant and solid exercise of charity. In addition, this consecration to God and men which transforms the existence of the spectator is rarely understood as something isolated, but seen as part

of all as an observable phenomenon, in its exterior dynamism, asks the source of this dynamism. These are two complementary and equally necessary points of view.

Holiness is to be understood only in reference to Christ, the source and pattern of all holiness. In Christ the principle and cause of holiness is the very Person himself of the Word of God, who assumes human nature. Moral holiness consists in the constant and perfect union of the human will with the will of the Father. The whole life of Christ manifests itself as inspired by a filial attitude to the Father. Doing the Father's will is Christ's only concern: it is the only thing which counts. When he comes into the world, he says, "Behold I come . . . to do thy will, O God" (Heb 10:7). Christ is Son, and it is for this reason that he always says, "I bless thee, Father . . . yes, Father, for such was thy good pleasure" (Lk 10:21).

The Father's will is the law of his *apostolic action*. In the desert, he opposes to Satan's three-fold temptation his faithfulness to the will of God (Mt 4:1-11; Lk 4:1-13). In Samaria, beside Jacob's well, he answers the disciples who bring him food with, "My meat is to do the will of him who sent me" (Jn 4:34). His real family is made up of those "who do the will of God" (Mk 3:35). His disciples are those whom the Father has "given" him (Jn 17:6). And the prayer that he teaches revolves about its central petition, "Thy will be done on earth as it is in heaven" (Mt 6:10). The Father's will is the law of his *teaching*. Nothing is dearer to a man than his ideas, his programme, his doctrine. And yet Christ says, "My doctrine is not mine, but his that sent me" (Jn 7:16). He is only the faithful witness to the Father (Jn 8, 26 and 38 and 55). "Whatsoever I speak therefore, even as the Father said to me, so I speak" (Jn 12; 50). At the end of his life he can say to the Father, apropos of his disciples, "I have given them the words which thou gavest me" (Jn 17:8). The Father's will is the

of the life of the larger community which carries it, that is, the community of those who belong to Christ and the Church. It is a question of a social and collective holiness.

law of his *mission*. It is from the Father that he has received his mission of salvation, his mission to be the Savior of men (Jn 8:42; 7:28). "For I have come down from heaven, not to do my own will, but the will of him who sent me. And this is the will of him who sent me, that I should lose nothing of all that he has given me, but raise it up at the last day. For this is the will of my Father, that everyone who sees the Son and believes in him should have eternal life" (Jn 6:38-40). Finally the Father's will is the law of his *sacrifice*. Christ is the Good Shepherd who gives his life for the sheep, because this is the will of the Father (Jn 10:17-18). Christ desires the hour of sacrifice willed by the Father, which will be the greatest manifestation of his love. All his life tends towards this supreme hour fixed by the Father (Jn 12, 27-28). The hour of Christ is the will of the Father leading him through the willed stages and stations to the final sacrifice. As he leaves the Cenacle to go to Gethsemane, he takes the opportunity of revealing to his disciples his inner dispositions: "I will no longer talk much with you; for the ruler of this world is coming. He has no power over me, but I do as the Father has commanded me" (Jn 14: 30-31). Jesus will be immolated, but the real cause of his death will be his free will, his loving obedience to the Father in accomplishing his mission of salvation. In the agony, in spite of the revulsion of the flesh and the emotions, Christ says, "My Father . . . not as I will, but as thou wilt" (Mt 26:39). When he entered the world he had said: "I come to do thy will, O God" (Heb 10:7). His last words, on the cross, were "It is finished" (Jn 19:30), that is, through his obedient sacrifice, the redemption of the world. "Father . . . I have finished the work which thou gavest me to do" (Jn 17:4). Christ was obedient even to the death on the cross.

The Father's will is for Christ a reality which lives within him: it is the Father himself who is always in him. The Father's will is the Father's love within him. Christ is in the midst of mankind, but at the same time he is nourished by a good which is imperceptible to men: the vision of the Father. Of this continuous contemplation is born a love which never slackens, and which carries him unceasingly towards the Father. This love is a participation in the uncreated love with which the Father and Son love each other, and this love is the Spirit. In the last analysis, if Christ always does his Father's will, it is because he is the Father's Son, who has all the Father's love, and because the Son returns eternally to the Father the love he receives from him. Christ is Son and nothing but Son, the Amen of the Father. The Spirit of Christ is a filial Spirit, a Spirit of love. The Father and the Son in the innermost depths of the Trinity, live one and the same life of love, and the Spirit is the pouring out of the mutual love of the Father and Son.

Christ is Son by nature. But the wonder of wonders is that we are called by grace to share in this great mystery of the filiation of the Son. God "has predestined us to be his adopted sons in Jesus Christ" (Eph 1:5). God has predestined us "to be conformed to the image of his Son, in order that he might be the first-born among many brethren" (Rm 8:29). "See what love the Father has given us, that we should be called children of God; and so we are" (1 Jn 3:1). "When the time had fully come, God sent forth his Son ... so that we might receive adoption as sons. The proof that you are sons is that God has sent the Spirit of his Son into our hearts: the Spirit that cries 'Abba, Father' " (Gal 4:4-6). Christians are those who have the Spirit of Christ in them, and who are led by this Spirit (Rm 8:14). If we are sons, it is because we have the Spirit of the Son, the Spirit of love through whom the Father loves the Son and the Son the Father, and who brings about in us what he brought about in Christ, the continual and perfect accomplishment of the Father's will. Since the Spirit of Christ is a filial Spirit, it is in leading a filial life, that is a life wholly submitted to the Father's will as expressed by Christ, that the Christian is a true son of the Father. Only those who do the will of Christ, as Christ did the will of the Father, really have the Spirit of Christ. "If you keep my commandments, you will abide in my love, even as I have kept my Father's commandments and abide in his love" (Jn 15:10). And again "He who has my commandments and keeps them, he it is who loves me; and he who

loves me will be loved by my Father and I will love him and
manifest myself to him" (Jn 14:21). Doing Christ's will develops in us a filial spirit which unites us to Christ as Christ was
united to the Father.

The saint is he who always and in everything does the will
of God, moved and led by the Spirit of adoption, who is a
filial Spirit.[41] His good, like Christ's, is to do the will of God,
and like Christ he says in everything, "Yes, Father, for such is thy
good pleasure." Because the Spirit is within him, as the source
and principle of a new life, inspiring and directing all his living,
and introducing him into the life of the divine Persons, all his
behavior is that of a new creature. He follows the rhythm of
the divine life: he thinks God's thoughts and has God's love.
Through *faith*, he sees everything in the revealing light of
the Father; he sees and understands everything as God sees
and understands it; he judges everything according to the measure and criteria of God himself; for he has new eyes, the
Father's gift, the source and principle of a new way of looking
at the world. Apparently nothing is changed: trials, work, lack
of understanding, all remain the same. His life is made of the
same stuff. And yet everything is different. To the eyes of faith,
the dull landscape of daily life is smiling and full of light. All
things and all values are transformed by Christ and reveal an

---

41. The only criterion of holiness is the constant and perfect doing of
God's will in the precise context of a given life. The Church, in her
canonization processes, recognizes no other criterion of heroic virtue.
According to Benedict XIV, "Heroic virtue" consists "solely in the
faithful and constant fulfillment of individual and personal duties" (AAS
14 [1922], 23). Benedict XV, in 1916, said, "holiness properly consists
simply in conformity to the divine will, expressed in the constant and
exact fulfillment of the duties of one's own state of life" (G. de Ste-
Madeleine, "Normes actuelles de la sainteté," in *Trouble et Lumière,
Études Carmélitaines,* Paris, 1949, pp. 175-188). In actual fact, it is
impossible to fulfill the divine will exactly, constantly and perfectly
without being habitually under the influence of the Holy Spirit who
helps to overcome the weaknesses and inconstancies of human nature.
This habitual submission to the Holy Spirit is the mark of a soul which
has reached the stage of complete spiritual maturity, or sanctity.

infinite depth. In the *love* of God which has been poured into his heart through the Holy Spirit (Rm 5:5), the saint loves everything as the Father loves it: for charity acclimatizes him to itself. He has God's tastes and inclinations. Because the Spirit of love lives within him, he is opened in the same impulse to God and to men (Jn 13:34-35). The love with which he is inspired transcends the divisions and distinctions made by human egoism. In the charity which has been given him there is no one any longer who is a stranger to him. For the actuating principle of the saint's love is the love of God. His charity proceeds from a source where there is no question of *I* as opposed to what is foreign or *other*, where all is a matter of the Father and his Son Jesus Christ and his adopted family; it proceeds from a source where there is only Christ, and the members of his mystical Body. In short, the saint is the human being who lives in perfection, even here in this world, the life of a child of God, a new creature wholly vitalized and inspired by the Spirit of Christ, who is that Spirit of love in whom the life of the Father and Son consists. Christ is the Son come into the world to give this filial life to us, and the saint is he who lives this life fully, sharing already in the perfect life of the divine Persons. The saint is then, *the new man*, the new creature, regenerated by God, given life by his Spirit, endowed with a new principle of knowledge and love. The child of God disclaims being the center of the world. God's love is in his heart, and this is his gift to God and his gift to men. "The love which consumes him," said Bergson, "is not simply the love of a man for God, it is the love of God for all men. In God and through God he loves all mankind with a divine love." [42] One can see how the sight of this new type of human nature, this new life consecrated through the love of God and men to the point of being in a perfect state of oblation, constitutes an extraordinary paradox which excites astonishment at the same

---

42. H. Bergson, *Les deux Sources de la morale et de la religion* (Paris, 1932⁹), p. 249; trans., *The Two Sources of Morality and Religion* (New York, 1964).

time as it exerts over men in whom the same Spirit of love is
in travail, a secret and irresistible attraction.

4. *Observable characteristics of holiness*

If it is true that the Christian, and even more so the saint,
is in the world as a new creature, given life and transformed
by the Spirit, dwelt in by love of God and men, this new reality
must be accompanied by a new sort of behavior, by new attitudes, which can be discerned by the eyes of an observer. What
then are these facts capable of leading the man who contemplates
them to understand that *salvation* is in our midst, and that the
saint is the witness to its accomplishment?

1. What is most characteristic of the sign of holiness, especially if it is compared with physical miracle, is its unobtrusiveness. The saint demands nothing, asks nothing: he has not
so much as to speak except in that he exists, expressing in his
whole life the supernatural reality in which he is bathed. "The
saint" says Bergson, "is aware of truth operative within him
as an actuating force. He would no more hinder its diffusion
than the sun would refuse to shed its light. Only it is not simply
by words that he spreads it." [43] Holiness acts without violence.
Its power to attract lies in its very unobtrusiveness. Apparently
the most fragile of all signs it is perhaps also the most effective;
for it acts at a personal level and appeals to each man's moral
experience.

Holiness presents itself first as a *value*, or rather as an
ensemble of values; for in the saint being triumphs over having,
mind and spirit over mere instinct, love over hate and egotism,
life over death, God over man. In offering itself in the guise
of a common life, where the saint welcomes others by opening
himself to them, where all egotism is consumed in the fire of
love, holiness appears as a *good*, eminently lovable and de-
sirable, in which one wants to share. The saint bears witness

---

43. *Ibid.,* p. 249.

to the existence of charity and he evokes a taste for it. "Why
have the saints people who imitate them in this way?" says
Bergson again. "Why do men of great goodness draw crowds
after them? They do not ask for anything. And yet they get it.
They have no need to exhort, they have only to exist: their
existence is a challenge." [44] Holiness acts primarily then as a
value, by exerting attraction as a *good.* It reveals to the man
who meets it a quality of life which, without it, he would
not have suspected to exist, and which he secretly desires to
share. It shows him, in a life like his own, an ideal which is never
wholly absent from his own heart. It does not explain the
value of Christianity by means of a rational demonstration or a
panegyric: it shows Christianity *present and at work* in a life
which it has transformed.

If it is true that the highest values are those which leave
the greatest room for freedom (the pressure of a value being
in inverse proportion to what one might call the *value* of its
value), the highest values must attract precisely because they
are high.[45] In this respect, the sight of holiness arouses, in those
who do not close their eyes to it, a lively desire to share it.
Holiness is an *appeal* or *challenge,* not a pressure: it presents
itself to a man as a promise of the fulfillment and transcendence
to which he already aspires. Julian Green often returns to this
idea in his *Journal:* "At twenty-six one used to want quite simply
to become a saint. One was right." [46] Few men make any effective response to this appeal; for it is an appeal to a new style
of life, a style acquired only at the price of hard sacrifice. That
this is so does not, perhaps, matter very much: silently, without
seeming to do so, holiness awakens attention, arouses sympathy,
and sets in motion without forcing it the impulse through which
perhaps a man tears himself from inertia and turns his face
towards God. From this time onwards the question is before

44. *Ibid.,* pp. 29-30.
45. J. de Finance, "La valeur morale et son idéal," *Sciences Ecclésiastiques,* 10 (1958): 295-319.
46. J. Green, *Journal IV, 1943-1945* (Paris, 1949), p. 67. *Diary,*
1928-1957 (London, no date). *Journal,* 7 vols. (New York, no date).

him. "Is he going to prefer a life according to the love of which he has just, through the mediation of another, had a personal revelation, is he going to test the attraction and, as it were, temptation, or is he going to prefer the old egotistical life? The choice remains open: he is entirely free .... But he has been rescued from his indifference, and put face to face with a decision which he cannot escape." [47]

2. On closer inspection, holiness reveals an *accord*, a *harmony*, between an ideal and life. In the concrete, this ideal is the Christian ideal, brought by Christ and recorded in the gospel. Holiness gives it body and existential life. It enables us to see the gospel in operation. Thanks to holiness, we have the gospel before us as a living and lived reality, incarnate in men of flesh and blood. In the saint, truth and life echo each other and coincide. The gospel is communicated by transparency, truth shining through life, *message* taking body in *witness*, the salvation announced becoming present. The saint is an ocular—and by this means a rational—*demonstration* that the gospel can transform human life. This concord between message and life, between salvation announced and salvation contemplated, is in itself a sign of truth.

It needs to be remembered that if Christianity is to draw men to itself, this accord between gospel and life is a necessity which follows from its own nature, and this for three reasons.

First, Christianity is not simply an intellectual system, which can be communicated by means of an instruction which involves neither teacher nor taught, but a message of salvation, bound up with an event which has changed the meaning of the human condition and calls in question the life of whoever accepts it. The gospel tells us that man, in Jesus Christ and through Jesus Christ, is saved, that we are the children of God, and that already we share the life of the divine Persons. Hence if Christianity were unable to illustrate this change in the human condition proclaimed by the gospel, it would confess its failure.

47. Y. De Montcheuil, *Problèmes de vie spirituelle*, pp. 34-35; E. Barbotin, *Le témoignage spirituel*, pp. 195-200.

The saint, in living his life as son of the Father, witnesses to the truth and efficaciousness of the gospel as proclaimed.

Secondly, the essence of the Christian message is the revelation of the infinite love of God for man in the love of Jesus Christ. But how is a man to believe in this love unless he has before his eyes someone who has already been won by it? In the saint's love for God and for men, he can contemplate both God who is loved and God who loves. He can discern a harmony, a deep accord, between the announcement that this divine love has come among men in order to create love, and the living spectacle of a love which is open and self-giving. Man's love becomes the sacrament of God's love, the visible expression of God's love for him.

Thirdly, the gospel is the revelation of a new form of existence, a new *style of life.* But since this style of life in which God wishes to form men is at once sublime and new, how could God teach it to men except by means of concrete presentation and example? That is why Christ, the Son of the Father, is not only he who reveals to men their filial condition, but also he who initiates them into this filial life by leading among them himself the life of the Son. And that is why the saints in their turn perpetuate in the Church this filial life revealed and illustrated by Christ.

3. There is accord also between the gospel and the life in which holiness is realized, in their *going beyond* human nature: the ideal outstrips human nature and the reality outstrips human nature. In a world in which sin, division, egotism, and jealousy reign, the saint emerges. Often saints have lived within this world of sin from which they have with difficulty disentangled themselves. Although made of flesh and passions like ourselves, they rise above the level of our mediocrity. They breathe a purer air. In the actual historical universe, and in relation to man's concrete and habitual way of acting, they represent a transcendence. We know that men can be generous, but the

generosity of Peter Claver towards the Negroes, of Vincent de Paul towards the poor, of Jean de Brébeuf towards the Hurons, of Charles de Foucauld towards the Touaregs goes beyond any common measure. We know that men can be pure, but the purity of Stanislaus Kostka gives us a sense of vertigo. The moral universe has its constants, less precise no doubt than those of the physical universe, but such as the sociologist and moralist are able to establish. To say that a way of behaving goes beyond the common human manner of acting, it is necessary, it would seem, to find in combination, the following characteristics: a certain psychological wholeness and intensity, expressed in a sacrificial love of God and men; a continuity in duration and constancy of will; a certain sociological dimension such as is manifested in the Church.[48]

It is important to stress that this transcendence is not a simple and vertical transcendence as the heroism of the martyr may be, but a *paradoxical* transcendence which takes many forms. As a great Chinese convert, John Wu, rightly puts it, the saint is a living synthesis of apparently opposite characteristics. In St. Thérèse of Lisieux, he points out, there are in combination at one and the same time, "humility and audacity, freedom and discipline, joy and suffering, duty and love, strength and tenderness, nature and grace, boundless enthusiasm and genuine prudence, poverty and abundance, life and death, conformity and originality, limitless zeal, and unshakable humor."[49] The life of the saint reproduces in miniature the paradoxes of the life of Christ. Present in the world which surrounds him, present in all its poverty and wretchedness, the saint nevertheless gives the impression of living in another universe or of returning from foreign parts with their exotic products. Wholly given to God, he is at the same time full of tenderness to men. Unfathomable in his humility and simplicity, he is often fiercely intrepid in speaking of God, and claiming God's rights. Though he radiates purity and penitence, he is nevertheless convinced

---

48. P.-A. Liégé, "Reflexions pour une apologetique du miracle," *Revue des Sciences philosophiques et théologiques*, 35 (1951): 253-254.

49. J. A. O'Brien, *Roads to Rome*, p. 164.

that he is the greatest of sinners. To a resilient and creative originality he joins the most filial obedience. Such a transcendence of apparent opposites excites astonishment and questioning. What is the source of this inexhaustible charity and unfailing energy? From what center of unity do these rays which shine in all directions come? What is the clue to the riddle? In the charity of the saints man divines the action of an infinite love, transforming human nature and lifting it above itself.

To sum up, the observable realities can be reduced to these: (a) a value which attracts, and evokes the desire to share it; (b) a deep harmony between the message of the gospel and the life lived; (c) a transcendence in the human subject which corresponds to a transcendence in the message, a transcendence which is not simple, but complex and paradoxical.

5. *The dialectic of the sign of holiness*

These realities demand an explanation, a sufficient and commensurate cause. How are we to explain the presence, in our world of poverty and wretchedness and sin, of this new sort of man, this new creature dwelt in by the love of God and men, that we call a saint? How are we to explain this spiritual energy constantly renewed, which raises the saint above the level of other men? How are we to explain the coexistence in him of apparently opposite virtues?

The saints themselves attest that all that they are comes to them from *Christ* and the *Church*. Ignatius of Antioch, Augustine, Athanasius, Paul, Francis Xavier, Bernard, Benedict, Francis of Assisi, Vincent de Paul, Francis de Sales, all refer themselves to Christ as the model and mediator of all holiness. All that is great, admirable or extraordinary in them, comes not from themselves (for themselves, they confess their own nothingness and sin) but from Christ, the Light of Light, the source of all holiness. "Be imitators of me, as I am of Christ," says St. Paul (1 Cor 11:1). Christ is not merely their model: he lives in them. "I live, yet not I, but Christ lives in me," says St. Paul again (Gal 2:20). It is the Spirit of Christ who acts in them, purifying,

sanctifying, transforming, configuring them to Christ (Rm 14:
7-8). In the same breath, the saints attest also, that all that
they are comes to them from the Church. They do not look
to find Christ except in the Church and through the Church.
Not for a moment do they conceive that Christ can be disso-
ciated from the Church. They no more think themselves able to
dispense with the mediation of the Church than they think
themselves able to dispense with the mediation of Christ. They
draw on the source of grace which comes from Christ but is
offered by the Church. The saint is the Father's son by the
grace of Christ, but his soul as son, as child of God is formed
in the Church and by the Church, through whom he is born
and nourished and strengthened, in whom he grows and becomes mature. That is why the saint is, as it were, a living
epitome of the Church's doctrine.

This then is the explanation that the saints give of themselves. By themselves they are nothing. What they are comes to
them from Christ and the Church. Such an explanation is not
to be rejected without examination, since it seems the only
explanation adequate to explaining the phenomena observed.
If it is allowed, everything becomes lucid and intelligible:
the transcendence in which holiness consists, its fruitfulness in
charity, the attraction which it exerts and the paradoxes which
accompany it. If not, holiness remains a riddle. A fortunate
temperament, a favorable social context, a particularly tenacious
will, these could not account for sanctity taken in the concrete
with all its characteristics. Considering the importance of these
facts, it is rationally safe to believe the witness of the saints:
Christianity's power to sanctify comes from its divine origin in
Jesus Christ, the Son of God.

This conclusion is the more reasonable in that there is an
extraordinary harmony between the message of the gospel
offered by the Church and the life of the saints. The message
of the gospel and holiness are on the same level, one in the
order of the ideal, the other in the order of existence. The
gospel says that Christ is the Son of God, come into the world
as Light and Life, to save mankind. Through his death and

resurrection he has made us children of the Father, called to lead a filial life and share Christ's glory. And in the saint, this new type of human nature proclaimed by Christ, this human nature completely impregnated with charity, appears, living and acting under the influence of the Spirit. The saint is *the new man* announced by the gospel, with a new heart and a new spirit, born of God, regenerated by God. He is the living realization of the gospel. He *allows us to see* the spiritual renewal of mankind proclaimed and effected by Christ. The gospel and life, truth and being, are in perfect harmony. This harmony, this accord, this consistency in transcendence, is in itself a new sign of the truth of the explanation offered.

One can conceive then that the man who contemplates this harmony in transcendence, this intensity, this fullness of life, this constant fruit of charity, experiences a desire to communicate in this world of values which holiness reveals. The sight of holiness disposes him to hearing the gospel and acknowledging its truth.

Holiness is a true sign, but one which makes us immediately conscious of the plenitude of its scope. We are confronted by a reality whose power of signification is many-sided, and is exercised in different ways. The apologetic conception of a sign in the sense of a mark, like a trademark, and of a knowledge which proceeds by way of syllogisms, is then incapable, here more than ever, of taking account of the rich and fruitful dynamism of the sign.

The sign here is inseparable from the person: it is of one substance with him and emanates from him. And before any meaning which is not immediately perceptible, that is to say, before any knowledge of its identity in depth, holiness is an *expressive sign of love*. A consecration to God and men in which love is concentrated, it attracts as a light attracts in the dark, or as a spring of running water attracts the thirsty; for as man is made for truth, so also is he made for love. Holiness manifests itself as a good, as a value, and as such it attracts. But it attracts also in that it is an expressive sign *of a greater love*, that is, of the infinite love for which man is made without knowing it, and which he desires without power to possess. Holiness appears in our world of hatred and egotism, as *a rough sketch* of the absolutely pure love which is the divine love. That is why it disposes the soul to recognize this personal divine Love which has a Name and a Face, which has been revealed to us in Christ; for in Christ the *Agape* of God, that is, "the kindness of God our Savior and his love for men" has "appeared" to us (Tt 3:4). God is Love, and this Love has been revealed to us and given to us in Jesus Christ.

In relation to the gospel, holiness is *a sign of the gospel*, in the sense that it gives it substance in the order of existence. The gospel is incarnate in the saint and lives in him and through him. The salvation accomplished and lived allows us to see *shining through it* the salvation proclaimed. Holiness is the gospel's face, the visible presence of salvation in the world. Not only is there a coherence between the sign and the reality signified, but the sign is itself charged with this very reality. It is not a question of expressing holiness in terms of concepts and propositions; for that would be to repeat the gospel, to abandon what is lived for what is thought. Holiness does not give a rational demonstration of the gospel, it *reveals* it in operation, in the act of existence. It reveals a soul which is dwelt in by the Spirit and which has *become* what the message of the gospel proclaims, a child of God. The light of the gospel, contemplated in the gospel as *lived*, is in itself and of itself a sign of truth.

Finally holiness as *transcendence* is a sign not so much in the sense of a sign which proves as in the sense of a *sign to be interpreted, a riddle to be read, a mystery to be solved*. That is, holiness, envisaged as a higher synthesis, is a real problem and calls for explanation. And, as has been suggested above, the honest mind which considers this problem cannot fail to notice the admirable *consistency* which exists between the witness of Christ, the Church and the saints on the one hand, and the facts observed on the other; between the sublime level of the gospel on the doctrinal plane and the sublime level of holiness on the existential plane, between holiness itself and other illuminating characteristics which often accompany it—miracles, the gift of prophecy, mystical graces, for instance; and between holiness and other notes of the Church (unity, stability, permanence). Holiness introduces us to an *ensemble* of data at once complex and coherent. And the founding of Christianity by Christ, the Son of God, come into the world so that men may be saved and regenerated, certainly seems to recommend itself as the only acceptable interpretation of these data, and the only adequate explanation for phenomena at once so extraordinary and so coherent. The reason for holiness is the personal power of Christ acting through his Spirit. The sign, in this case, is not so much an argument as an enigma, for which we must find a sufficient explanation. Such a process of thought may seem less compelling, but it would appear more in conformity with the nature of the phenomena observed. One thing is sure: it leads to a solid certainty, which is rationally safe. Holiness is a sign *valde suasivum* of the divine origin of Christianity.

This dialectic or intellectual process by which we pass from the signifier to the thing signified, theological reflection takes to pieces and subjects to analysis, as in a film in slow motion, in order to isolate and describe the details which go to make it up. This is a completely legitimate procedure, but we should never allow it to make us forget that in the sphere of a concrete discerning of the sign, and in the experience of actual life, things are usually rather different: it is enough then that there should be a synthetic perception in which Christianity appears as a divine reality and its message as worthy of belief. In this experiential and intuitive awareness, it is not necessary to represent the sign conceptually, or to analyze the process by which the mind is led from the sign to the reality: in a single operation, in a sort of direct vision, the mind penetrates, through the sign, to the reality it signifies.

6. *The efficacy of the sign and subjective conditions*

It is important to stress before every other consideration, that, in the concrete, the discerning of the sign of holiness, like that and even more than that of other signs, takes place in a climate of grace.⁵⁰ How, indeed, could it be imagined that the God of love, after establishing an economy of revelation and supernatural faith, both of which are themselves directed towards a supernatural end, would give man signs of this economy of salvation without helping him *efficaciously* to read the signs? Since holiness is the sign of the supernatural *par excellence*, the perceptible irruption into our world of the invisible action of grace, how is it conceivable that this same grace should not be at work to help man understand and appreciate the new universe into which the sign of holiness introduces him? Could he not say, like Candace's minister of state, applying himself in vain to understanding the scriptures, "How can I understand what I am reading unless someone guides me?" (Acts 8: 30-31). It would be contrary to God's wisdom and goodness to call on men to orientate their lives and their thought towards a supernatural end, while refusing them the very help capable of leading them there.⁵¹ The signs of revelation are situated in a context of salvation, and therefore of freedom and grace. And holiness, the sign of salvation present and accomplished, is bound up, more than any other sign, with the gift of grace. Its discerning therefore is instinct with grace, which clarifies the mind, ensures the intellectual honesty of mental processes, and enables the will to face bravely the question ineluctably posed by the perception of such a sign: that is, the question of a supernatural salvation connected with the intervention of God in history, and of a decision which involves the whole of life.

---

50. L. Monden, *Le miracle, signe de salut* (Bruges-Brussels-Paris, 1960), p. 84; G. De Broglie, *Les signes de crédibilité de la révélation chrétienne* (Paris, 1964), pp. 5-8, 77-78; trans., *Revelation and Reason* (London, 1965).

51. Since the signs of credibility are made solely in order to lead men to supernatural faith, observes Fr. de Broglie, "the only minds capable of grasping and using them completely and normally are those in which reason is not left simply to its own natural resources, but given the complementary light of grace" (G. De Broglie, *Les signes de crédibilité de la révélation chrétienne*, p. 8; trans., *Revelation and Reason*).

The action of grace thus clearly maintained,[52] it remains true that holiness does not, any more than the other signs (miracle, prophecy and so on), act *ex opere operato*. The sign is given, but a man is not always prepared to interpret it. A logical proof imposes itself of its nature, independently of the dispositions of him to whom it is addressed. A sign, on the other hand, is understood only by those who can discover its meaning.[53] So one can see a prodigy, without *discerning* the miracle, meet with holiness and see in it only a fact which disconcerts. The signs are given by God, but they can be perceived as signs, that is, not only as unusual phenomena but as divine action, only under certain conditions. They have an objective existence and they are objectively capable of putting us in touch with God, but they attain their end only if they are met by certain human dispositions and attitudes. "A man who is carried in the wake of his prejudices, or driven by his passions or his ill-will, may refuse not only the evidence of external signs, but

---

52. This effective historical presence of grace obviously does not mean that human reason left to its own devices is incapable of perceiving and evaluating the sign. Apologetic reflection can show that nothing in the dialectic which leads from the sign to the thing signified is strictly beyond the power of reason. What is meant is simply that *in fact* the grace of God is at work the moment we are concerned with a salvation which is properly speaking supernatural — and therefore in the signs as well as in revelation and faith. It is in this perspective of man in the real and historical sense that the First Vatican Council takes up its position, when it says that God has given us both exterior signs and interior grace: "so that the acknowledgment of our faith should be in conformity with reason it was God's will that the inner help of the Holy Spirit should be accompanied by the external evidence of revelation" (DS 3009).

53. "To know by means of signs is to discover in and through a concrete *ensemble* of phenomenal data some concrete truth whose content goes beyond the data. This obviously presupposes that the data should be susceptible of leading us to the truth, but it also presupposes the calling into play of a certain intellectual power of interpretation which all human minds possess but which, on the other hand, they possess only very unequally, according to a diversity of matters in relation to which they may be more, or less, well-endowed" (G. De Broglie, *Les signes de crédibilité de la révélation chretienne*, p. 17; trans., *Reason and Revelation*.

316 of 348 CHRIST AND THE CHURCH

also the awareness which God infuses within us" (DS 3876). And the attitudes and dispositions needed to discern the sign of holiness are more numerous than in the case of miracle.

First of all, certain *intellectual* attitudes are necessary, in particular an openness to the hypothesis of divine action in man, capable of raising him above his own powers and transforming him. Anyone who refuses to admit the possibility, through divine help, of spiritual resurrection and spiritual ascent, will always be able to invoke, when confronted by holiness, the argument of unknown psychological forces or a naturally heroic temperament. We have to presuppose, moreover, on the part of the subjective human being confronted by holiness, a certain experience and awareness of the finite, fragile and deceptive character of man, incapable of keeping his promises, and ready in all situations to throw up his commission.

But above all certain *moral* dispositions are necessary. For we know from the gospel that there are those who are voluntarily deaf, who stop their ears lest they should hear, and those who are voluntarily blind, who refuse to see. Those who shut themselves up in a closed world, a world of wealth, or pleasure or power for instance, will not be able to perceive the signs of God. Imprisoned in the material, walled-up alive in a world of shadows, they will be impervious to light from beyond. Christ came among us, the living and thrice-holy God, "holy in the sight of God and of man," and yet the Pharisees accused him of having a devil (Jn 10:20), and of casting out devils through Beelzebub, the chief of devils (Mk 3:22; Lk 11:15). Holiness attracts some and gives scandal to others. It attracts the well-disposed but provokes the proud. The greatest obstacle to the action of the signs and particularly to the action of the sign of holiness, is, in fact, the exaltation of the self, the claim to complete autonomy, the arrogant pretention to have no need of anyone else. Such a disposition paralyzes the action of the sign. To the self-sufficient, holiness is irritating. Self-sufficiency, whether it is religious, philosophical or cultural, gives birth to contempt, disdain and inattention. Holiness seems by its brilliance to violate and reduce the brilliance of the proud. The consciousness, on the other hand, of *our own sorry condition,* our own want and poverty, disposes us to recognize the fullness of charity which the saint represents. Man has to give up his assumed self-government in order to give himself to God.

To be precise, the following dispositions seem to be needed, at least in an elementary state, if the sign is to have any chance of operating. First of all a genuine *sincerity* is necessary, an authentic desire for truth (Jn 18, 37) and light (Jn 3. 19); for it can happen that men prefer darkness to light. There is also a necessity for that minimum degree of *humility* which consists in not attributing to oneself the glory of God (Jn 5, 44) and not constituting oneself the center of the universe. A certain *sense of moral values* is necessary, a certain capacity to recognize them and appreciate them. In this connection, an inordinate attachment to money or pleasure, a one-sided education orientated towards the technological and quantitative, a philosophy impregnated with materialism or naturalism can prevent one seeing what is there and recognizing its value. A certain spiritual depth is also necessary, and a certain incipient magnanimity.[54] There are, that is, certain minds which seem to be born in a state of poverty, congenitally incapable of seeing in other people anything but deficiencies. In the Curé d'Ars, they will see only his lack of culture and the limitations of his knowledge. In Benedict Labre, they will see only his sordid lack of cleanliness. Such an attitude acts as a sort of filter, preventing the light of holiness from reaching the eyes. Magnanimity is the more important, in that the saint, even the great saint, retains the defects of his temperament, and weaknesses which affect his judgment.[55]

---

54. It is not claimed that *all* these conditions are absolutely necessary for the sign to be effective. It can happen with the help of grace — always at work in this process of discernment—that, in spite of rather unfavorable dispositions, the shock of the sign operates with an accelerated rhythm. But it can also happen that the absence of a *single one* of the dispositions cited puts an obstacle in the way of the sign. What is being said is simply that the dispositions described above are the normal context in which the sign operates.

55. It is noticeable that the efficacy of the sign of holiness varies

Finally it needs to be remembered that if the sign of holiness presupposes certain dispositions on the part of those to whom it is made, it demands also a certain stress on the part of those who give it. Holiness does, of itself, make-a-sign, but as has already been suggested, a certain *sociological* dimension seems to be necessary for the sign to communicate. There is no doubt whatever that holiness in a state of isolation already constitutes a sign, but how much more convincing the sign is if the holiness in question is an affair not only of a few but of many, that is of a whole community. "It is necessary that holiness should have a collective character," observes Fr. de Montcheuil, "if it is to present itself to everyone, and impose itself on the sight of all, so that it strikes the eyes of the indifferent, and can be no more excluded from its *milieu* than reduced to it."[56] In an egotistical world, the existence of groups ruled by charity will always be astonishing and attractive. "See how they love one another," people said of the first Christians. It therefore depends on us whether the sign of holiness attracts more, or less, attention, and is more, or less, infectious. It depends on us whether charity becomes the sign by which Christ's disciples may be recognized (Jn 13:35). The Church needs in all ages and in all contexts, to shine with the light of charity and bear the fruits of the Spirit; for any diminution in her common spiritual life makes the brightness of the sign of holiness grow dim. The poet Tagore used to say, "If your lives were like the life of Christ, all India would be at your feet." Heroic sanctity cannot be really effective unless it appears as the

---

according to whether it has to be read outside the Church, without the Church's help, or as presented by the Church, who explains and brings out all its value.

---

56. Y. De Montcheuil, *Problèmes de vie spirituelle,* p. 45. P.-A. Liégé points out that "the presence and divine power of Jesus Christ, which we proclaim, should shine through the common life of those who call themselves Christians.... The fact of holiness should constitute the great and permanent miracle which the Church has at her command in her missionary presence in the modern world" (P.-A. Liégé, *Vivre en Chrétien,* Paris, 1960, pp. 117-118; trans., *What is Christian Life?* (London, 1961).

apex of a broad pyramid whose base is constituted by ordinary holiness, that is, by the witness of a really Christian life. "We are the salt of the earth; if mankind corrupts it is because we have not fulfilled our vocation." [57] The world is waiting for saints. If saints and sanctity are nowhere to be seen, men live in darkness and die of cold. For, in the end, what gives force to the apparently fragile sign of holiness is that it is a sign of the supernatural which transforms man. And the sign here is the very *splendor of the transformation brought about.* We pass directly from the reflection to its source. In holiness the supernatural is in act, and in operation within our own world. In miracle, nature alone is affected; here man himself is changed and given life by the Spirit of love. It is the promise of the living God fulfilled. "I will give you a new heart, I will put a new spirit within you.... I will put my spirit within you" (Ex 36:26-27).

---

57. Y. De Montcheuil, *Problèmes de vie spirituelle*, p. 47.

INDEX OF PROPER NAMES

Adam, K., 274
Adrian VI, 146
Aeby, G., 177
Aimé, D., 296
Alfaro, J., 43, 44, 100
Alszeghy, Z., 138
Amann, E., 180
Anselm, saint, 140
Antón, A., 129, 157, 225
Athenagoras, 152
Aubenas, R., 191
Aubert, R., 32, 191, 198
Augustine, saint, 59, 64, 139, 140,
    228, 229, 262, 297

Ballerini, 110
Balmes, 109
Baraúna, G., 108, 221, 263
Barbero, G., 175
Barbotin, E., 285, 306
Bardy, G., 175, 292
Barth, K., 118, 143
Bauer, J. B., 217
Baum, G., 116, 157
Bautain, L.-E., 109
Bea, A., 151
Beauduin, Dom, 151
Bellarmine, R., 48
Bellucci, D., 151
Benoit, P., 83
Benedict XIV, 302
Benedict XV, 302
Bergson, H., 303
Bernanos, G, 119
Blanchard, P., 287, 289
Blet, P., 187
Blomjous, 123
Bloy, L., 289, 293
Bonhoeffer, D., 118

Bonnefoy, J., 118
Bonsirven, J., 167
Borromeo, C., 148, 262
Bossuet, 97, 108
Bouyer, L., 118, 207
Boyer, C., 151
Brown, R. E., 82
Brox, N., 91
Bulst, W., 108
Bultmann, R., 40, 56, 85, 136,
    196
Burdach, K., 191

Canisius, P., 148
Cerfaux, L., 217, 221, 224, 226
Chenu, M.-D., 120, 121, 203
Chesterton, G. K., 293
Chieregati, F., 146
Claudel, P., 295
Clémence, J., 46
Clement XI, 212
Congar, Y.-M., 108, 118, 120,
    145, 151, 157, 183, 200, 202,
    203, 207, 217, 221, 234, 235,
    236, 239, 292
Couturier, 151
Cristiani, L., 148
Cros, P.-L. J.-M., 60
Cyprian, saint, 139

Daniel-Rops, 184, 191, 293
Danielou, J., 118, 167, 175, 177
Davis, C., 116
Dawson, G., 180
De Bovis, A., 233
De Broglie, G., 43, 44, 49, 53, 58,
    67, 68, 314
De Certeau, M., 138
Dechamps, 109, 123, 124

Decourtray, A., 89
De Finance, J., 305
De Foucauld, C., 280, 291, 292
Dejaifve, G., 228, 233, 234
De Labriolle, P., 175
De Lagarde, G., 198
De la Potterie, I., 91
De Lubac, H., 118, 120, 198, 207, 220
De Montcheuil, Y., 291, 306, 318, 319
Denzinger-Schönmetzer, 5, 10, 16, 17, 30, 31, 32, 41, 42, 43, 51, 58, 76, 78, 80, 82, 109, 211, 212, 213, 256
De Ste-Madeleine, G., 302
De Vaux, R., 167
De Vitoria, F., 60
De Vogel, C. J., 295
Dommershausen, W., 217
Dostoievsky, 119, 289
Dulles, A., 256
Dumas, A., 180
Dumont, C., 45, 50, 70, 153
Duns Scotus, 139, 140
Dupanloup, 110
Dupont, J., 169
Dupuy, B.-D., 157
Duquoc, C., 205

Eugene IV, 145, 149
Eyt, P., 118, 206

Fénelon, 109
Féret, H.-M., 280
Feuillet, A., 84
Fliche, A., 175, 191, 198
Flick, M., 138
Francis Xavier, saint, 60, 148
Franzelin, J. B., 109
Frauenfelder, R., 296

Gaetan, saint, 148
Gaudemet, J., 175
Gauthier, P., 117
Génicot, L., 184

Ghéon, H., 294
Girault, R., 294, 295, 296, 298
Gleason, R. W., 66
Grand'maison, M., 125
Green, J., 287, 305
Gregory VII, 181, 182
Gregory X, 145, 149
Gregory XIII, 149
Gregory XV, 149
Gregory XVI, 192, 193, 194
Grillmeier, A., 263
Guitton, J., 183
Gutwenger, E., 286

Hamel, E., 167
Hamer, J., 128
Hocedez, E., 198
Holstein, H., 115, 131

Ignatius of Loyola, saint, 24, 59, 148, 262
Innocent III, 149, 263
Irenaeus, saint, 108

Jarry, E., 198
Jeremias, J., 167
Jerome Aemilius, saint, 148
John XXIII, 34, 109, 114, 115, 151, 198, 287
John of the Cross, saint, 24, 148
Jossua, J.-P., 138
Journet, C., 61, 229, 230, 231, 232, 233, 236
Julius III, 149
Justin, saint, 139

Kallas, J., 84
Kempf, F., 180
Ketteler, 197
Kierkegaard, 119
Kleutgen, J., 109
Knowles, M. D., 180, 184, 191
Kuhn, G., 217
Küng, H., 111, 117, 118, 145, 147, 215, 221, 226, 240, 241, 242, 252, 263

Lacordaire, 109
Lacroix, J., 39
Laffoucrière, O., 40
Lamennais, 192, 193
Landgraf, 228
Langevin, G., 203, 221
Langevin, P.-E., 83
Latourelle, R., 10, 12, 14, 27, 42, 44, 47, 85, 90, 91, 106, 109, 128
Laurentin, R., 118, 120, 121, 122
Lefèvre, A., 100
Lelotte, F., 293, 294, 295, 296
Leo XIII, 109, 149, 151, 197
Lepargneur, F. H., 57, 63
Leyvraz, R., 293
Liégé, P.-A., 286, 308, 318
Lonergan, B., 177
Luther,, 145, 146, 147, 190, 191, 229, 261

Macaulay, Th. B., 274
Malevez, L., 123, 124, 125
Malmberg, F., 231
Manaranche, A., 94, 108, 207, 256
Marcel, G., 292
Maritain, J., 293
Maritain, R., 293
Marrou, I. H., 167, 175
Martelet, G., 9, 80, 239, 261
Martin, 71
McGoldrick, P., 227
McKenzie, J. L., 118
Menoud, P. H., 84
Mercier, 151
Merton, T., 294
Metz, J. B., 39, 117, 205
Molinari, P., 287
Mollard, G., 123
Mollat, D., 91, 100, 101
Monden, L., 44, 47, 52, 66, 314
Mouroux, J., 71, 72
Mühlen, H., 108, 226, 276, 284

Nédoncelle, M., 294, 295, 296
Neri, saint P., 148

Newman, 151

Obolensky, D., 180, 184
O'Brien, J. A., 292, 293, 297, 308
Orbe, A., 177
Origen, 108
Ortiz De Urbina, I., 177

Palanque, J.-R., 175
Papini, G., 295
Pascal, 36, 46, 49, 65, 67, 108, 184, 295
Pastor, L., 191
Paul III, 148
Paul IV, 148
Paul VI, 14, 45, 137, 150, 152, 198, 199, 254
Pax, E., 217
Péguy, C., 118, 289
Philips, G., 138, 142, 232
Pius V, 148
Pius VI, 212
Pius IX, 76, 149, 192, 193, 194, 195, 197, 285
Pius X, 109, 151
Pius XI, 109, 151
Pius XII, 109, 212
Pinto De Oliveira, G. J., 138
Post, R., 147
Poulet, C., 293
Pousset, E., 282
Prestige, G. L., 177
Procksch, O., 217
Prusak, B. P., 157
Psichari, E., 289
Pusey, 151

Rahner, K., 35, 56, 117, 120, 124, 138, 141, 203, 205, 207, 232, 236, 237, 238, 240, 241, 242, 247, 270, 273
Ramsey, 152
Ratzinger, J., 10, 238
Ricard, R., 191
Richard of Saint-Victor, 140

Richardson, A., 84
Richardson, W. J., 108
Rogier, L. J., 191

Salaverri, J., 229
Savonarola, 108, 190
Schafer, B., 294, 295, 296
Schillebeeckx, E., 55, 90, 107,
  120, 138, 205, 277, 290, 292
Schlier, 245
Schutz, R., 146, 261, 262, 280,
  281, 283
Shepherd, M. H., 175
Simon, M., 168
Six, J.-F., 291, 292
Smulders, P., 108
Spanneut, M., 177
Stein, E., 296
Stern, K., 293
Stöhr, J., 232, 238
Suarez, F., 59
Suganami, L.-P., 294

Tagore, 318

Teresa of Avila, saint, 148, 297
Tertullian, 108
Thils, G., 129, 150, 157
Thomas Aquinas, saint, 42, 139,
  140
Thomson, P. Van K., 295
Trépanier, B., 91

Undset, S., 295
Urban VIII, 149
Urdanoz, T., 61

Vanhoye, A., 91, 103, 104
Van Imschoot, P., 217
Von Balthasar, H. U., 50, 118,
  207, 215, 237

Wattson, P., 151
West, M. L., 118
Willaert, L., 148
Witte, J. L., 108
Wu, J. C. H., 297, 308

Zaccaria, A.-M., 148